"NO WORRIES"

A Secular
Western
approach to
Buddhism,
Meditation, Life
& Actuality

B. CUMMING

Copyright © 2016 B. Cumming

ISBN: 978-1-925590-03-6

Published by Vivid Publishing
P.O. Box 948, Fremantle
Western Australia 6959
www.vividpublishing.com.au

Cataloguing-in-Publication data is available from the National Library of Australia

Introduction

The content of this book is simply a communication of a current theory of actuality that was realized within a period of meditation on the 13th June 1980. This was followed by an actualization process throughout the various schools of Buddhism over the course of twenty five years and then within a secular western context which is still on-going. This journey was an attempt to make intellectual sense of the experience so it could be communicated to a new secular western audience without recourse to religious dogma, institutionalised belief, or other cultural influences.

The communication of the Dharma has never been about the communicator. It has always been about the communication. It has always been communicated so that it can be tested, challenged, refuted or realized within direct experience, without the need of any belief aspect imposed by the confused and conditioned, self-biased mind.

If, by engaging with this book, it helps you to move away from the mind state of worrying towards the mind state of contentment or peace of mind, you can be assured it is the Dharma. If it does not, then it is suggested that you discard whatever you find unhelpful.

B. Cumming

Acknowledgments

It would possibly fill this entire book if everybody who has contributed in some way towards its development were individually acknowledged. There have been so many teachers within each of the main traditions of Buddhism, both formal and informal. There have been so many mentors along the way, many of whom are still in contact. There have been so many Dharma friends who have been there, supporting and encouraging this journey, that it would take a lifetime to be able to express the depth of gratitude that is owed to each and every one of them. They know who they are and so do I and that is all that really matters.

I am indebted to the kindness and dedication of Bodhidasa (Troy Shier) Taradeva (Barbara Warren) Dhivajri (Emma Watt) of the Darmadatu Sangha and my friend and fellow journeyman Chris Johnys. They have somehow painstakingly managed to untangle my uneducated scribbling into something that sounds possibly half intelligent and have apparently put all the dots and squiggly bits in all the right places. Thanks also to Buddhist artist Garava of the Triratna Buddhist Order for permission to use his water colour 'melancholy skeleton' for the front cover of this book and to Shaktidana (Michelle Mainwaring) of the Dharmadatu Sangha for creating the back cover.

This book is dedicated to the memory of my late parents, who provided me with the opportunity of human life and encouraged me, from a very early age, to be a critical, free-thinking, creative individual and to my wife Mudita (Julia) who has been there supporting me every step of the way since the age of 13.

Contents

Chapter One: The Secular Western Context

"No Worries." It's possibly the most iconic phrase used in Australia and, more than likely, every other western culture has its own version of it such as **'no problems.'** If you are not Australian, for the purpose of this book, where you see the words **'worry'** or **'worries,'** just replace them with the words that are used in your own country and the concept will work in the same way.

For Australians, and those that have a preconceived idea of what Australia is, (based on what they have seen and heard from others) a country that conjures up an image, perhaps, of a care-free nation that is so laid back, the problems of everyday life pass them by. Considering it is one of those countries that appears to have more creatures living there that have the ability to kill you, or cause you serious injury, or illness compared with anywhere else in the world, at times it is difficult to understand how this image became a part of the popular portrayed view of Australia.

Australia seems to present an image, inwardly and outwardly, of being a nation at ease with itself. This iconic phrase **'no worries'** communicates the idea, perhaps, that Australians spend most of their lives surfing at the beach, throwing a shrimp on the barbie (BBQ) or knocking back a stubbie (small bottle of beer also known as "piss") on the veranda with a few mates. Yet, it seems clear that everything is not always as it seems in this amazing and diverse country that is Australia, nor, I suggest, any other western society.

According to published statistics from the Australian Health Department, Australia has one of the highest levels, per head of capita, of mental illness in the form of depression, stress and anxiety disorders, in the developed western world. These statistics indicate that it is increasing at an alarming rate, as is the rate of suicides. It would seem that in actuality, Australians do quite a lot of worrying and it is suggested here that it is very much the same within most other western cultures.

The aim of this book is to explore how the teachings of the Buddha, when understood on the basis of their practical application, are possibly more relevant today than they were over 2,600 years ago. But only if they are approached on the basis of one's own cultural conditioning and with a willingness to adopt and engage fully in a particular lifestyle change, to alleviate or eradicate the worrying aspects of life, without recourse to religious dogma, or institutionalised belief.

It is acknowledged from the outset that there will always be some benefit experienced by engaging with Buddhism and its practices that have developed in cultures that are not our own. There may even be some benefit experienced even if any of those developments appear to have become entrenched in religious dogma, political elitism, or are not aligned with current scientific knowledge that was not known previously. This book is not in any way an attempt to undermine, or be disrespectful, towards any form of classical Buddhism. Neither is it an attempt to undermine the faith, or disrespect the beliefs of millions of Buddhists world-wide who practice the Buddha's teachings to make the world a kinder place for all of us to live in. It simply sets out an alternative approach that has been found to be helpful within a western culture.

Before we go any further it is vital to have an understanding of the context in which this book will be exploring Buddhism. Context is an essential component of the process and is there to create focus. We are living today in a particular time in history and in a particular culture that is vastly different from ancient India and the many diverse cultures where the teachings of the Buddha later developed. For the Buddha's communication to be effective for us it is helpful to address the issue of context from the outset.

We live in a rapidly evolving secular western society which brings with it unique difficulties which arise from the way we have been conditioned to live. It is the human conditioning process that lies at the centre of everything the Buddha communicated. In his original communication he used the language of his day. He used the existent belief systems, current ideas and concepts and even the superstitions of the local populace as a means of showing them how unhelpful they were.

It is suggested here that it could be unhelpful for us to cling to things that have no relevance for us today. For the Buddha's teachings to be of use to us, it is helpful to use our own language. It is helpful to draw on information and knowledge that is available today and information and knowledge that may become available in the future. It is unhelpful to be afraid of letting go of practices, traditions, rites and rituals that no longer have any practical use within a modern secular western world.

The motivational intent behind this book is simply a way of setting out an approach to Buddhism that aims to be practice led and based on living within an ever evolving secular western society. The basis of this is an understanding that it is only when you are prepared to take a long hard look at your own cultural conditioning, with an integrity that is not influenced by someone else's ideas, that you will come to see the journey as it was meant to be seen by you and where it can be of most help to you. Whilst doing this there is a clear requirement to remain loyal, as best as one can, to the essence of the original communication. This is the challenge that has been taken up by those organisations and individuals who are engaged in this latest reformation that has come to be known as secular western Buddhism.

The primary consideration of this approach is to explore what works now, rather than what should be believed in because of an ancient tradition. The journey of the modern day, secular western, Dharma practitioner, is to seek to answer three principle questions.

1. What works to free this thing we call the mind from worrying?

2. What works to accomplish the development of compassion?

3. What works to awaken us to the way things are in actuality?

As a newcomer, or even if you have engaged with classical Buddhism before, at first you may find it difficult to let go of the language, the spectacle and the romanticism of what you may have previously understood Buddhism to be. That is to be expected, considering the way it has been portrayed historically in the public domain. Sadly, as we will come to see, nothing is ever as it seems.

The secular western approach to the Dharma is not about dilution or dummying down the Buddha's message. It is about the restoration and revival of his practical method of living. It will serve to enliven and refresh a valuable communication which at times has got stuck in the ancient past. A modern secular western society relies heavily on the scientific method of discovery rather than beliefs in mysticism and magic. The ancient texts and the development of Buddhist thought over the last 2,600 years provide us with a secure legacy for which we are assuredly grateful. But, it is helpful to be aware that we are not beholden to it just because it is called Buddhism if we are to make progress within the journey.

The practical and systematic approach that is set out within the context of this book is centred on three self-supporting and equally important methods of development and they will be explored in detail in later chapters of this book. The first method is that of meditation. It is promoted here as the means to develop clear thinking and a sense of emotional well-being. The formal sitting meditation practices that are suggested within the context of this book, bring a very light form of discipline into your daily life and practice and can be traced back, through Buddhist literature to the Buddha himself.

Progress is measured by the significant helpful changes in your psychological mind states and overall sense of emotional well-being over a period of time. There is a core concentration practice that uses awareness of the breath as its focal point and there is a more explorative and experience-based practice that uses a range of people who you regularly come into contact with as its focal point, in order to develop a kinder approach to life for you, others and the world around you.

The second method is about developing an ethical lifestyle that is not dependent on externally imposed rules and regulations. You will be encouraged to consider adopting a set of ethical guidelines and to use them as a means to work towards becoming proficient in observing your habitual patterns of thinking, speaking and behaving and then taking responsibility for them without recourse to blaming others or external events. There are five basic ethical training principles that are promoted here within this context and they will be explored in depth in a later chapter.

I undertake the ethical training principle, to avoid wherever possible, doing harm and to practice loving kindness.

I undertake the ethical training principle, to avoid wherever possible, taking anything that is not freely given and to practice generosity.

I undertake the ethical training principle, to avoid wherever possible, engaging in sexual exploitation, or manipulation and to practice stillness, simplicity and contentment.

I undertake the ethical training principle, to avoid wherever possible, unkind speech and to practice truthful and kindly communication.

I undertake the ethical training principle, to avoid wherever possible, anything that will tend to decrease the clarity of the mind and to practice keeping the mind clear and radiant.

The third method is the effect of practicing the other two self-supporting methods. This is the development of insight. This is not an intellectual, knowledge based pursuit. It's not about being clever, intelligent or knowing stuff. It is about developing levels of concentration, within the meditative process that will eventually give rise to irreversible transformation. It is about seeing through our conditioned beliefs about whom we are and how we came to be that way. It is about moving away from the worrying mind to one that is at peace with itself, others and the world around it.

When reading this book it may be helpful to understand the founding principle of this secular western approach to Buddhism. At times, when, and if, you experience anything of an unhelpful reaction to what you read, it is suggested that you come back to this page and re-engage with this founding principle as it sets out clearly your personal responsibility. It is based on an early Buddhist text and is one that is considered to be of vital impor- tance in this approach. It moves the individual away from blind faith or belief, towards their own direct experience and is promoted as a safety precaution against coercion or manipulation, which, it is sad to say, goes on quite a lot within some Buddhist organisations.

Buddha's Charter of Free-Thinking and Critical Inquiry

It is unhelpful to simply believe what you hear just because you have heard it for a long time.

It is unhelpful to follow tradition blindly, merely because it has been practiced in that way for years.

It is unhelpful to listen to rumours.

It is unhelpful to confirm anything just because it is stated in a scripture or text.

It is unhelpful to make assumptions.

It is unhelpful to draw conclusions by what you see and hear.

It is unhelpful to be fooled by outward appearances.

It is unhelpful to cling to, or become attached to, any view or idea just because you are comfortable with it.

It is unhelpful to accept as fact, anything arrived at by logic.

It is unhelpful to be convinced of anything out of respect or reverence to your chosen Dharma communicator.

It is helpful to go beyond opinion and belief.

It is helpful to reject anything that, when accepted, tried and tested with integrity, leads to worrying in the form of want, not want and confusion.

It is helpful to accept anything that, when accepted, tried and tested with integrity, leads to the practice of loving-kindness, contentment and clarity.

This advice is a guide to what may be of benefit when developing criteria for what is and what is not conducive to making authentic progress on the Dharma journey.

If we understand the charter correctly, we will have noticed already that the Dharma is not a belief based system. It is a thing to be tested and challenged in relation to our own lives. It is a thing to be tested and challenged within our own direct experience, so that we can move towards the alleviation and eventual eradication of our worries. It is a thing in action. It is a thing to do. It is a thing to practice. It is a thing to live.

So, as we can see, there is no room for belief on this journey. What is a belief? Within the context of this book, a belief is something that has arisen within us from our conditioned experience. Perhaps it has something to do with the way we were raised, our education, the media, or even in some circumstances a direct or apparent mystical experience, or maybe a combination of a number of those things. No matter how this belief arose, it is with us now. It has become, for us, a kind of personal truth. We don't know why, we just know it's the truth. We can't prove it's true to a third party because their conditioning factors were different to ours, so it becomes our individual truth. The problem with this is that we then build a wall around this belief because it is ours. We have become closed to it not being accurate and when anyone challenges our belief we react strongly in an unhelpful way. Make no mistake the Dharma journey is wholly confrontational, not in any kind of hostile way, but it challenges long-held beliefs and confronts us with the actuality of them.

It is suggested here that it is unhelpful to use the words 'truth' or 'true.' Those words appear to have been significantly responsible for the worst excesses of human behaviour throughout history and contributed to the deaths, mutilations and untold misery of so many beings. It seems apparent that the moment any one person or group believes they know a truth, then some other person or group who believe they know the truth will need to fight the other to prove one is right and the other is wrong and to the death if necessary.

Within this context it is suggested that it is not even helpful to promote the idea that the Buddha taught the truth. It is suggested here that it is helpful to consider that he communicated a 'current theory of actuality' that invites people to test, challenge and either realize it for themselves or refute it. What is amazing is that in 2,600 years, the brightest minds of each age have gotten nowhere near refuting it. Another consideration as to why it is not helpful to use those terms is that for something to be true, it must become fixed and static forever and that is the total opposite of what the Buddha communicated. What is suggested here is that we turn away from truth and look for 'facts.' Facts can be 'established,' whereas truths are believed. In doing so, it is suggested that it is helpful to adopt an attitude of what is referred to as a 'transitory view.' A view may well have arisen within the same set of conditioning factors as the belief, but it is only relevant to this moment in time and is subject to change if circumstances change. This approach plays a significant role in stopping us from getting bogged down in the dogma of fixed beliefs. If we remain closed to the inevitability of change we remain in the world of beliefs, but if we stay open, at least to the possibility that our individual truth may not be what we believe it to be, we open up the opportunity for realization.

So, what are these worries and how do they arise and cause us on-going difficulties? To explore this from a secular western perspective we will need to start at square one with an understanding of how Buddhism began.

Chapter Two: The Origins of Buddhism

Buddhism is not what you think. Buddhism is how you think, why you think it and what happens as a consequence of the thought process. It is about developing ways to integrate the pre-conscious, biological, nature aspect of being and the subconscious, psychological, nurture aspect of being into conscious awareness, so that this thing we call the mind can be at peace. The pre-conscious aspect includes all inherited or evolutionary genetic and other biological influences which would include the four primary drives of:

1. To survive
2. To replicate the species
3. To seek pleasure
4. To avoid pain

The subconscious aspect is the sum total of all the stored sensory data input since conception and birth that is called the conditioning process.

In its most simplistic understanding Buddhism is about developing ways to enable the thought process to move from causing harm to you, others and the world around you, towards the development of contentment, peace of mind and compassion for all living beings. It is about developing a way of life that can be lived fully without the drama of worries that arise in our everyday worldly lives that spoil it for us.

It is about taking 100% responsibility for everything you think, say and do and paying attention to the quality of your mind state and emotional experience in each moment and learning from that experience. It follows a basic principle of **'cause and effect'** that is aligned with doing the least amount of harm possible in any situation to yourself, others and the world around you. The good news is that in secular western Buddhism you do not have to do the guilt thing, beat yourself up or give yourself a hard time when you make mistakes, (as you surely will) because none of us will ever be mistake free.

Buddhism didn't actually begin until long after the death of the person on whose communication it is based. The name Buddhism itself was developed sometime around the early twentieth century within western society. It is derived from the words **'Bodhi'** or **'Buddha'** which means something like: **'one who is awake to the way things are in actuality.'**

It could be said that the story of the Buddha and Buddhism is all about worrying. To get to grips with its actuality we really do need to let go of all the intellectual and mythological stuff that appears to have been added in. It may have been added in to possibly give it a greater credibility, but more likely it was as a means of keeping it within an institutional religious set up. It never required anything added in. It has always been credible enough in its down-to-earth, practicalities. The very basis of the Buddha's story could easily be set out as:

1. **He worried about stuff**
2. **He noticed that he worried about stuff**
3. **He left his home life to seek out why he worried about stuff**
4. **He found out why he worried about stuff**
5. **He found a way to stop worrying about stuff**
6. **He suggested a way that you too could stop worrying about stuff**

The life story of the Buddha could be said to be, in many respects, an important teaching in itself. It shows clearly that this is a human process and not one created by an external, divine, higher intelligence, entity or energy. This is a very human story about human potential. When you think of the Buddha or see an image of the Buddha you are being invited to witness your own potential as a human being. When you see that serene pose and gentle smile it sings out to you, **"yeah this guy knows what it's all about."** And what usually comes next is. **"I want some of that."**

What you may not know however is how to get it. The likelihood is that for most of your life you have been looking in all directions for an external experience that would match that expression of the Buddha. What you will eventually come to realize, when you engage with the Buddha's teachings with integrity, is that your dream can never be fulfilled by external sources no matter how hard you try.

The historical figure, Siddhartha Gautama, we are told, spent over forty years travelling around Northern India attempting, as best he could, to communicate an experience that was realized in the concentrated states of sitting meditation. This experience is referred to here as **'clarity.'** This experience of clarity involved no element of faith or belief. Those things would automatically fall away within that awakening experience. What was realized within the experience and later communicated by the Buddha has come to be known as the **'Dharma,'** which in its most simplistic description would mean, **'the way things are in actuality.'**

As the Dharma spread to other countries and different cultures, it began to absorb local customs, traditions, beliefs, superstitions, rites and rituals. This was inevitable. There really is no other effective way to communicate the Dharma, without reference to what exists culturally and historically. It seems clear that the Buddha did that throughout his teaching life. He used Indian culture and the pre-existent religious belief systems to communicate what he had discovered within that experience of clarity.

Today, there are so many different Buddhist traditions, schools, sectarian groups and organisations. Many who choose to explore it for the first time in Australia, or other western countries, appear to struggle to understand what it is to be a Buddhist or what Buddhism is. The whole Buddhist arena is now so large and diverse, it has become very difficult for people to know what is and isn't Buddhism outside of the cultural context of where it is being taught and practiced. For the average westerner this can be very confusing. They think they are being drawn towards Buddhism, but what they find is that they are inevitably being drawn towards a particular form of classical and often religious Buddhism that is associated with a culture that is alien to them. They then have to try and distinguish what is the Dharma from what is actually Indian, Tibetan, Japanese, Chinese or other Asian religious culture and this can take forever and can, for some, be a crippling and time consuming distraction.

The form of Buddhism taught and practiced within each of these different expressions of the Dharma are equally valid and perfect for those whose conditioning is dependent on that culture. But it provides, it is suggested here, limitations for anyone else, other than as an intellectual or religious pursuit. The methods, as taught by the Buddha, could be described as the developmental model for the authentic human being. One who is free from their own cultural conditioning, group think and behaviour. It is a journey of transformation, of change and is not for the faint hearted. It is an on-going living process. The institutions of culturally specific classical Buddhism may well go to great lengths to blind you to this fact. That is just the nature of institutions and there is nothing malicious going on within that. You are invited here to take the blindfold off from the outset and to keep it off.

It can be quite difficult to pinpoint when Buddhism actually began. During the lifetime of the Buddha there were no Buddhists or Buddhism. There was just him and his motley crew of fellow wandering beggars, living off the hand-outs of local villagers or being sponsored by wealthy and influential patrons. This was quite the norm in ancient India then and to some extent, it could be said, very little has changed in this respect throughout the classical Buddhist world.

Despite early reservations about being able to communicate the Dharma effectively, the numbers of his followers grew very quickly, despite his apparent non-evangelical approach to teaching. It would appear that the vast numbers that are often referred to in Buddhist texts, are something of an over exaggeration of the actuality of the situation according to archaeological surveys and some scholastic investigations. So, it is always helpful to bear in mind that 'nothing is ever as it seems' within Buddhism.

One of the difficulties that arose over time is the use of the word Buddha. This is because not only does it refer back to the historical human Siddhartha Gautama but it also relates to the 'awakened mind' of any other being that has realized the same experience as the historical Buddha.

It is suggested here that what we have now that falls into the umbrella category of Buddhism, is a number of new expressions or communications of the Dharma that have evolved at different points in history and communicated by other awakened minds, who may or may not have walked the original Dharma journey that was set out by the historical Buddha. They may well be linked by the realization experience of clarity, but the practices and methods communicated as the Dharma journey are poles apart. We also have expressions or communications of the experience of clarity that do not even have the word Buddhism attached to them at all, yet still point towards the same experience, but via a different method, which then complicates things even further.

For instance, (I'll give you an exaggerated example to show you how ridiculous it all is) if I, as a Dharma practitioner, was waking through the park eating an orange and clarity was realized, I would become a Buddha. What I communicated following that would then be considered to be Buddhism. It is likely, that as part of my communication, I would link the experience to both walking in the park and eating an orange and would possibly suggest that what you would find helpful to do to realize clarity is to walk in the same park as I did and work towards finding the right orange that will assist your breakthrough into actuality. So, it comes as no surprise then that the Buddha promotes meditation as the primary key to unlocking the experience, as that is what he was doing at the moment clarity was realized.

In many respects it may have been more helpful if new names were created at each new communication point so it was not too confusing and misleading for people. For this reason where it is necessary to refer to different periods of development within this book the following terms will be used:

1. Theravadanism

2. Zenism

3. Tibetanism

4. Pure-Landism

5. Shingonism

It is made very clear here that this secular western context is not being dismissive or disrespectful to any of these great traditions by doing this. This book is about trying to cut through the institutionalised developments of classical Buddhism to try and find a way back to its roots. It is fully recognised that all of these developments have equal validity as expressions of the Dharma. The secular western approach does not subscribe to the historical one-upmanship that has been going on within the world of Buddhism throughout its history as each period of reformation happened.

If we were to peel back all of the multi-layered developments of Buddhism, so that we were back to its roots and then put to one side what was then Indian culture we would be left with the Buddha's Dharma. This is what we will be attempting to do, as best as we can, in this book.

The life story of the historical figure we refer to as the Buddha plays a significant part in our understanding of what it was he was communicating over 2,600 years ago and the reasons he did so. It is a constant reminder, not only of the simplicity of the message, but also that what was realized back then, can be realized right now by us, if sufficient effort is made. The story itself plays a crucial role in understanding our own connection with the Buddha in the 21st century.

One of the difficulties we have when doing this, is that we have very little actual verifiable information to go on. There does not appear to be that many written records available from that period. What we do have is a traditionally handed down story that contains so many inconsistencies when viewed on the basis of plausibility. It also contains inconsistencies from a historical perspective based on what we now think we know about that period in history due to advances in science and technology. Added to this problem is the tendency of religious story tellers and writers to create myths and legends of mystical and magical proportions to promote the story and Buddhism is no exception.

In reflecting on his life we have to accept that we can never know with any certainty what details are accurate accounts of what actually happened back then. As long as we are aware of this fact and proceed along the lines of whether or not something is provisionally acceptable, even on the balance of probabilities, we shouldn't be troubled too much by doubt and indecision. This is always one of the major stumbling blocks for making progress on the journey. This means that it is helpful to tread carefully as we try and find a route through the maze and the fog so we can arrive at what is relevant today.

It could be said that if, at some point in the future, a scholar or historian provided credible evidence, or even on the basis of the balance of probabilities, evidence that would suggest that no such character as the historical Buddha actually existed, it would not make much difference to the validity of the communication of the Dharma that is presented in his name. It has never been and never will be about the communicator. It has always been and always will be about the communication. There is a well known image within Buddhism that illustrates this point. It is a picture of a finger pointing towards the moon. The moon represents the Dharma, the realization of actuality and the finger represents the awakened mind that points towards it.

The life story of the Buddha is full of symbolism and inspiration that helps us to see why the communication of the Dharma in a secular western Buddhist context is as relevant for us today as it was back then. The single most important point about the story is that Siddhartha began his life as an ordinary human being the same as you and I. There was no divine intervention. There were no pre-ordained special circumstances. He arrived on this earth simply as a result of the human birth process that resulted from his parents having sex. Anything other than this plain and simple fact can only ever fall into the category of a blind belief of some kind.

Chapter Three: The Birth of the Buddha

The traditionally handed down story of the birth of the Buddha suggests he was born in a place called Lumbini, which is now situated within the borders of Nepal. As was the custom back then, his mother was making her way back to her own place of birth so the baby could be born there. En-route she went into labour and had no option but to give birth on the spot. The birth story itself (like many other stories within Buddhism) is of epic proportions and makes claims that can only be engaged with on the basis of irrational belief or blind faith, if the symbolism of them is taken to be literal.

We know for instance that there hasn't been a single credible report of a newly born human baby being able to walk by its own effort from birth. Yet here in the story we find the new born Buddha-to-be striving off in all directions. The birth itself is described as a difficult one and the baby, we are told, was born from the mothers' side and not the womb. Often, within classical Buddhism, this is pointed out to be of some higher significance. It is suggested here, that was done to support the later deification of the Buddha as a divine being and to give religious credibility to what eventually became Buddhism.

It is being suggested here that we need to explore, or at least consider other possibilities from those that are found in the traditional stories. Not out of mistrust or disrespect, but to try and find an actuality aspect to them that is based on rational and critical thinking, rather than just accepting something blindly. If we looked at this scenario on the basis of what we now know about modern birthing methods, it is possible at least, if not likely, that the difficulties that prevented the baby from being born from the womb were resolved by performing some kind of primitive caesarean section in order to save the life of the baby. We are told that the mother died a few days later. Wouldn't, or couldn't, this possibly be as a result of an infection considering the birth took place out in the open in primitive conditions and with no medical facilities? To many classical Buddhists just thinking in this way would be tantamount to Buddhist heresy.

Following the death of his mother the young Siddhartha, we are told, was raised by his aunt who later married his father. In the traditional story we find the Buddha-to-be elevated to the status of royalty and declared a prince with his father named as King. With what we now think we know of the history of this particular region and period of time, it is suggested that it is more probable that his father would have been the head of a local clan. This may well have afforded him great wealth, prestige, privilege and power, but there would have been no royal status as we understand it to be in the west. There is some suggestion that his fathers' position as head of the clan was even an elected one with no line of succession as there is with royalty.

It is suggested here that it is the wealth and privilege that is significant to the story and this provides us with another opportunity to align our own position with that story to see its relevance for us today. Within Australian culture and possibly other western cultures, no matter what our individual personal or financial circumstances, we are, materialistically speaking at least, far better off than the young Siddhartha would ever have been. We have free education and free medical care. We also have the provision of a social security safety net. In comparison with possibly the majority of the world's population, those who live within western culture are materialistically richer now and way beyond the wildest dreams of anyone 2,600 years ago.

Within the traditional story we are told that shortly after the birth of Siddhartha, his father sought the advice from some kind of apparent holy man, or prophet-come-fortune-teller. This person told the father that his new born son would either grow up to be a great ruler or a great religious leader. On the face of it, considering he would have been aware of the family history and its circumstances, he was pretty much on safe ground in making that prediction, considering they could have actually meant the same thing. Although this kind of superstitious nonsense was quite prevalent and in big demand in those days and to some extent still persists today, even within western culture, it would almost be as effective as predicting that the outcome of a pregnancy would result in a boy or a girl.

That aside, we are told that this prediction was of great concern to the father who took the decision to hide all of the unpleasant and harsh realities of life from his son and to keep him engaged in a life of perpetual pleasure. If we reflect on this part of the story, from the perspective of our own experience, we may come to the conclusion that what his father apparently attempted to do would be little different from what our parents tried to do for us, or even as parents ourselves, what we try to do with our own children. Parents, naturally it seems, want the best for their children and want to keep them free from harmful influences and maybe we might even consider that just as his fathers' decision may seem a bit over the top and reactive, we too can be a little overprotective at times.

Little is known about the early life of Siddhartha. It is likely at least that he would have been trained in the skills of war such as archery, sword-fighting, spear throwing etc as that is what the role and function of his particular clan was. He would probably have been schooled in the various customs, beliefs, superstitions and traditions of his clan. Much of what he learned would have been passed down by word of mouth, as there is no evidence to suggest that he ever learned to read and write himself and this will be of some relevance later in the story. As to any religious input, although at that time in history there were many diverse religious influences that may eventually have amalgamated to some degree into what we now call Hinduism, the prevalent religion of the day had apparently yet to travel to the area where Siddhartha grew up as a child and his clan are now understood to have been followers of a sun-worshipping sect.

When we reflect on this part of the story we can see, just as Siddhartha from an early age was conditioned by the culture of his time, so have we been by ours. Again, if he could break free from the unhelpful influences of that conditioning, then there is no reason why we can't break free from ours. He would have been educated or trained in what was considered important for him back then, just as we have been educated and trained to fulfill our expected or projected roles within our own society. In so many different respects, his early life would have matched ours with personal relationships, job, family, social network and an on-going pursuit of things that we like, whilst trying to avoid things we don't like.

There is one significant incident from his early childhood that is worth mentioning now because it becomes of important significance later on in the story. It is a recollection by the Buddha of a time when he was a very young man sitting under the shade of a tree in the hot sun, whilst his father took part in a ritualistic ploughing of the field for the sowing of the first seeds of the year. He says that he became engrossed with the slow movements of the process and found himself experiencing a deep level of concentration that he had never experienced before. It is this memory that is said to have been the influence as to why he eventually sat under the Bodhi tree at Bodh Gaya, with the resolve to bring an end to his worries. Quite unintentionally it seems the young Siddhartha had stumbled into the world of meditation.

Chapter Four: Going Forth

At about the age of 16 Siddhartha married a cousin. Although it would have been the custom for it to have been an arranged marriage, we are told, in the traditional story, that it was a very loving relationship and that they were well suited. As the story of his early life unfolds we hear that Siddhartha was spoilt rotten by his father, who indulged the boy with access to the greatest pleasures that were available at that time. It's said that he bought him three mansions in different regions of India so that he could live comfortably in the hot, cold and wet seasons. These homes, it is said, were apparently alive with dancing and singing all hours of the day and night. Servants were on hand 24/7 to attend to any of his wishes. Of course there is no actual evidence to suggest that this actually took place, but it is never in the best interests of story tellers to allow facts to get in the way of a good story.

By the age of 29 things for Siddhartha appear to have begun to take a turn for the worse. Despite all of this pleasurable experience, underlying worries began to creep into his mind. The birth and naming of his son may give us a possible indication as to the extent of that worry. Although apparently overjoyed at having a son, he chose the name '**Rahula**' for his first born. Rahula means fetter, which is something that is getting in the way, or a burden. It was, as if at this stage, he had already recognised to some degree, that he was being held back by the pursuit of pleasure.

Here he was, happily married with a young son who he loved to bits. He wanting for nothing yet he was still not happy. He couldn't, it seems, find a level of contentment that could be sustained for any length of time. He began to notice that no matter how much he enjoyed his life of pleasure, even the short-term bursts of pleasure eventually subsided and he was left sad, bored or restless. To overcome this all he knew was to engage in something pleasurable again and of course this became a bit of a vicious circle of **'pleasant'** and **'unpleasant'** experience and this caused him to worry that something was wrong. He began, for the first time to reason with himself that there must be more to life than this. He began to dwell on such things as the meaning and purpose of life.

In the traditional story we are given a series of events that symbolise, it is suggested, the worry that the young Siddhartha was going through. It is accepted here that for many classical Buddhists this appears to have been adopted as a factual series of events, but when you explore this part of the story with a critical eye it simply doesn't add up. We are told that during this period he convinced a trusted servant to take him outside of the compound in which he was living where, it is said, he was kept from seeing anything unpleasant.

On the first trip out, it is said, that he came upon, for the first time ever in his entire life, a human being in physical pain suffering from **'sickness.'** The person is described as coughing and feverish. When his servant explained that everyone at some stage in their lives suffers in this way Siddhartha was apparently overcome with worrying at the realization that his family, friends and he himself could, at any moment, experience such pain and misery with this thing called sickness.

During the second trip they met with a human who was bent double, walking with the aid of a stick, hair grey and face wrinkled. The servant explains that this is an **'aged person'** and that everyone ages. This news apparently served to add another layer of tension and worry to the mind of Siddhartha.

As they made their way out for the third time they came across a funeral procession where the **'dead body'** was carried in plain sight to the cremation grounds. When his trusted servant told him that this was a dead body and that everyone had to die, Siddhartha was apparently devastated. Within the story we are told that the combination of these three sights affected Siddhartha so deeply that he could barely think of anything else as he reflected on the very purpose and meaning of his own existence.

Although it is suggested here that this is just a symbolic story, within the context of the story just imagine what it would be like if you came across something that you never knew existed before. It's hard to imagine for us how things such as sickness, old age and death caused so much difficulty for Siddhartha because we see so much of it in our own daily lives. But try and imagine coming across something that you had never seen before for the very first time. For instance, you're walking down the road and a pig flies overhead. You never knew they could do that. You'd be really shocked wouldn't you? Although, the way we are genetically engineering almost everything these days maybe not.

In the story, this is how it is for him but much worse because the things that he apparently saw for the first time related to him, his family and friends. On the fourth journey he noticed a homeless wanderer, an apparent holy man. This was a very common sight in India, as it still is to some extent today. But for Siddhartha this was his first encounter with such a person. He was, we are told, immediately struck by the calm demeanour and the sense of stillness in the way this man went about his daily life. The ever curious Siddhartha asked the wanderer what his purpose in life was and he was told that he had given up the life of a householder to go in search for an end to the suffering of the world and within the story, we are told, that Siddhartha immediately knew that this too was to become his quest.

When we explore the story on the basis of rationality and a critical eye to try and find an aspect of actuality, it is suggested here that much of it simply does not stand up to close scrutiny. He clearly was never in total isolation so it would have been impossible to avoid noticing the ageing process all around him. He would have experienced not only his own ageing process but also how his father was much older than himself. Is it realistic to accept that in India 2,600 years ago for the entirety of his 29 years of life, Siddhartha never had a moment sickness or never noticed anyone around him being ill? Was he never told that his mother died? It is suggested here that by clinging to the literal version, instead of exploring its symbolic meaning, we actually distance ourselves from the actuality aspect that the story is trying to point out to us.

This part of the story is all about us, not him. The entire story, from birth, right up until the experience of clarity under that tree is there to show us our connection with why we worry, what we worry about and the pointless things we do to stop worrying. Its symbolism is telling us that the catalyst for change for Siddhartha was finding himself worrying about the stuff that is an essential part of being born a human being. There is an aging process, there is sickness and death and that meant that he too would age, get sick and die and so would everyone else he knew and loved. If that became the intense focus of your thoughts that would be quite depressing for anyone, which is why, for most of us, we choose to ignore these facts and hide them away somewhere. We try to keep them out of sight so we can get on with our day-to-day lives of distracting ourselves from having to face up to these issues. If we took the realistic circumstances of this story and related them to our GP today, it is likely that we would be diagnosed as suffering from clinical depression on the spot, prescribed medication and packed off to see a psychologist or therapist of some sort.

When we reflect on this part of the story with some integrity, we will see, once again, how we are connected to this story and how it is so relevant to us today. It is suggested here that at some point in our lives a huge question mark will arise in our minds, usually in the form of 'what is the purpose or meaning of life?' It may be prompted by a whole range of different things such as losing someone close to us, be that by death or the end of a relationship. We might lose our job or the house goes into negative equity or any other moment of personal crisis that makes us take a step back and take a look at the bigger picture. It may even be, for some, that niggling background worry that we can't seem to find the reason as to why we can't seem to be happy.

Where it is a bit different for us today is that we have so much more available to us to distract ourselves away from this sense of worry that arises when we experience the big questions bubbling up to the surface. Some people turn to drink or drugs to avoid the worry that is there in the mind. Others become ill and require therapy or counseling or other medical intervention. Some throw themselves into hedonistic activities or hobbies and some just become couch potatoes and watch junk T.V whilst consuming junk food at the same time.

However we may have arrived at this moment of noticing our worries it can go two ways. For some it is crunch time and can be a trigger, a catalyst for a change in direction. For others it will be a missed opportunity. Those that ignore the opportunity will try to suppress the experience, or ignore it and hope it goes away. They will seek to rationalise it or justify why they are ignoring it and will continue to go round and round in the same habitual cycles of pleasant and unpleasant experience because, it is suggested here that in the background there is some kind of **'fear of change.'** For many, it is clear that there is an apparent comfort blanket effect in clinging to what they know, even if it hurts them, rather than be prepared to step outside of that comfort zone and explore something else.

It certainly was a crunch moment for Siddhartha and for him there was a cultural tradition that was custom made to provide the opportunity to explore these questions, but it came at a price. For many, the thought of leaving our family, our friends, job or our home would be the last thing we would do and there are those today that think what Siddhartha did next was a bit of a cop out or showed a lack of responsibility. But this was quite normal in India at this time. It is clear that both his son and wife were well taken care of during his absence and they were all reunited again later on.

Fortunately for us, because of his decision to go in search of an answer to the problem of the worrying that he was experiencing, we do not have to do so. He did much of the hard work for us. As a result of his journey we now have a practical method that can be applied in our daily lives, whatever our chosen lifestyle that will help us to arrive at the same conclusion. There is now no need to put ourselves through everything that he did. Nevertheless, it is not going to be an easy journey that's for sure. We live in a very different world and have very different things to overcome, but essentially, what he communicated is that we too can arrive at this experience of clarity by our own efforts in whatever life circumstances we find ourselves in.

Having made the decision to leave home, it is said that he snuck out one night under the cover of darkness without telling his family, gave away his possessions to his servant, shaved his head and donned the rag robes of a wanderer. These two acts are known within classical Buddhism as **'going forth'** and **'renunciation.'** Again, thankfully, today in the 21st century we do not have to consider giving all our things away, nor having our heads shaved. There is not a problem with having stuff. We need a certain amount of stuff in our lives so that we can function in the everyday world. What going forth means to us is a change in direction. What renunciation means for us is to take a good hard look at our stuff on the basis of **'do we need it'** or **'do we want it.'**

It is helpful to explore what drives us to hold on to so much stuff that we no longer have a need for. This is a great practice in itself. It provides us with an ideal opportunity to be generous, perhaps by letting go of some of the stuff we have, to give it to somebody who actually needs it. What the Buddha is pointing to here is that less is actually more. The more we simplify our lives, the less worry there is. Quite a lot of that worry we experience is as a result of being attached to something, or even someone in some cases. Lurking behind that attachment to stuff is a fear that we might need it later on, so we'd better keep it just in case.

That's why there are three pairs of jeans hanging in the wardrobe that you wouldn't be able to get into until you have had lap band surgery. You know this. You just can't let go. Every time you see those jeans hanging there on the rail up pops a worry, "**I really should lose some weight so I can wear those jeans**". Not a helpful thought like, "**I should lose some weight because it might be healthier for me or it might prolong my life,**" but a worrying thought that I'm experiencing guilt because I've spent all that money on something I can't use, or convince myself to give away.

I began making plans to move to Australia way back in 1998 following an initial trip to visit my younger brother. To facilitate this I sold my five bedroom house and moved into a one bedroom flat in London to raise the funds to build, in advance, what I planned to be a meditation retreat centre in a rural bush setting. Transferring the contents of a five bedroom house into a one bedroom flat meant that for over five years the garage under the house was stacked from floor to ceiling with boxes and boxes of stuff. Stuff that I had no use for in that entire period. When it came to move to Australia, at great expense, all of those boxes of stuff were transported by sea container and sat there awaiting my arrival. When I arrived in early 2006 and began the unpacking it became clear that I did not need any of this stuff that had been packed away for over five years. I had just kept hold of it because there was an attachment to an idea of '**just in case.**'

To deal with this my wife and I spent the next few weeks attending a weekly swap meet/boot sale and tried to literally give it all away for free. In three weeks we had not managed to shift a thing and the bay was actually costing us $10 each time. Finally, an Australian woman took pity on us and told us that nobody would take it for free and that we would need to put a price on it. So, we duly labeled up everything at the most absurd low prices. We were swamped with offers and here's the thing. The moment we put a price on it, even though it was a ridiculously low price nobody would buy it unless they knocked us down by half. What an amazing opportunity to explore attachment generosity and greed all wrapped up in the one experience.

This clinging or attachment can be even more worrying when it comes to personal relationships. It's said that when a man enters a new relationship he subconsciously thinks that the women is never going to change and of course she does. So, he worries because he got it wrong and now has to live with the consequences. On the other hand, it's said that when a women enters a new relationship she subconsciously wants the man to change and of course he doesn't. She starts to worry also because she got it wrong and has to live with the consequences.

If you add into this mix society's pressure to conform to the expected norm of long-term relationships, children, financial stability etc is it no wonder that just being in a relationship that is based on an attachment to the ideal of the perfect partnership just doubles the amount of worries? That's not to say that healthy long-term relationships don't exist. Of course they do, but just like the Dharma journey they are an on-going work in progress. A process that is based on mutual respect for each others individuality amongst other things.

So, we find that the young Siddhartha has gone forth and become a homeless wanderer. If we reflect on this part of the story from the perspective of our own lives, we come to the spot where culturally biased classical Buddhism tells us that we can go no further unless we go forth in the same way that Siddhartha did. In Theravadanism, which is one of the earliest forms of Buddhism that still exists, we have two choices: we can become a monk, or nun (if that is allowed in that particular country and the majority don't) and work towards our own experience of clarity, or we can remain a householder, a lay practitioner, whose primary role is to support the monks/nuns and thereby earn merits towards a more fruitful and promised apparent future life for ourselves.

Within that form of Buddhism there is so much cultural baggage that has been accrued over the years that it is hard to find anything much that is of practical use to our western society, other than the Dharma teachings themselves. In many cases, even those have been often misrepresented as a means of controlling the local population and to keep the institutions alive. The same can be said about Zenism and Tibetanism, the latter having possibly the greatest inclusion of local cultural traditions and customs within their teachings and many that appear never to have been taught by the Buddha at all.

Thankfully, once we have put to one side all of the institutional and conventional pressure to conform to what each school believes is the only truly authentic version of Buddhism, we can perhaps understand why, as westerners, we need to go beyond classical Buddhism, so that we can engage fully with the Dharma from within our own culture. In doing so, it is important to develop and retain a sense of immense gratitude:

1. To Siddhartha for doing the groundwork and pointing us all in the most helpful direction
2. To all of the Dharma practitioners, of the various schools, who, over the past 2,600 years, have kept his communication alive

Because of their work, secular western Buddhists can now benefit from the entire teaching body, but are able to separate the actuality of the Dharma from cultural influences and therefore utilise the teachings within the context of our own western conditioning as a means of reducing our worries or eradicating them altogether.

It's always helpful to keep reminding ourselves that this is what Buddhism is all about and nothing else. The Buddha was not interested in worrying himself over the big questions of life such as how did the universe start and how does it work, is there a creator entity or what happens after death. He just wanted to understand why he worried, what caused him to worry and if there was a way to stop worrying.

For Buddhists today, going forth takes many different forms. There are those who choose to live a full or partial monastic life and those who ordain outside of the monastic system. Some of those will choose to live within Buddhist communities or within family units. Fundamental to all those options is a willingness to change. There is a willingness to leave something of our old self behind us so that we can make progress on the journey. Perhaps within our own lives we may have experienced some resistance from friends and family members when we tell them we are taking an interest in Buddhism. This is quite normal. It's amazing what strange ideas are out there about what a Buddhist is. Being a Buddhist is about change and human beings don't like change. It brings up far too many worries for them. They'll be wondering about things like if you have to have your head shaved, or are they going to have to watch their P & Q's when they are around you? They will wonder if you're going to get all holy and precious or run off to a monastery. The list is endless. It's OK. That is quite normal. It's called fear of change.

For the next six years he lived as a wandering beggar. During this time he met and aligned himself with all of the apparent holy men or apparent spiritual masters of his day on his travels. One thing to bear in mind here is that there were many such people doing this kind of thing at this time and all seemed to have their own band of followers and devotees. We are told that he was an enthusiastic and ardent student, who tested and challenged everything to the max and was often invited to join various communities as an equal to the teacher. He declined all invitations because, although he gained a great deal from everything he was being taught, he found that the answer he was looking for, which was the cause of worry and how it could be ended was never answered by them. With each new method, doctrine or technique, he found that even when he pursued it fully with 100% integrity it always fell short in one way or another.

Having done the rounds and tried everything that was on offer, he turned to taking up austere practices that included almost starving himself to death or subjecting himself to extreme physical pain. Back then and even today in India there was and is some very weird stuff going on. The range of bizarre and crazy looking practices engaged with by those who think they are on some kind of apparent spiritual quest is amazing. There is histori- cal data that suggests these may well have included things such as emulating a cow, chewing grass and mooing. He might have been found hanging upside down from a tree, emulating a fruit bat. He might have wandered naked, covered from head to toe in smelly mud. Others spend years standing on one leg or with one arm raised in the air. All of these behaviours and more were being practiced in India at this time. Two of the most popular practices were self torture and starvation and, according to the story, he surpassed everybody in his dedication to these practices.

This part of Siddhartha's story mirrors that of so many apparent or would be Buddhists in the west today. However, there is a significant difference. Whereas Siddhartha moved on because he had learned all there was to learn from a particular teacher, today, many students move from teacher to teacher to bolster their own sense of importance. For many, things such as credible lineages and celebrity status are now more important in a teacher than what they are teaching. The slightest challenge to the fixed beliefs that are held sacred by the seeker is enough to send the students off in search of another teacher who will tell them what they want to hear, rather than what is helpful to know. Of course in our western world of non-acceptance of personal responsibilities and with our tendency to point the finger of blame elsewhere, it will always be the teacher's fault and not the student's.

Some of the most insightful and realized Dharma communicators throughout history have been abandoned by their students because they were not seen as perfect human beings. When the teacher is seen as not perfect then the student worries what people might think of them if they hang around with this imperfect teacher. So off they go in search of the perfect teacher because it is their self-biased mind that has been hurt. Others would rather just cling to a teacher who smiles, says all the right things that you want to hear, but can only recite from a book or a text and appears to know everything. And all the while these crazy games get played out because the student has yet to realize that it is nothing to do with the teacher. All a teacher does, if they have any real value, is point in a particular direction. They are rarely, if ever, infallible.

When we reflect on this part of the story, perhaps we can recognise something of ourselves in it. How many times have we dabbled in a never ending range of activities that promised us the happiness we sought? Perhaps we too have tried mainstream theistic religion in its various shades, fortune telling, astrology, psychics, stone therapy tantric sex or colonic irrigation. What fortunes have we spent on self-help books or the latest DVD by our never ending range of celebrity gurus? How often have we apparently been healed by crystals, reiki, gongs, mantras or prayers only to find that we are quickly back at square one? How many different meditation practices have we tried and decided that they didn't work after a couple of sessions?

How many apparent teachers have we found and dismissed because they did not match our expectations or projections, or as is usually the case, because we didn't like them or what they had to say? Are we inclined to try out anything or anyone new that comes onto the market? It's really helpful to be honest with ourselves about this because this kind of thing is exactly what Siddhartha was doing for six years and it got him nowhere. There is a massive message within this part of the story for us if we take a good look at it and learn to laugh at ourselves.

This is the world of the perpetual seeker, always on the look out for the next thing out there that will bring them peace of mind no matter what the cost. People pay a fortune for all this stuff. Yet, if you offer them something that has been tried and tested for over 2,600 years and shown, beyond reasonable doubt, to actually work they seem to see little value. Why? Because with these other things, someone else is promising to do the work for you, promising to heal you, promising to make your troubles go away, but they never do, do they? As soon as that short-term flush of pleasure fades, up pops the same worries and you're back at square one.

Life back in India over 2,600 years ago was very different to life in Australia in the 21st century or any other western nation. The big three worries of sickness, ageing and death haven't changed, but the day-to-day worries for people have increased dramatically and continue to increase as the pace and pressures of modern living gets ever faster and takes a heavy toll on the minds of those living within western countries. This culture of materialism and consumerism, which fuels our search for perpetual pleasure, immediate gratification and short-term satisfaction, is destroying us and the planet. This is why, it is suggested, that the teachings of the Buddha are more relevant now than at any other time in history. It's because they provide a practical, sensible, common sense way of living that leads to the peace of mind that we all search for. It starts with our mind. It starts with us. We cannot save the world or change any other being on the planet, but the choices we make can effect and influence others and the world around us.

According to the Buddha all things that are physical, emotional, psychological or a combination of those things will change. No thing ever stays the same. Human beings are themselves an ongoing process of conditioned change. We are an amalgamation of blibs and blobs that, due to preceding causes and conditions, ended up as 'us.' However, because we have this thing we call mind to contend with, we have to actually do something, to make changes to our lifestyle, if we are to take advantage of our

43

potential to realize peace of mind. Some things about us will change automatically. We will grow old, we will get sick and we will die and there is nothing we can do about it. We can swap a few body parts, dye our hair, inject poisons into our face, eat nothing but muesli and manipulate our bodies into all manner of weird and whacky positions, but there is no way we can avoid the big three.

The moment that you accept that fact, as it is, without fearing it, you actually give yourself your first real opportunity to experience a taste of peace of mind. All the while you resist it, because you fear it, you will continue to worry. That is why this is called a journey. It is a gradual process. You have to make the journey. You have to live it. Nobody can do it for you. For the most part though, we will live our lives in denial of actuality, on auto pilot, repeating familiar behaviour patterns that have been formed as part of our on-going conditioning process.

Siddhartha's motivation for making such a change was the realization that he was worrying about not experiencing peace of mind. If we reflect on this from our own perspective we will see that we are no different from Siddhartha in this respect. We do have moments of great happiness, joy and a sense of satisfaction but these experiences are equally matched by periods of unhappiness, sadness and dissatisfaction. It is as if we live our lives on a see-saw, going up and down, up and down, when what we really seek is to find a balance that lets us sit in the middle at rest.

Chapter Five: Worrying

Worrying is found in this thing we call mind. It's where all of our problems are processed and troubling thoughts arise. This in turn causes us and others harm, when we talk or do things on the basis of that worrying mind. So, what is this worrying all about? What do we mean when we use the word worry, worries or worrying here? To explore that, it is helpful to create a definition or an understanding of what we mean by it, so we can all be on the same page. People tend to create their own definitions and understandings of words that are quite often very different from each other and certainly not ones that align with dictionary definitions. The traditional Buddhist word for this experience is dukkha.

But that doesn't really help us here in Australia. Dukkha is the name that is given to a product that is crushed nuts that you dip pieces of bread laced with olive oil and balsamic vinegar into. Now, whilst I'd be the first to accept that the severe pain of crushed nuts would be a bit of a worry for the male of the species, we do need to find a more useful definition of what a worry is, if we are all going to understand fully what it is and more importantly, how we can deal with it.

Imagine one of those lottery machines that have lots of numbered balls inside. You begin by erasing the numbers from the balls and replacing them with words that are helpful in defining what worry or worrying is. You could write suffering, dissatisfaction, anxiety, angst, pain, un-satisfactoriness, emptiness, boredom, malaise, grief, stress, depression, pain, discomfort, fear etc. In fact you could write down almost any word that represents to you an unpleasant physical sensation, an unpleasant emotional reaction, or unpleasant thought experience. It could be any word that describes what it is you are experiencing when the mind does not seem to be at peace with itself, others and the world around it.

Once you have done that, in your imagination you switch the machine on and the balls begin to bounce up and down and crash into each other. The only difference here is that once one ball comes into contact with another, it joins together to form a larger ball, and so on until all you are left with is just one huge ball and on that ball is the word 'worry.'

Underneath the word worry we find a simple sentence that is possibly the most helpful phrase to fully understand what worrying is all about. It reads, **"I want my current experience to be different to what it currently is"**. By adopting this understanding of what a worry is, we can recognise it in a practical way so that it can be dealt with effectively in our everyday lives. If we look at the bare state of any unpleasant experience, assigning no blame or guilt, we will find that what we really want is for the experience to be different than it is. This is us worrying.

Worrying arises in three different ways. Its causes are either physical, emotional or psychological. At any given moment of our existence all three of these experiences are present simultaneously. Physical experience is always present because we are subject to the laws of gravity and therefore a physical part of us is always in contact with something else and we can become aware of a physical sensation. Emotional experience is always present because we are continually reacting or responding to things that are experienced by the five senses of sight, sound, taste, touch and smell.

These experiences are then processed by this thing that we call the mind so we can make sense of them. Without us being aware most of the time, there will be a judgment within the pre-conscious aspect of being that the experience is pleasant, un-pleasant or neutral. Neutrality is quite rare and even when it is present, it doesn't stay long as it very quickly turns to a 'want' to make the experience into something pleasurable. Whatever the current experience is, it will bring forth a physical, emotional and psychological reaction or response that arises in the most part from our subconscious. This is our conditioned, habitual behaviour kicking in. The mind process or the psychological aspect of us, which includes thoughts and the activities of the physical brain, are working 24/7 both consciously and subconsciously.

Worrying has three distinctive elements. The first type of worrying arises in response to our on-going, moment by moment, physical, emotional and psychological experience in our everyday lives. This is the kind of generalised worrying that we think we have to put up with because we can't find that peace of mind that we so desperately want. The second type of worrying is hidden, just under the surface of that general worrying and is an aspect of actuality that we are possibly unaware of to any great extent. This is because it can only be fully understood when the self-biased aspect of the mind is either suspended or eliminated, usually during the meditative process.

Having said that, we have to start where we are at and that is with an intellectual understanding at least. This hidden fact behind some of our worrying is the actuality that all conditioned things are impermanent. Every thing is subject to change. Even when we are in the happiest state of mind we think possible, it has an inbuilt element of worry because it is impermanent. When that moment of happiness ends, as it must, it can only be replaced with a degree of unhappiness and we start to worry again because we have lost the happiness and we want it back. Even the most blissful states in meditation contain within them an element of worry because they are not permanent.

The third type of worrying is hidden, even deeper than the actuality of impermanence and is the actuality of no-thing-ness. This aspect of actuality can drive you crazy, even when you tackle it with the intellectual mind. So, for now, we'll leave it alone and deal with it in depth later in the book. There is very little point in getting weighed down in all the heavy duty, mind-boggling stuff until you have at least got enough tools in the bag to tackle the job. Of course to do any repair job properly, you also need to study the manual. The problem here is worrying and the manual is the teachings of the Buddha.

Worrying as we shall find later, is an essential component of human life. So although we call it a problem, it is actually quite normal. If you're one of those people who have got this far into the book and are thinking to yourself **"It's OK I don't worry,"** then I suggest you read on. I'm sure that along the way you might find a few tips that will be helpful, otherwise you'll only start worrying that you're not worrying enough and begin thinking that you're being left out, which is a worry in itself.

This is quite normal. That's what we do. That's what all self-biased minds do, whether they want to admit that to themselves or not. We worry about things all the time. It could be said that we're not happy unless we're worrying, because if we ever stopped worrying, we'd be worried that we had stopped worrying. That's how normal this worrying thing is. We're not doing anything wrong by worrying. We have no concept of the notion of sin in secular western Buddhism. We also recognise that guilt is possibly one of the most unhelpful emotional states you could ever engage in. It does nothing but cause more worrying and needs to be avoided at all costs as it's like trying to swim with a pair of concrete boots on your feet.

Chapter Six: Awakening

The second major turning point for Siddhartha was again as a result of a crisis point. He had been such an extremist it took him to the brink of death before he finally acknowledged that he was worrying more than he ever had. In effect, he had more or less just wasted six years of his life, as he was further now from his original intent than he ever was. The crazy thing is that the more he put himself through different levels of pain and degradation, the more people began to follow and admire him. The reason for this, (and very little has changed) is people want someone else to do it for them. They think that if someone else can do all the work somehow it might rub off if they hang around with them. So many Buddhists still fail to understand the significance of the picture of the finger pointing towards the moon.

This cannot be repeated often enough. It is not, and never will be about the teacher. The teacher only points you in the direction of clarity and offers the Dharma journey as your guide. The rest is up to you. It is often said within Buddhism that the most authentic and helpful teacher you will ever have is the one that you have the most serious problems with. The Dharma journey is about you resolving your issues, not the ones that you perceive that they have.

Having experienced and exhausted the two extremes of behaviour, namely living a full-on hedonistic life of endless pleasure and the other extreme of austerity, he realized that it had got him nowhere closer to the answer he was seeking. It gave rise to the idea that there must be a middle way. This middle way idea came to be very prominent throughout his communications. He decided that if he was going to continue to search for an answer to the problems of worrying and how to end it, he had no option but to start eating regularly again, so he could rebuild his strength. This decision did not sit well with his companions, who took the view that he had gone soft and given up and so they abandoned him.

This episode highlights a situation that continues to this day. People attach themselves to a particular teacher and even if they gain immense benefit from what they are being taught, they are prepared to throw it all away if the teacher does or says anything that bursts the bubble of specialness that they have created around them and projected onto them. The thing that is never understood is that it is part of the teacher's job to burst those bubbles, just as the bubbles were burst for them by their teachers. The bursting of a bubble is a gift, not an imposition. It gives you the freedom to take the next step on the journey.

It was inevitable that these kinds of reactions would occur when the teachers who brought the Dharma to the western world began to detach from culturally biased and institutionalised Buddhism. It is very clear that the western understanding of Buddhism has been seriously conditioned by the cultural and institutional worlds of classical Buddhism, who have no intention of rocking the status quo. The average Buddhist monk is automatically accorded the same level of respect that we would give to a vicar or a priest within our own culture because that is what we have been conditioned to do.

Although we have come to recognise the failings of our own apparent spiritual leaders as they continue to fall from grace with one apparent scandal after another, we still project far too much onto those with grandiose titles within the Buddhist world. Many of whom, it is sad to say, are also caught up in similar unhelpful behaviour worldwide. The Buddha never taught that there should be a hierarchal structure, but pointed to the individuality of Dharma practice. Even at the point of death he refused to name a successor, despite there being others who had also apparently realized clarity within his group of followers. If we blindly follow the instructions of the teacher, without testing the actuality of his words for ourselves, then we have once again attached ourselves to the finger and not the moon and we are no different to the Buddha's companions who abandoned him.

Siddhartha found himself alone again. It was now six years since he had left his home. The motivation to find the answer that he had been seeking was as strong as ever. He had tried all the usual apparent spiritual or religious practices, plus many of his own conceptions to no avail. But he was not about to abandon the search. It was, as if he had realized the futility of being a perpetual seeker that continues to seek an answer in anything, or anybody that is external to his own mind. After all, that was where the worrying was taking place. In effect, what he had been doing for the last six years was searching for something that he had never lost. How fortunate are we that he finally worked that out.

He stopped to rest in the shade of a large fig tree, which was situated on the bank of a river. The name of this place was Bodh Gaya and it is now the major destination for Buddhist pilgrims from all over the world. It is within the state of Bihar in Northern India. It was here he recalled that memory from his childhood about his father, the plough and the state of concentration he entered into. This sets the scene for an epic battle with this thing we call the mind. Everything he had ever learned, all of the intellectual knowledge he had ever amassed, all his beliefs, views and opinions were going to be released, so he could enter into a state of meditative concentration that would lead to irreversible insight into the nature of actuality that would reveal why he worried and how he could stop worrying.

It is said, within the legendary account that it was at this stage that he made a vow to himself that he would remain on this spot until such time as he found the answer that he was seeking. No indication has been given as to the amount of time that passed between his making the decision and the realization of clarity. He could have been there just a few hours. Of course, if we are going to build the awakening experience into something magical and mystical in the way it is portrayed in the story, then we could be led to believe he sat there for days, weeks or months.

The fact is, it doesn't really matter. The experience itself would have been outside of our conditioned understanding of the concepts of time and space. Symbolically at least, it could be said, that the actual time factor is based directly on the amount of effort made. It seems evident from the story that he was supported with food from a nearby farm and given fresh grass to sit on by a grass cutter. We know scientifically he would have needed to urinate and sleep etc, so he retained some contact with the outside world during this period, however long it lasted.

Over the course of 2,600 years the experience of clarity has, it is suggested here, been over complicated. It has been over complicated to the point where the institutions of classical Buddhism have created an unattainable state of being that appears to be out of reach to anyone except the self-created, apparent spiritual elite within the institutions and often not even them. This goes totally against what the Buddha communicated within his teachings and the symbolism of his own life story. Although the lead up to this breakthrough realization experience will be different for each person, the end result will always be the same. It is simply a different vantage point. It will be a different way of knowing and understanding the nature of actuality and will lessen or eradicate our worries so we can live a full and active life with a greater level of contentment with the way things are.

Siddhartha's breakthrough came during a period of meditation. But let's be clear that it was just the breakthrough moment. It didn't end there. The actualization of that experience was an ongoing process and this becomes clear when we see how his communication developed over his lifetime. He was still physically subject to ageing, sickness and death. If he stubbed his toe on a tree stump he would have experienced physical sensations that would be painful. Maybe he wouldn't have been inclined to run around, hopping and swearing, but to pretend that somehow because of this experience he would float over the tree stump or not experience the consequences is bordering on the ridiculous. It could be said that the breakthrough was a change in direction. It moved him away from reacting against everyday experiences to responding to them in a way that was helpful. Because of the nature of the insight what was always helpful would be compassion.

From the moment he sat down, it was all about meditation. No tinkly tinkly music playing in the background, no pan pipes, no sounds of dolphins singing. There was nobody talking him through a journey or down the garden path. No banging gongs for him to tune into, no chanting of secret mantras. There were neither amazingly detailed images with which he could entertain himself, nor was he lying on his back with his knees raised and his head supported by a soft cushion. He was seated in an upright position, his spine straight, his legs folded to create a stable base. He was ready to do battle with his conditioned and confused self-biased mind.

The legendary account of this plays out as some kind of cosmic drama in 3D technicolour and Dolby surround sound and moves in the direction of creating a mythical fantasy. Many within cultural Buddhism do still accept it as a literal account, but in actuality what was happening, as any experienced meditator will know, was that he had begun to do battle with the self-biased mind of the separate ego-personality. There is much to reflect on and understand within the story, but again, it would be more helpful for us to look at the symbolic nature of the story as it unfolds. It would be fair to assume that in normal everyday circumstances, to do battle, we would first need an opponent. In this case, it was given the name **'Mara,'** often referred to in classical Buddhist books as **'The Evil One.'** This, in turn, whets our appetite for the obligatory fight between good and evil which is such a strong part of our conditioning. If we accept this rationale it will lead us in an unhelpful direction. Those who have dabbled in the world of meditation will know from their own experience that the only battles going on are the ones raging in their own minds.

According to legend, as Siddhartha sat in meditation he was surrounded by all manner of hideous creatures. Many were armed with grotesque weapons and were intent on doing him mortal harm. Some were breathing flames like the mythical dragons of medieval times. Siddhartha is reported to have been stoned and by that, I don't mean being out of his head on wacky backy. In some versions, these monsters were throwing entire mountain ranges at him. They threw spears and fired flaming arrows at him. And all the while, Mara was seen standing on the sideline, like a world war one general, directing operations from the safety of the tea tent. Meanwhile, Siddhartha simply remained seated, surrounded by the golden light of serenity, blissfully unaware of what was occurring as the various missiles turned to flowers as they came in contact with his aura, and fell to the floor.

If we reflect on this part of the story and our own experience of meditating, we may recall that the first thing that we had to contend with, after finding a comfortable sitting position, was to face up to the unhelpful parts of ourselves and the guilt that arose in connection with that. Guilt and lack of self-worth are such a huge part of western conditioning. Perhaps we can see now the important link between ethical conduct and meditation. If our thoughts, words and actions are based on kindness, generosity and compassion, it is going to be easier to settle down into concentrated meditation as less of the dark and disturbing stuff arises to distract us. Like Siddhartha, we can sit unaffected by it.

Having failed at the first attempt, Mara sent in reinforcements in the shape of his three daughters who danced seductively around Siddhartha, only to be ignored. If we look to our own meditation experience perhaps we will recall times of wanting to drift off into the world of fantasy, sexual or otherwise. Within the story, nothing Mara does can distract Siddhartha, and eventually he gives up and lets Siddhartha continue with his meditation. You might have discovered already that in meditation when we don't engage with something, it soon moves on.

Anyone who has taken up meditation practice, at any level, and with any consistency will know from their own experience, that the battle to be won is with their own self-biased mind. That is our own personal Mara. It will intercede and try and distract us in many ways, pleasant, unpleasant and neutral. This thing we call mind does not want to be tamed and it will fight for its survival and supremacy. In an ancient Buddhist text it says words to the effect:

"Though one may conquer in battle, a thousand men, a thousand times, he who conquers himself has the more glorious victory".

That sums up what Mara is all about.

As each level of meditative concentration arises there are new experiences to contend with and work through. This process is one in which the pre-conscious, biological, nature aspect of being and the subconscious, psychological, nurture aspects of being begin to integrate into conscious awareness. This is clear thought that is unobstructed by the self-biased mind. It begins at a point in the meditative process that follows a period of thought-less-ness that some refer to as bliss. This can be very misleading for meditators who have yet to work out the difference between thought-less-ness and a loss of attention that can happen when the mind has moved into a relaxed state. We will be exploring the meditative process in depth in a later chapter.

Having defeated Mara, the way was clear for Siddhartha to enter into ever deepening states of concentration. One of the biggest dangers in reading too much about these states is that it can often influence you to try and align your experience with that of the author or the third party under discussion, instead of relying on your own findings. Practically speaking, you will find that a sustained meditation practice will eventually lead to deeper levels of concentration, and when sufficient effort has been made, insight will automatically start to bubble up.

The word **"insight"** is another of those problematic Buddhist words. Over time, it has been used to indicate an experience of unique or special character. But the use of the word often does little but bolster the ego-pride of the individual who is being discussed. In essence, it means seeing through to the actuality of something. It's that moment when the light bulb switches on in the head or the penny drops. It's that little a-ha moment. Something suddenly makes sense for the first time. We get it! It is suggested here that these insightful experiences happen far more often than we are led to believe, and when it happens, in that moment of direct discovery, there is no aspect of faith or belief involved. This kind of low level, insightful experience can happen any time, any place, anywhere and is not directly related to meditation practice or even Buddhism. Even within the world of meditation this level of insightful experience does not remain for long. Because of the conditioned nature of our minds we seek to label the experience, give it meaning and then add it to our set of core beliefs.

Insightful experience brings forth change. Whatever the experience, it will move us forward. As we develop deeper states of concentration in meditation, the insightful experiences will become more frequent, stronger and they will last longer before we return to perhaps a slightly weakened version of our old behaviour patterns and conditioned reactions.

Quite often the very thing that is stopping our progress is our want for success. Even the want for awakening, which is often referred to within classical Buddhism as a helpful want, is actually quite the opposite. It is unhelpful because it arises in the self-biased mind and that will always get in the way. In many books you will read that Siddhartha achieved or gained awakening. This terminology leads us to believe that there is something to be gained, when something is actually lost. It is helpful to lose the false beliefs that our self-biased mind holds on to.

The realization of clarity has, it is suggested here, been blown out of all proportion over time. It has been replaced, by intellectualism and institutionalised protectionism. In texts recorded up to five hundred years after the death of the Buddha, it is stated that even during his lifetime, many of his followers realized clarity. It didn't seem that difficult back then. The excuse given for the present day lack of clarity is that there were fewer distractions around in the Buddha's days, compared to the modern day practitioner who has so much more in their busy lives to divert their attention.

There seems to be so many flaws to this point of view. If you take into account the large numbers of individuals who have reportedly turned their backs on the modern world to live as monastics, then where are all these awakened monks? If clarity was realized as a result of meditation, is it not possible to meditate anytime, anywhere, or any place? That is not to say that creating helpful conditions is not important, but realistically if it was meditation that triggered the experience of clarity then it follows that it can be realized outside of a controlled environment or any particular choice of lifestyle.

There are two factors to reflect on when we are considering the realization of clarity. The first is that we have been conditioned to believe that we need to replicate all aspects of the historical Buddha to realize clarity. How on earth are we ever going to replicate the perfection of the Buddha as he is portrayed in literature and in classical Buddhism? When we read the accounts of the Buddha's life, we are told that he never got angry, never experienced pain and was perfect in every way, after he realized clarity. Could this be why we struggle to identify or recognise the awakened mind these days? We compare likely candidates to this unrealistic model that has been created. The second factor to consider is that the institutions of culturally biased classical Buddhism cannot survive without the creation and the protection of a hierarchical structure, but that was never a part of what the Buddha taught.

It is suggested here that when the Dharma was turned into a religious belief system, which was to be overseen by the apparent spiritual elite, the essence of the Dharma as a living, organic method of transformation for every individual, was lost, in favour of the broader purpose of building and supporting the various religious institutions of classical Buddhism. In this respect, Buddhism has much in common with theistic religions. Just as Christians await the return of Jesus Christ for their salvation, so too do many Buddhists, who await the arrival of the future Buddha Matreya for theirs. Christians are guaranteed a place in heaven and eternal life and Buddhists are promised a favourable new life, depending on how much merit they have accrued in this life. In both these and other belief systems, you have no option, but to rely on a third party negotiator, who, by virtue of his learned status, will always be closer to the creator entity or clarity than you are.

Why on earth would he make so much effort to break free from one religion just to create another? If he wanted to create a Buddhist hierarchical empire why did he refuse to name a successor? The Dharma is about liberation not subjugation, which is such a strong feature of mainstream theistic religion and also, sad to say, religious Buddhism. The Dharma he taught was simple. It had to be. In the main he was not teaching to the educationally elite. The vast majority of his followers would have been poor and uneducated. That was what India was like at that time. We really do have to put the experience of clarity into its plausible context if we are to stand any opportunity of realizing it.

Early Buddhism created and promoted the idea that after realization, the Buddha became so perfect that he did not experience any worries. They also cloaked the experience of clarity in mystery and intrigue far beyond that which can be achieved by any human being and so the very essence of the Buddha's teaching is lost. Once again, as in other systems, it becomes all about the teacher and not what he taught.

The insight that was realized in that breakthrough moment of clarity is the basis of everything that the Buddha ever communicated. It is vital to remember that all he was concerned about was understanding why he couldn't find lasting satisfaction with anything and why he was worried as a result. He was concerned with finding out what caused him to worry and he was seeking to find a way to stop that worrying. That was his single goal throughout his journey, from the moment he left home until he sat under that tree.

So, what was this experience of clarity all about? What was realized? How did this realization experience of clarity end the

Buddha's worries? It's said within Buddhism that there are something like 84,000 teachings of the Buddha. Each and every one of them points back to this one experience on which the entire Dharma journey points towards. In essence there is only one teaching. Crack this one and peace of mind is realized. Quite often, even today, on archaeological digs all over the Buddhist world artifacts are discovered with a variation in wording that point to this source realization. One of the most common is this: '

'Those things conditionally arisen, the realized one has told their cause and the ceasing of them too.'

The source teaching of Buddhism is known as Paticca-samuppada in the Pali language and Pratītyasamutpāda in Sanskrit. It has been translated or interpreted to mean dependent arising, dependent origination, conditioned existence, conditioned co-production, conditionality, or, as it will be referred to in this book as **'conditioned causal continuity that is no-thing-ness'** and for ease of reference **'causality.'**

It is suggest that this interpretation, although wordy, can be more helpful as it sets out all three aspects of the experience in its totality and can be broken down into three smaller parts to make it a bit easier to get to grips with. It then gives a term that lies at the centre of the experience itself. This is, after all, us making our best effort to unpack an experience rather than being stuck on language. When we first engage with this source realization of the Dharma it seems to make some sense on an intellectual level. Things arise on conditions and cease again when their conditions cease. But when we begin to explore its implications, we will eventually be dumbfounded, or at least confused by its complexity. This is because the complexity of this source realization goes beyond the capabilities of the confused self-biased mind, but it is one that has to be tackled if we are to realize peace of mind and bring our worries to an end.

In the story of the Buddha we are told that he sat with this experience for some time after its realization, trying to decide if he was capable of communicating it to others, such was its complexity. A direct consequence of the experience itself was the expression of infinite compassion for all beings that motivated him to find a solution to the communication problem.

From this moment on everything the Buddha ever taught and everything that was later expanded upon by others and will continue to be expanded upon with each new generation of Dharma communicators, can be traced back to this single moment of realization of the way things are in actuality. The substance of this realization is the filter for everything we explore on the Dharma journey. When we begin to explore the full range of teachings of the Buddha, at times we may lose sight of the source realization, so it is imperative that we keep bringing it to mind to remind ourselves that it is central and takes precedence over everything else he ever taught. It appears throughout Buddhist texts and is communicated in a range of different formulations and we simply can't get enough of it if we are to realize clarity for ourselves.

The Buddha was not a mystic. Neither was he a divine being. The experience of clarity was not a shattering revelation that revealed to him some esoteric knowledge of how the universe ticks. He talks about it in terms of a freedom of heart and mind from the compulsions of wanting things to be different than they are. He awoke to the immediacy of experience in the transitory flow of current experience. He did not present himself as a saviour of the world or a religious leader worthy of veneration and worship.

In an early text, we find the story of the Buddha meeting with a religious wanderer who challenges the Buddha with a question about knowing the past, after being disappointed with the answers of a number of other well-known apparent spiritual teachers. The Buddha is reported as saying, words to the effect:

"Let the past be, let the future be. I will teach you the Dharma: this being, that becomes; from the arising of this, that arises. This not being, that does not become; from the ceasing of this, that ceases."

We can see from this story two things. The Buddha is encouraging the wanderer to be aware of the present moment experience only. To notice how it comes into being as a result of causality and also that it is more valuable to understand or realize this than to spend time comparing teachers. Sometimes the traditional formula can be quite hard to get to grips with so if we were to try and put it into a modern context, what it is saying is, that every thing that exists has come into existence as a result of preceding causes and conditions and at any point when those causes and conditions end the thing that depends on them will also end.

Immediately this throws up one very big question. What is a thing? A thing is any physical matter, any emotional experience or psychological thought process or a combination of those things. One of the most helpful exercises is to try and find a thing that does not fit into one or more or a combination of all three of those categories. Many have tried and as far as I am aware all have apparently failed. When you work on it yourself it tends to boost a level of trust, so it is recommend you give it your best shot. It is saying that no thing can come into existence independently and of its own making.

This is probably going to sound a bit frustrating but the Buddha points out, that although the formula of causality might seem relatively simple, it is actually beyond the intellect or reason and cannot adequately be expressed in either words or concepts. It is purely experiential, a direct seeing and knowing of the way things are in actuality. Despite this, it still remains our entry point onto the Dharma journey. This source realization will be explored in depth in later chapters of the book in relation to the many and varied ways in which it was communicated. For now, I will give a brief overview to help us move forward to a stage where we will be ready to get into it at some depth later.

The first component part of actuality that the Buddha points out is that all things are conditioned. This means that for any thing to exist right now there must have been some thing that preceded it that gave rise to its existence. To be conditioned also means that for any thing to continue to exist it can only do so if it is supported by its current conditions. Here is another different version of the formula that you might find helpful:

"When there is this, then that arises. When there is not this then that does not come to be. When this comes to an end, then that ceases to be."

Within this first component of actuality it is also helpful to note that no first cause or condition or end effect of any thing can ever be found.

The second component of actuality that the Buddha points out is that all conditioned things that are experienced are in a constant process of change. Physical, emotional and psychological experiences are never stationary and are forever in motion. No conditioned thing can ever be permanent. That is the actuality, but of course, that is not what this thing we call mind is telling us. It is telling us that there is some degree of fixed-ness or permanence and as a result we cling to, or become attached, to personal beliefs or individual truths that we then need to defend. We find ourselves taking everything personally because we cannot see those subtle changes in progress. As you are reading this book, if you take a look around you, you can't see that everything is changing, including you. But in each moment bits of you are flaking off onto the floor and if you're at home, maybe the next time the carpet is cleaned, bits of you will disappear up the nozzle of the vacuum cleaner. Even the carpet will be in a constant process of change, wearing out with each contact with a human foot or piece of furniture and once it ends up in landfill or incinerated, its component parts just continue in some other form.

This second component of actuality has the strongest connection to the fundamental problem that the Buddha was trying to resolve. We live in a disposable society. We know that. But look what happens to our state of mind when anything breaks down. We experience worrying. That's because, subconsciously, we want things to be permanent and to give us lasting satisfaction and of course, in actuality, no thing can do that. We may buy the latest mobile phone because it will have everything we will ever need, but then three weeks later a newer model comes onto the market and we become dissatisfied and want a new one.

As far as physical things are concerned our conditioned mind finds it difficult to cope with the actuality of impermanence, so we go round and round in circles, repeating the same scenario over and over again. We do this because we are driven to seek what is pleasant and avoid that which is unpleasant and these pre-conscious drives are behind almost everything we think say and do. This is our knee jerk reaction. It is our habitual patterned reactionary mode of being.

The more we look at things in light of the impermanent compo-nent of actuality, the greater the opportunity we have to let go of the clinging to an unrealistic expectation of things. But there is one area of this component that we simply do not want to accept under any circumstances. This is the fear that we experience when we ponder the fact that we too are impermanent. It doesn't matter how many times we dye our hair, have a face-lift, eat muesli, drink cabbage soup, do yoga, Tai Chi or meditation. It doesn't matter how well off we are financially or how poor we are. It doesn't matter if we are well known or a complete nobody. At some point we are all going to get sick and die and with every breath we are ageing.

The inevitability of death and the uncertainty of its timing play a significant part in creating our worries. It is the inherent survival drive of the pre-conscious, biological, nature aspect of being that creates a fear of non-existence. That drives us to engage in all manner of irrational belief systems, which provide us with an apparent comfort blanket or a sense of security, usually in the form of a religion in which classical religious Buddhism is no exception.

The third component part of actuality that the Buddha points out is no-thing-ness. This, without any doubt, is the most confusing and mind-boggling aspect of this realization because it goes beyond the conditioned rational mind and can only be realized directly, once it is experienced. This does not mean we give up trying to engage with it on an intellectual level because this will still be of great benefit to us. The Buddha recognised that the human condition is driven by wanting things that we like, which often translates as wanting any experience to be other than it is. Similarly, it is driven by trying to avoid or change things that we don't like. It is driven by an overall confusion about the actuality that we are not a fixed or separate and enduring ego-identity, personality, individual, self, soul, spirit, essence, mind-stream, conscience, energy, vibration, inner, outer, or any other thing than can be identified, labeled or established as being you, me or I. We will be exploring the subject of no-thing-ness in a later chapter.

Chapter Seven: Conditioned Causal Continuity

When we begin to explore our day to day, or even moment by moment human experience, through the filter of causality it can be both challenging and exciting most of the time. This body that we consider to be ours only came into existence and exists now, because of preceding causes and conditions. We have the condition of conception, the condition of birth and the condition of growth. We are currently being sustained by the air we breathe, the food we eat, by the complex inner working of all manner of things that are contained within this amazing human body.

Inevitably, it will all come to an end when the conditions that keep the whole thing going come to an end. Even our dreams, our memories, our wants, our individual sense of being, exists as a result of preceding causes and conditions such as our education, nationality, culture and general upbringing. We exist like a tiny spider, sitting at the centre of a complex web that connects every thing to every thing. We can accept perhaps, intellectually at first, the interconnectedness of every cause and condition but we struggle to experience directly how, or why, any particular thought or emotion arises.

The physical nature of our bodies affects what kind of mood we are in. Our emotions affect our thought process and everything we think, say and do affects us, everybody else and the world around us. We can understand, even on that level, that this thing we call 'us' is connected, in some way, with every other thing on the planet. In light of this understanding it can, at first, seem a bit scary. If we are really just this interconnected thing, what can be found that has any degree of permanence? What is there that we can cling to that isn't in a continuing process of change, a flow of arising and subsiding of just experience? This throws up that all important question that lies at the centre of all our worries. How on earth are we going to find peace of mind in such an apparent crazy world that is governed by causality?

We will experience what we think of as the good times. We will experience joy, fun, laughter, romantic love and all manner of other things that we like. But the fact is that no matter how hard we try, or how hard we want it to be different, none of these things have any degree of permanence. They will end when any of the conditions that created them change. No thing is permanent. With the pleasant times, we need to accept that there will be the unpleasant times and this too is governed by causality. Sometimes it can just be helpful to understand that this thing we call life is not under our control and the universe doesn't care. Thankfully, the Buddha provides us with a very practical way to begin to cope with this fact and uncertainty by encouraging us to adopt a gentle and calm look at the way things actually are and not how we believe them to be.

It's important to keep reminding ourselves that the Buddha was born into this same world of uncertainty and impermanence as we were. It was his worries that set him off in search of an answer to that problem and it was his realization of causality that brought them to an end. He wasn't particularly interested in how the world came into being, how the universe works, how the world around him worked or even what happened to him after he died. Throughout the early Buddhist texts, we find him wandering around India repeating the same thing over and over again to the effect of:

"I teach only worrying, the cause of worrying, that it can be ended and here are a few suggestions, that if you adopt them as a practical way of living, it might be helpful for you to end them and realize peace of mind,"

Although much later on, in different expressions of the Dharma, a greater emphasis was placed on understanding the no-thing-ness of all things and whether things ultimately existed or not, it seems clear that the Buddha seemed more focused on what he considered being the practicalities involved in understanding the human experience. At the time of the Buddha, there were many different schools of thought in India, but there were two principal ones. The first proposed that there is an eternal and unchanging mode of being called Brahmin and all you had to do, through meditation, was to gain access to this unchanging inner self and merge with actuality. The second proposed that the world operated as a result of a random combination of elements so you might as well get on with it the best way that you could. The Buddha's proposal cuts through the middle ground and was unique to him. As all things arise as a result of preceding causes and conditions, then by understanding the nature of these causes and conditions it becomes possible to develop helpful conditions and to eradicate unhelpful conditions through conscious choice and effort.

A really good example of the Buddha's approach is found in a story in one of the ancient texts. It is about a member of his community who threatened to leave unless the Buddha answered the following questions.

1. Is the universe eternal or not eternal?
2. Is the universe finite or infinite?
3. Is the soul and the body the same or different?

4. Does a Buddha exist or not exist after death?
5. Does the Buddha both exist and not exist after death?

These kind of questions seem to pop up all the time and I guess we would also want to know the answers to these and other big questions like is there a creator entity? Or is there life after death or life on any other planet?

The Buddha's response is one of those teachings that we would do well to remember as it will come in useful when, at times, we may experience doubt or a lack of confidence or trust that we have found the right journey or communicator for us. The Buddha told the community member words to the effect:

'You are like a man who has been shot with a poisoned arrow, but will not let the doctor remove it unless the doctor tells you first about how the arrow came to be poisoned, what the poison is, who fired it, where it was fired from and then insisting on seeing the doctors qualifications, in writing, in triplicate, signed by those who trained him.'

Ooops! Too late. You're dead! What the Buddha is basically saying here is that the answers to these and other big questions are irrelevant in the quest for clarity and peace of mind. In fact, he is saying that to pay too much attention to them will actually cause you to worry.

Let's take a look at one of the most common and debilitating conditions in western culture in the 21st century and see how we can apply the principle of causality to it. One of the biggest types of worries is this thing that has been given the label stress. What is stress? It is suggested here that it is an unpleasant thought pattern that arises when life becomes too demanding, or we find ourselves faced with adverse life conditions. Its symptoms could include such things as physical pain or discomfort, muscular tension, headaches, poor sleep and even nausea for some.

If we explore stress on the basis of causality, we can learn to see that the symptoms arise because of certain conditions. Maybe we think we've got too much to do. Perhaps we're just very tired physically or emotionally. Maybe we think that somehow we haven't got control over our own life. It could be a whole range of things, but until such time as we go in search of the causes and conditions, we can't really understand why we keep finding ourselves stressed out. The difficulty we have is that if we don't go and look, we might find that the symptoms begin feeding themselves in a cyclic fashion. We have a sense that we are sick and we get stressed, but then the stress makes us want to vomit. We have a sense that we are tired and get stressed and start worrying about being tired which keeps us awake at night. Whatever the experience is, the good news is that it is not something that will stay the same. It will change as conditions change. Even the experience itself is in a constant process of change.

One thing to bear in mind when exploring causes and conditions is that just as we are represented by that spider at the centre of the web of interconnectedness, the causes and conditions of our stress are themselves an integral part of the same interconnected web. Our stress may not just arise as a result of one cause or condition. There may be many factors and those will be connected. For instance, if our current experience is unpleasant, it's unlikely that we'll be in the mood to get out of the house into the fresh air and do some exercise, so we'll just lounge around on the sofa or lie in bed being sorry for ourselves. It might be the lack of exercise itself that contributes to that unpleasant experience.

So, how do we deal with stress in a helpful way from a Buddhist perspective? We first need to explore and identify the conditions and then, either make changes or remove them altogether. We might only have to change just one condition for it to have a knock on effect to the others. Perhaps just doing a bit of exercise might actually help us sleep better. With a bit more sleep, we won't be so tired and have a bit more energy to do what needs to be done. All of a sudden, just by making one small change we alter a whole range of other conditions and we find ourselves less stressed or not stressed at all.

So, here's the advert:

"No alcohol, illicit substances or prescribed medication was used in the making of this non-stressed out individual."

All you did was take a good uncluttered look at the actuality of your experience and how it came into being as a result of causes and conditions. We have begun to practice **'awareness.'** Paying full attention to our physical body, our emotional experiences and how our thought process works in connection with both of those things. The development of awareness, primarily through meditation practice, gives us the tools to do the job. It enables us to make conscious choices rather than running around like a demented rodent, trying to catch its own tail on auto-pilot. It helps us to stop reacting on the basis of our conditioned habitual patterns of behaviour. Understanding causality, even intellectually, allows us to step into the current moment of experience fully so we can explore it fully.

Let's turn our attention now to the first two aspects of causality so that we can get a clear understanding of the different processes involved. There is a significant distinction to be made between what is a cause and what is a condition and it's helpful to understand this otherwise we won't know where to start looking. A cause could be said to be something that has a **'now'** aspect to it. It's something that triggered the effect to happen in this moment. A condition, on the other hand, is any number of supporting factors that may have led to the cause and then the effect moment. If someone dropped dead at your feet and was taken off to a hospital they will be given a cause of death, perhaps a heart attack. So, the immediate cause of the death was a heart attack. The conditions that led to that cause could be endless. It could be genetic, diet, lifestyle or whatever, but each will play their own little part in creating the conditions for the **'now cause'** to arise. If just one of those conditions were not present then that effect could not take place. It might well have taken place with a completely different set of conditions, but that is a different story. If we now apply this to our problem of worrying, we will already have worked out that there is not one single cause for our worry, but a number of conditioning factors that give rise to the cause and then effect.

Your own direct personal experience is one of the major conditions that will enable you to engage with the Dharma journey towards the realization of clarity. Conditions that will hold you back are believing that you just need to hold the right set of beliefs, as in a religious approach to Buddhism, or that you have worked it all out intellectually, as in a philosophical approach to Buddhism or even that you have tried to force this thing we call mind to be free of worrying by making continual strenuous effort, as in some kind of ascetic approach to Buddhism. The Dharma journey is the continual exploration of ways where we can meet our direct experience head on, with full awareness and see it for what it is and how it arose. It's helpful to be aware that the development of awareness initially can lead to an increase in worries because we are starting to focus and pay attention more intensely on our experiences. The Dharma journey itself is reflected well in the words of the Talking Head song 'Road to Nowhere'

We're on the road to nowhere
Come on inside
Taking that ride to nowhere
We'll take that ride

This is not a path with a beginning and an end. The Dharma journey isn't a linear thing. It is an all-embracing journey, a voyage of non-self discovery.

As we develop our awareness of the transitory flow of continual experience, there will be something of a shift that takes place. We will gradually become less reactive to our experiences and the world around us and we will become more responsive to them. Generally speaking, most people tend to live their lives in a reactionary way. Something happens and they do the same thing they always do. When this happens, this is the reaction. This is the result of our life-long and on-going conditioning process. We develop habitual patterns of behaviour that are automatic, precisely because there is no awareness present. This is us in 'reactive mode.' Each time we react habitually, we reinforce the habit and it establishes a significant part of our personality or identity. This is the re-conditioning process.

It could also be said that it will define who we are to others who engage with us on the basis of knowing in advance what our reactions will be. When we are in reactive mind mode we are not aware of the conditions that have given rise to our current experience. This mode of thinking is a major contributory factor in how we can go through life on auto-pilot without ever questioning our beliefs, or patterns of behaviour and as a result will never realize the opportunity to understand why we worry, or more importantly, how we worry.

The 'responsive mode.' is very different and is the basis for living with awareness. Here, our life itself becomes a learning space. Not one of taking in information, but observing, paying attention, noticing what is going on in our physical bodies and its sensations. It observes the emotional experiences that arise in connection with those sensations by paying attention to the sense experiences of seeing, hearing, smelling, tasting and touching. But most important of all, we observe the thinking process that is linking all of these things together. When the mind moves from reactive mode to responsive mode, it gradually becomes free of its reactive shackles and allows itself to experience a new-found freedom that is somehow more alive, spontaneous, creative and is expressed through the practice of a kindly response for self and other.

When our mind is operating in reactive mode, what we are doing is creating the conditions that give rise to worrying. When we begin to develop a responsive approach to life through the practice of awareness, those conditioning factors become more and more self-evident, which then gives us a genuine opportunity to make the changes to our way of life and the way we think, that will decrease our worries considerably.

Before we move on let's remind ourselves of the source principle in a different formulation and take a look at a few practical examples of how we can see it being applied in our everyday lives. The principle is:

"When this arises, then that also emerges. When this ceases, then that also ends. When this is, then that also comes into being. When this is not, then that cannot come into being."

By exploring the following examples we can see how easy it is to apply this principle to our everyday life and reduce our worries just by being aware of the source principle.

1. When there is expectation, then there is bound to be disappointment. When expectation is not there, then disappointment cannot be experienced.

2. Whenever there is self-biased mind present, there is bound to be a wounded self-biased mind. When self-biased mind is not there, the wounded self-biased mind cannot be experienced.

3. Whenever there is anger, then there is bound to be conflict. When anger is not there, then conflict cannot be experienced.

4. When there is perception, then there is bound to be misunderstanding. When perception is not there the misunderstanding cannot be experienced.

5. When there is birth, then there is bound to be ageing, sickness and death. When birth does not happen, then ageing, sickness and death cannot be experienced.

6. When there is wanting things to be other than they are, then there is bound to be worrying. When that want is not there and there is the acceptance of the way things are, then there are no worries.

7. When there are worries, then peace of mind cannot arise. When those worries are not there, then all there is, is peace of mind and compassionate action.

Chapter Eight: The Decision to Teach

Following that initial realization experience, the Buddha didn't suddenly rush around shouting **'eureka,'** or anything like that. He knew that it was impossible for him to contain what he had realized within the experience, within himself, as the effect of the realization had answered the question of why he worried and what caused it. It had resulted in an overwhelming response of compassion. If we were to put this scenario into a modern day context, it would be like someone discovering a cure for cancer. A self-biased mind would immediately patent the formula, sell the rights to the highest bidder and make a vast fortune from those that can afford to buy the product. They might, later on, donate something back, but often, it could be said, it would be the result of a twinge of conscience. The awakened mind that operates on the default of compassion would simply share the knowledge and not be concerned about any fame or fortune aspect of the process. The end result would be the same but the motivational intent would be the opposite of each other.

One of the difficulties we have with trying to understand what this experience is all about is that we do not have an **'awakening product'** to buy and sell. Although, absolute fortunes are spent by the seeker who fails to recognize this is an internal exploration and that there is no clarity pill or elixir. All that we do have is a number of very practical suggestions from the Buddha that we might find helpful for us to realize the experience for ourselves.

Another problem we face is that it is practically impossible for anyone to convey what the experience actually is and that is so frustrating for so many people. We want to know what it's like. How is it experienced? Will we walk and talk funny or have a fixed grin on our face all the time? Will our voice become a gentle soft whisper? Will lotus flowers really spring up in our steps as we walk? When we pass wind will it really smell like sandalwood? Do we get to choose the colour of our aura? For those living within a materialistic, consumerist western society, it seems that we want to see an end product that we can give a value to before we are prepared to commit ourselves fully to it.

If you think about it, how difficult would it be for you to explain an experience you had to anybody else so that they could know the experience for themselves? How could I tell you what the experience of eating an orange is, so that you would know that experience if you had never eaten an orange yourself? This is why the Buddha and other communicators use different methods to point toward it. Because realistically that is the only way it can be done.

Because the reliance on belief and faith systems are in decline within western culture, we appear to be left drifting in a never-ending cycle of searching for an external answer as to why we worry that we can't find lasting satisfaction with anything. No matter how many times we are told that the answer can only be found within ourselves and by our own effort, because nobody can show us the end product, we seem reluctant to make that effort. This then throws us back into our habitual patterns of behaviour. This will include a reliance on beliefs and external influences that will include teachers who we want to do it for us. They can't. If you don't drop this mind-set from the outset it will mean more teachers, more books, more therapies and more worries.

This is why, for many, the Dharma journey will not be about realizing the experience of clarity. Often, within western culture, it will be about learning ways in which we can make our day to day life a little bit happier. It will be about becoming a better person, a nicer person. It will be about belonging to a network of others who seem to be of a similar mind-set. Within cultural classical Buddhism, it will primarily be about making merit in this life to pave the way for a promised better apparent life next time around. There is nothing wrong with these approaches. In themselves, they bring some benefit to the individual and society. But these approaches are not what the Buddha set out as being the things that will alleviate or eradicate your worries.

After the initial realization of clarity, the Buddha let it settle down for a bit and then started to try and make sense of it on an intellectual level so he could communicate it to others. We have no idea how long this process actually took. But it seems that it was an on-going process throughout the remainder of his life when you consider how many different and varied ways he communicated the same realization.

During this period, he would have evaluated the risks involved in communicating something that went against the flow of the pre-existent belief system of his day. He would have been aware that he would be considered mad by some and maybe locked away for his own good or that of society. He knew that if he rocked the status quo of the religious or political institutions of his day he could be and was at times, in physical and mortal danger.

He knew that his every word would be under intense scrutiny by those who would seek to undermine what he had to say. He would be accused of being a fraud, an idealist, an egotist and a fool. Despite all of this, he knew that he had no option but to try, as best as he could, to communicate this for the benefit of all beings. It is no different today for any new communicator of the Dharma. Why? It's because, yet again, people will look towards the communicator and not the communication. It becomes a personality issue that is fuelled by the imposed belief that nobody can actually realize this so, therefore, they must be making false claims.

There is a symbolic story within classical Buddhism that tells us something of this reflection period. It is said that the Buddha brought to mind the image of a lotus pond, which for him represented the human world. He considered that the majority of human beings would be so bogged down in unhelpful mind states, or so trapped within the confines of individual belief systems, that they would either not hear what he had to say, or would not be prepared to listen. He likened these individuals to the very root of the lotus plant. Without the roots, there could be no lotus plant so the roots were common to all beings and represented potential for growth. Lotus plants thrive in the layers of smelly mud at the bottom of the pond and that mud he recognized as being representative of the human dilemma of worrying.

He noticed that some of the plants had begun to grow shoots that had broken free from the mud and were now sitting there in the murky waters near the bottom of the pond. They were still being fed by the strong nutrients of the mud below them. This he likened to individuals who were no longer totally blinded by the mud but had begun to search for a way out of it. That dark murky water still meant that they would be confused and at times a bit scared to grow any further as it meant finding nutrients for themselves rather than being fed from below. He thought that this type of individual would be able to understand what he had to say in a limited way, but at least they had recognised that staying in the mud wasn't what they needed and was unhelpful and limiting, so there would be of some benefit for them.

The Buddha noticed that once the lotus plant had broke free of the mud they began to grow upwards towards the clearer water at the surface. There was nothing pulling them upwards. They were growing at their own pace and by their own effort. It was as if the lotus was experiencing for itself how healthier and happier it was with each step of the growing process as it experienced directly the ever clearer water on its upward journey. He noticed that each and every lotus in the pond was at a different stage of development. It seemed that the more they relied on finding their own nutrients, the faster they grew and the more they relied on the nutrients beneath them, it slowed them down. He likened this to the letting go of beliefs in favour of the direct experience of the situation, the move from external influences to internal discoveries.

This type of individual he thought would hear what he had to say. They would test and challenge what he had to say. They would commit themselves to breaking free of the water and to experience the warmth of the sun on their petals for themselves. They would be supported by the knowledge that there were many other lotus plants doing the same thing. They would be able to see above them that some plants had actually flowered. Even the remotest possibility that they could themselves flower one day was all that they needed to spur them on. This is also an inspirational reminder of the importance of support and how we can find inspiration and help from others who have made progress on this journey and are prepared to walk by our side with us.

Symbolically at least, this is the catalyst for the start of the Buddha's teaching life. He reasoned that there were human beings out there in the world with '**just a little dust in their eyes.**' He considered that there would be many who would benefit from just '**a gentle eye wash.**' He began by using a well-known four-part formula that was used within the field of medicine that was known to him then and is still current today.

1. **The problem, disease or illness was first diagnosed**
2. **Then the cause was identified and recognised**
3. **It was then established that it could be cured**
4. **And finally, the cure would be prescribed for the patient to take**

Chapter Nine: The Four Principal Assignments

The first public communication of the Buddha was made to a group of five former companions who had abandoned him earlier when he took the decision to end his starvation and bring to an end the period of extreme asceticism. It is said to have taken place in a deer park at Sarnath. Although it is of major significance, as it is the first teaching he gave publicly and sets out the journey in its entirety, it is, in fact, just one of a number of attempts or formulations he used to communicate the source realization of causality.

It is known within classical Buddhism as the '**Four Noble Truths.**' It is also known as the first turning of the Dharma wheel. The given title can, for some, lead to distractions and confusion. Many Buddhists get caught up in the specialness of the word '**noble.**' They tend to see themselves as something special or important or take on an elitist attitude towards the Dharma journey and this is never helpful. Actually, the term noble, in this context, means that it wasn't directed at the ordinary man in the street, but was the preserve of the self-appointed apparent spiritual elite. It is suggested here that the term itself crept in during the first reformation period.

The word truths in the title can also be problematic. It is clear that is has fed the move towards creating yet another belief based religion, which is clearly not what the Buddha intended. Often this has led people down blind faith alleyways because the word truth is contained within the title. They adopt an idea that somehow the Buddha is asking us to believe in them because they are true and when you explore them in relation to the ancient texts, it is clear that there is a contradiction within the title itself.

If taken literally, as they invariably are, the Buddha says that birth is worrying, ageing is worrying, sickness is worrying and death is worrying. That is what he sets out in the first apparent truth. Then he says that it is true that it can be ended. If you think about that for a moment, on the literal level of understanding, it is a total contradiction because even if you were awakened you are still going to age, get sick and die, just as he did. So, on that level, it clearly is not true. As we will discover later, in a chapter that will explore this in depth, what the Buddha was actually saying was not within the context of everyday life and that these four principal assignments he set out are expressions of actuality, not truths to be believed in but things to test, challenge and realize.

As suggested previously, it is really helpful for this word truth to be eradicated from our language if we are really going to make progress. First, because it causes far too much harm and second because it actually goes against what the Buddha was actually communicating. How many more people will have to die and suffer before anyone realizes that there is no such thing as a fixed truth. There is just an experience that you have chosen to believe as being true. Actuality is actuality. It is what it is. There is no need to believe in actuality, because it is always there. It is just perceived to be different things by different people as a subjective reality. As we will discover later it is our view of actuality that is at the core of our worrying. For these reasons it is suggested and encouraged that we leave well alone the word truth or truths and maintain a transitory view based on verifiable facts.

In this first communication, the Buddha sets out four principle assignments for his followers to engage with. Therefore, to avoid any conflict about beliefs in our Dharma practice, it is helpful to understand from the outset that this teaching is about something to do. It is something in action and not merely something to be believed in. The real basis for this teaching is that the Buddha is asking us to understand the actuality of our situation and the cause of so much worrying in our lives. He suggests that we find ways to cultivate a way of life that will either eradicate or significantly lessen those worries and advises us on the ways in which we could do that, so that we can experience the alleviation or eradication of our worries.

The first of these principle assignments is to own up to the fact that we are not happy and contented all of the time. If we were prepared to be totally honest, we would admit that we are not happy and contented for most of the time. There seems to be this underlying worry that is always there about not being whole or complete in some way. We have an idea that somehow we need just one more thing to make us happy. This actuality is what we call here worrying. This first assignment is a massive challenge for us to understand. It really questions almost everything we have been conditioned to believe throughout our lives. The actuality of sickness aging and death are reflected back to us like a mirror and we can't avoid them no matter how many times we look away, smash the mirror or kid ourselves it's not real.

In classical Buddhism and its books, the term most often used is suffering. In the west it is not uncommon for people who choose to explore Buddhism to not get past the first few pages because as soon as they read something like 'life is suffering' which is a very common statement that is used, they think it's not for them. After all, how many of us think that our lives are full of suffering in the usual way we understand that word?

Worrying is at the centre of what Buddhism is all about. It is what set the Buddha off on his journey and was the catalyst for the identification of its origins and the way to deal with it within the experience of clarity. When we fully understand that our worries are caused by our attitudes to our own experiences, we will be moved to explore the teachings more deeply because, as human beings, we are driven to find peace of mind. Eventually we will discover that this current moment of experience is defined by an infinite number of conditioning factors and a cause. This current experience of mind will always be as a result of what we think, what we say, or what we do in the previous moment.

Human beings tend to have an amazing capacity for self-deception. We close our eyes to how thing actually are and simply hope they will change for the better. We build up expectations and that inevitably leads to disappointment. We will go to almost any length to avoid looking directly and honestly at the way in which we live our lives. We seem to stumble from one unsatisfied state to the next in search of happiness. Like a hamster on a wheel, we chase after sensory experiences, never finding lasting fulfillment. Gain turns to loss, happiness gives way to sadness. We always think that final complete satisfaction is just around the corner. **"If only I can do this, or get that, then everything will be OK and I'll be happy."** We do almost anything to distract ourselves from facing the actuality of our situation. We may reach for recreational drugs, alcohol, holidays, a fictional or romantic pulp novel, un-reality TV, even a Dharma course. At least this last option might give us an opportunity to realize, that although we can't change what happens to us, we can choose our responses which in turn will make a huge difference in the way we experience our lives. There is nothing wrong with these things. What we need to explore is: are they helpful?

If we ask ourselves why am I taking an interest in Buddhism? Then look beyond the superficial answers to a deeper purpose, we will discover that the motivational factor behind our decision to take a look at Buddhism is likely to be rooted in our worries or the absence of peace of mind. Worrying is such a huge part of our daily lives because we find it almost impossible to find satisfaction with the way things actually are at any moment. We always want things to be different. We build up expectations of things and people, that can never be fulfilled and we inevitably end up disappointed. Of course we have moments of happiness, even joy, but they never last. We get pleasure out of many things but it is too often short-lived and this causes us to worry.

We save up all year to go on our holiday overseas. We build up our hopes and expectations but long before we get there, even as we're about to board the airplane, we start to worry if the hotel is going to be any good. Will the food be OK? Will it be sunny enough for us to top up our tans? Even if our expectations are met when we're there and we have a great time distracting ourselves from our underlying worries with shopping expeditions and lovely cocktails during happy hour, the moment we return home to our daily routines, we experience a sense of loss. This is the cycle of worrying.

If we were to pay attention and examine in detail our moment-by-moment daily lives, we would come to see how much time we spend trying to distract ourselves from our worries. If we unpack the term worry a little more we would discover a multitude of facets. At the top end of the scale it would include depression, neurosis and stress, on the other end of the scale would be concern, anxiety or doubt. The balance point on those scales is the middle way of the Buddha. The point where we have learned to be OK with the current experience as it is.

What happens when we worry? We might try and shrug it off, or try to convince ourselves that it's OK, but more often than not we try to find something to replace it with. It does not work. We need to learn to be present with it, as it is and work our way through it there and then. If a large wave is heading straight for us at the beach and we try to avoid it we will find ourselves unbalanced and crashing into the sand and surf. But if we dive straight into it we discover it is only water. Similarly, to understand worry, is to know it calmly and clearly for what it is, something that is not permanent. The greatest challenge in this first assignment is to act before our habitual reactions kick in and move us back around the cycle of pleasure and pain.

If we can't recognise this problem within us, then we are either awakened, or we are trying to avoid facing actuality. From the very outset of Dharma practice there is a need for honesty with ourselves. Not the kind of honesty that weighs us down with irrational guilt. There is no room for this most damaging emotional state within the Dharma journey. If we really do want to overcome these worries about the way things are in our lives, if we really do want to find contentment and fulfillment and a greater sense of peace of mind, we have to begin from the standpoint of honesty and integrity.

The whole of the Buddhist tradition, no matter which school or sect, is based on the recognition of the inevitability of worrying within the un-awakened human state of existence. No matter how well adjusted we are, we are still going to get physically old, sick and die. These three things are inevitable. But if we know and see them for what they are, we do not have to worry about them. It is not compulsory. They are just an inevitable part of what it means to be a human being. All experiences that cause us to worry can be treated, lessened or eradicated, by first understanding what conditions or causes the worry to arise and by then taking steps to ensure that it doesn't have the opportunity to rise again.

The first assignment therefore, is to open our eyes to the actuality of worrying. We need to understand what it is and what it is not. We are not being asked to believe in the existence of worrying. We are being asked to examine it fully, explore it in minute detail and search for it from every angle within our own life situations. We are encouraged to pay attention to our own experiences on a moment-by-moment basis and to realize for ourselves that we could be so much happier if we were able to lessen or eradicate the unhelpful aspects of our lives. We are encouraged to do this by examining our thoughts and more importantly our habitual beliefs about them. This is what we do when the mind is engaged in responsive mode rather than reactive mode. This is living in awareness.

In the ancient texts the Buddha sets out seven factors that give rise to worrying. The first is that birth begins the worrying process. Despite modern pharmaceutical intervention could anyone realistically argue that the birth of a child is not a worrying experience for both child and the parents?

The second factor he sets out that gives rise to worrying is the ageing process. As we age, we become physically weaker and that often results in a loss of agility. We begin to forget little things. Our eyesight and hearing weakens. We become a bit more dependent on others. We are forever discovering new aches and pains. Bits of us break down and have to be replaced and we end up rattling with the amount of different pills we have to take to keep us alive.

The third is sickness. Whether its terminal cancer or a mild headache, all sickness is unpleasant. It's not just the physical aspect. It can give rise to a fear of helplessness and frustration. Even at the peak of physical fitness we can be affected by various forms of diagnosed mental health issues, especially within our culture that seeks to move us ever faster, to be more productive and achieve ever greater economic efficiency.

The fourth is death. Despite every attempt to kid ourselves it's not going to happen to us, you can be assured that it is inevitable and it is only its timing that is unforeseen. There will also be worries when people that we care about, or know socially die. Just thinking about the actuality of death, for some, can cause worry.

Those first four factors are the ones that we can't avoid or actually do much about, other than accept them as fact and as a result lessen or eradicate the worrying aspect of them. The three that we can do something about are the bread and butter of the work in progress that we call the Dharma journey.

The fifth factor is the recognition that worrying arises when we are in contact with something we don't like. The list of dislikes is endless. Although we have been conditioned to believe that there is some unbreakable blood bond within the family unit, it is actually very common for families not to get on with each other.

As a result it creates the worrying of going through the motions for the sake of peace and quiet. We might be in a job just for the money and hating every minute of it. We might get frustrated by environmental or political issues. To exist it seems that we have no option but to live amongst people and things that we don't like.

The sixth factor is when we are separated from what we do like. Sometimes this can be even more worrying. Divorce or the break up of the family unit is very common within our society. Children are often left under the supervision of just one primary care giver. Often children can be used as a kind of weapon when relationships become unpleasant. Here in Australia, we also have a developing problem with what is called fly-in-fly-out employment. This is where workers spend long periods away from the family home and that is raising serious concerns within the field of mental health, including a rise in the workplace suicide rate.

The seventh and final factor is not to get what one wants. Whether we have seriously coveted a gadget of some kind, or fall in love with someone, or failed to achieve some kind of personal goal that you set yourself, or a target that was set by others, worrying will arise in the form of disappointment.

What we are exploring within this first communication is the basic principle of cause and effect, or causality in action. We have an effect that we call worrying. Once we have worked through the process of assuring ourselves that we fully understand what worrying is, to the extent that we can recognise that it is inher-ent within all experience, we turn to the second assignment, which is to go in search of its cause. We now have to identify its cause so we can do something to prevent it or reduce it if we can. In doing so we will discover that there are an infinite number of interconnected preceding conditions and causes for all effects.

Within that process there will be things we can do and things we can't do to alleviate or eradicate the worrying aspect. For instance, within the context of the actuality of worrying that we have realized within the first assignment as **'death is worrying,'** death, could be said to be the effect of being born. But within that process, even before the birth there are an infinite number of conditioning factors. We can't do anything about the ones that led to birth, but we can do something about the ones that lead to death by taking good care of our health whilst we are alive.

'Ageing is worrying.' Birth could be said to be the primary cause and ageing an effect. It is a biological fact. It is apparent that we are now living longer than ever, but as yet this cannot be prolonged indefinitely. This longevity has a myriad of contributory factors such as advances in medical science and technology. There are all manner of things available to us today to assist living within the ageing process without the worrying aspect taking a hold. We have mobility devices, delivery meal services, social groups, residential homes and for many a pension to pay the bills.

'Sickness is worrying.' Birth could be said to be the primary cause and sickness is the effect. Again there are a myriad of causes and conditions within each bout of sickness. Some illnesses are said to be genetic, in which case the sickness would be linked back to a third party within the family lineage. Some of these skip generations and reappear later. A viral infection can be ingested just walking along a street minding our own business. The range of illness is vast and they will all have their own set of conditioning factors, some of which we can do something about and others we can't. Malaria, for example, is a water-born disease, but we also have to have the conditions that are suitable for the disease to appear, such as insanitary conditions. We also need the existence of the mosquito and of course we also need to be bitten by one that carries the disease. We can now visit Malaria ridden countries and lessen the worrying aspect because we can take suitable precautions.

In all of these scenarios and more, one thing is very clear. None of these things happen to us because we are bad people, or have done something wrong to deserve it, or are just unlucky. Contrary to what some classical Buddhists insist on telling people, that is not what the Buddha taught. In regard to sickness in particular all we can do is follow medical advice and take reasonable precautions. No amount of praying, monetary donations, lighting candles or circumambulations around deity figures and shrines will prevent sickness.

The second assignment the Buddha gave us was to realize what causes us to worry in its many different forms. This is the nuts and bolts of what the Buddha was trying to help people to understand. This is where we have to discover the cause of our unhelpful physical, emotional and psychological experiences. Within classical Buddhism it is usually recorded as either 'craving' or 'desire.' This can be a problem for us in the west because we have a different understanding of what those words mean. Craving, we tend to link to the world of addiction in experiences that involve cigarettes, alcohol, drugs, junk food, gambling or anything else that has become addictive in 21st century western culture. Also, in the west, we associate the word desire to romance and sex. In this second assignment the Buddha is asking us to understand that the root of our unhelpful experience is based in wanting things to be different to how they are.

Human beings live by sensory experience. We see, hear, taste, touch and smell. All of these sensory experiences are happening in every moment of our lives. The results of those sensory experiences are processed by this thing we call mind. We catch sight of something and an immediate decision is made. We find what we experience through our senses to be either pleasant or unpleasant. We hear something and we react in a way that is helpful or unhelpful to the sound, depending on whether or not we find it pleasant or unpleasant. We put something in our mouths and we either go **"mmmm - that's nice"** or we spit it out and go **"'yuck."** We touch something and it is a pleasant or unpleasant experience. We are drawn towards pleasant smells and are uncomfortable with unpleasant odours. We are aware that human beings have the ability to make choices but these instantaneous, reactive decisions, are far removed from actual choices. They are, in effect, out of our control because they are driven by the pre-conscious and then subconscious aspect of being, our conditioned self-biased mind which wants the experience to be pleasant and not unpleasant.

In those rare moments when we are not on auto-pilot and are simply reacting to our sensory experiences we do make choices, but even these choices are based on the two pre-conscious signals of experiencing something pleasant or unpleasant. We either like something or we don't. If we examine our daily lives we can see it going on all the time. We may have a particular circle of friends and may steer clear of others. We may order this off the menu in a restaurant and not that. We watch this TV programme and not that one. We listen to this kind of music and not that kind.

We buy this product and not that one. Underlying all of these decisions, and almost every other choice that we make, on a moment by moment basis, is the fact that we find something pleasant or unpleasant and that will ultimately inform the choice we make.

Generally speaking, worrying in the form of an unhelpful physical, emotional or psychological experience is not going to arise in any of the above circumstances, because the choices we are making are the ones in which we will experience pleasure. Worrying will arise though if the food we ordered hasn't been cooked properly, or the CD cover has the wrong CD in it, or the TV programme we wanted to watch has been shifted. In each of these scenarios we are no longer getting what we want or, we are getting something that we don't want.

Seeking pleasure and avoiding unpleasantness are the major causes of our worries. What this means, is that no matter what we get, no matter how good, we always want more. Or we want something else. Or we don't want something to stop. This behaviour sets the pattern of basic human behaviour. It defines us. We deceive ourselves into thinking we are fixed beings that don't change. We cling to our own myths and stories of who we are and what we do. We develop habitual patterns of behaviour that we cling to. I like this. I want that. I don't like this. I don't want that. Such is the predicament of the self-biased mind which gives rise to worrying that is driven by wanting experiences to be different than they are.

Just as the actuality of worrying is all about learning to understand it, initially we will get nowhere if we do not act on that understanding. This is our opportunity to begin letting go of the drives of the self-biased mind. Again we can use a set of scales to try and understand what this wanting is all about. On one side of the scale is egotism and selfishness, that deep seated anxious longing for security moving downwards to the fear of rejection by those we love, to the compulsion to have another glass of wine, bar of chocolate or a cigarette.

Whenever worrying arises, the habitual reaction is to indulge it, or deny it and both of these actions prevent us from simply letting go. It's helpful to understand that the term **'letting go'** does not mean putting an end to it by any means other than recognising it for what it is and understanding it. Letting go of our wants is not rejecting them, but allowing them to be what they are, simply a transitional state of mind. Like every thing, it has no degree of permanence. Instead of trying to force it away we need to realize that its very nature is to free itself. By continually involving ourselves in the human predicament of I want this, I like this and I don't want this and I don't like that, we heighten the intensity of the hold that self-biased wanting has over us and as a result we continue to worry. Instead of being a state of mind that you have, it becomes a compulsion that has you.

What the Buddha suggests is that if we really want to begin to eradicate the cause of this aspect of worrying, then we have to look inside ourselves with complete honesty. Not as a punishment inflicted on us by other people, life circumstances, an unknown supernatural force or creator entity. It has nothing to do with luck, fate or chance. He teaches that the worry that we experience, on a moment-by-moment basis, is directly linked to what we think, what we say and what we do. The more we can simply accept things as they are and not get caught up in our attachment to pleasure and our aversion to unpleasantness, the more we will find that worrying, caused by unhelpful physical, emotional and psychological experiences will subside and eventually may disappear.

Within this second assignment we are encouraged to explore the subject of attachment to things that are physical, emotional and psychological. Again, because of our very different ways of living, we may associate this word attachment with many things that the Buddha had never experienced. We may therefore often misunderstand what he was getting at. At the top end of this understanding we are asked to realize that we have an attachment to the confused belief of the self-biased mind that we refer to as "I" as a separate and enduring ego-identity. As a result, we hold on to the notion that there is a "me" that is independent from everything else that we believe is "not me."

Our assignment here is two-fold. Firstly, we can tackle the subject matter on a practical, moment-by-moment basis in our everyday world of self-biased subjective reality. Here we intellectually know we exist and we experience ourselves as being separate. Secondly, we can tackle the subject on an insightful basis, which will allow the gradual fading of the veil of confusion until, within the experience of clarity, it will be eradicated. This aspect of the second assignment will be explored in depth in a later chapter, when we look at the subject of no-thing-ness.

Attachment therefore, according to the Buddha, is another cause of worrying. It is this root cause that feeds the saplings of wanting things to be other than they are, until they become the weeds of a worrying mind. Most of our Dharma journey will be engaged in pruning back the weeds, trying to keep them under control or at least make them look pretty. We might even try an array of weed killers that have been skillfully advertised as the answer to our problems. These will keep our gardens looking tidy for a while, but eventually, we will learn that if we really want to eradicate the weeds, we will have to sever the roots so the weeds will not grow again.

Over the course of 2,600 years classical Buddhism has often used the word attachment almost in the same way as other religions have used the word sin. Apparent unworthiness through guilt supports the continuation of the spiritual elite, but this is not what the Dharma teaches. Many people who have been drawn towards Buddhism have been put off by this approach to attachment. They are told that to be a **'proper Buddhist,'** they need to have no attachment to people or material possessions. Celibacy is often championed as the apparent spiritual ideal. The monastic lifestyle is promoted as the only way to realize the experience of clarity. The actuality is that it is very easy to fool yourself that you have no attachments to material possessions if someone else is catering for your every need. How is the monk going to survive without someone else doing all the work to feed, clothe and house him? It's at the very centre of what that system is all about. Celibacy, as a method of suppressing sexual desire has led, throughout history, to a great deal of pain and suffering for others who have been either secretly abused or coerced into sexual relationships under the pretext of serving an apparent spiritual guru.

The public image and therefore perception of monastic life, very often does not match what is going on in the real world of Buddhism. As painful and disturbing as it is to acknowledge this, it is still far healthier to be aware of the actuality than to collude with the pretence by turning a blind eye to it. It is helpful to make this journey with our eyes open and to do as much as we can to prevent anyone in a position of perceived or imposed authority from abusing their power, position and trust.

What the Buddha is saying here is that possessions are not bad. Relationships are not bad. He's not even saying that sex is bad. What he is pointing to is for us to explore the internal motivational factors behind what we think, say and do in relations to things. It is absolutely possible to be in a loving, caring relationship with someone without there being an aspect of attachment. If we were to fully understand that what we refer to as **'love'** is, in actuality, an unconditional physical, emotional and psychological response to any given situation, we would understand that love can only really be present when there is no element of attachment involved. Generally speaking what we usually think of as love is wholly conditioned and therefore something completely different.

What is unhelpful, is giving ourselves too much of a hard time over this. The aspects of causality in relation to impermanence and insubstantiality will only be fully realized as insightful experiences. We can scratch the surface of them intellectually and conceptually and we do need to do that so we can engage with them in the practical way that the Buddha proposed. Our mission in our daily practice on the Dharma journey is to chip away at our habitual, unhelpful behaviour patterns, so that we can begin to detach ourselves from the beliefs that we have created in our worlds of self-biased subjective reality.

In effect we are engaging in the process of un-conditioning our minds and the integration of the pre-conscious and subconscious, allowing the insights to develop that will let us break through. To start the process, it is helpful to understand that there are two basic beliefs that we need to tackle.

1. That without a particular person, condition or thing being present in our lives, we can never be content
2. That we believe that we can't be content whilst a particular person, condition or thing is present in our lives

Quite often we are more attached to the belief than the person, condition or object. The belief drives us towards a state of tension or worry in our efforts to cling to this someone or something. If we do manage to hold on to them, we may well experience pleasure but because, subconsciously at least, there will be an underlying worry about losing the pleasant experience, our pleasure will be short lived and we will find ourselves back at the beginning.

We need therefore to develop a way to practice, through the filter of acknowledged attachment. We need to examine our attachment to our beliefs with critical thinking, precision and probably more importantly with total honesty. We need to experience for ourselves that, not only is it our confused beliefs that are causing our worrying, but more importantly, it is our attachment to them that is causing the most damage. For example, will money or success make us happy and give us peace of mind? Even when we experience for ourselves that they won't, we will often continue to pursue them because we still believe they can. Will another person make us happy? This is a little more difficult to understand fully because we, as part of our conditioning process, have developed a need to be appreciated, loved, secure or connected to others and we believe that someone else can provide all those things for us. As long as we relate to another person through the filter of the confusion that they can make us be a certain way, we will be setting ourselves up for a painful reaction and disappointment.

During our lifetime we will experience many losses. Things and people will be taken away from us at the most inopportune moments. The experience of loss quite often arises as a form of grief. It is painful. It is worrying supreme. We experience it as intense worry because subconsciously we are attached to a belief that things and people are permanent. No matter how many times we lose our job, no matter how many times our partner runs off with someone else, or the value of the house goes into negative equity or someone in our close circle of friends or family dies, once the grief period subsides we, subconsciously at least, will find ourselves believing that none of this is ever going to happen again.

It is helpful if this first communication of the four principal assignments is understood from a view point of practical and common sense. When we understand the nature of worrying and its cause and are encouraged to let things be as they are, what the Buddha is not saying is that when you are crossing the road and a truck is heading towards you at speed, or out of control, that you just stand there and say to yourself **"it is what it is"** without reacting because worrying will arise if you do. Just as he doesn't communicate blind faith, he also doesn't communicate blind stupidity.

The way to develop a more contented life, according to the Buddha, is to accept what you have and not want what you don't have. At first glance this might seem a little simplistic, or idealistic. But, if we take a deeper look into our everyday physical, emotional and psychological experiences we will discover for ourselves there is a lot to be said in the saying **"less is always more."**

Our starting point for understanding this is realizing the difference between a 'need' and a 'want.' In our materialistic and consumerist society, we over-use the word need. If the need is a genuine one, such as the need to eat and drink to survive, for most within western society this can be achieved without too much worrying. Worrying will only arise if we want that food product to be different than it is, or if we can't afford to buy the food we want. The same can be said of other stuff. Stuff isn't the problem. Sometimes we actually need stuff. What we have to do is to observe our hidden motivations and work out if it is a genuine need or a habitual want. Again, we have to take a common sense approach to this.

There is a lot of stuff in our lives that we don't necessarily need, and it doesn't fall into the category of 'want' either, because we can see it clearly for what it is, and have no unrealistic expectations around it. It has more to do with practicality than anything else. Do I need a car? The truthful answer is no. Is it more practical to have a car within my life circumstances? Yes it is. Does it matter what it looks like? No it doesn't. Will I be devastated when it doesn't start? It'll be an inconvenience for sure, but I'm more than likely to be grateful when it does start.

But again we have to be honest with ourselves about this. Many people will have walk-in wardrobes jam packed full with clothes, all in good condition. They've become bored with them or they're out of fashion and they want something new. Sound familiar? We tell ourselves that if we buy just one more shirt or dress we'll be happy. We can add into that all manner of fantasies. Perhaps if we buy a new shirt or a dress people might find us more attractive, or we think we will fit in better with people. In actuality, all we are walking out of the shop with is an unrealistic expectation of what this shirt or dress can do. It is a piece of cloth and nothing more. Are we still going to be happy with it when it fades, or rips or goes out of fashion and spends years hidden in our wardrobe with all the other stuff that we were once happy with?

As we develop a greater commitment to the Dharma journey and our practice of its teachings become more effective and established, it may well seem to those around us that we are becoming a tad colder, a little less emotional, a bit distant perhaps. Especially if our partner or the people in our many and varied social networks are not involved in the same process. We need to be aware that this is going to happen. It is a natural part of the un-conditioning process. Learning to become detached from our core beliefs can be a painful process, because it is all about change and those around us will not want us to change and will often resist that change. This is why it is helpful to have the support of like-minded individuals during our growth process. It is the essence of what being part of a Dharma community of like-minded individuals is.

In actuality, the process of becoming unattached will bring us ever closer to experiencing the unconditional aspects of themes such as love, compassion and generosity. Those experiences will be genuine, as opposed to their neurotic and superficial counterparts. Eventually we will realize that this thing we call peace of mind is not dependent on anyone or anything. It is a state of being that relies on our acceptance of the ways things are in accordance with the actuality of causality.

According to the Buddha there is a way out for all of us from the everyday problem of worrying and that is to eradicate its cause. He said in his first teaching words to the effect:

"It is the complete separation from and destructing of this very want, it's forsaking, its renunciation, the liberation there from and non-attachment thereto that will bring to an end worrying."

Following the experience of clarity, the Buddha knew instinctively that he had to find a way of communicating what had been realized in a way that the populace of largely uneducated people could understand. This is why he gave them a system to develop, understand and realize rather than relying on the inherent belief systems that had, so far, failed them. Although it is accepted that today, in the west, we are well educated, the initial problem of finding a way of communicating the teaching remains the same. We have become so self-centred and fixated on our absolute right to individualism that we resist any form of perceived external authority. In many ways, this makes the communicators' job even harder because, as a result of our conditioning, we have become closed to anything that might entail us having to actually change something ourselves. We have developed other ways that we hope will deal with our worries, namely prescription medication, illegal drugs, alcohol and consumerism in all its many disguises.

Until such time as we can accept that none of these things will alleviate our worries, we can't even start to begin the journey towards the experience of clarity. This, in effect, is the third of the assignments that the Buddha gave us. It's essential to understand that we cultivate both helpful and unhelpful thoughts, but if we follow his helpful suggestions, it will lead to the alleviation or eradication of our worries.

If we are going to embrace life fully and be as happy and con-tented as it is possible to be, then we need to do something to lessen and eventually eradicate those aspects of worrying that are able to be dealt with. We need to learn from within our own experience, the consequences of everything that we think, say and do. It is no use simply believing that what we are told will be of benefit to us. Just because something is written in an ancient text or discoursed by the Venerable, Geshe, Rinpoche, Master, Celebrity Guru whatever-his-name-is, doesn't mean that it's true. Even though these words have now become holy and revered by many, it doesn't make them any more valid. This belief approach will just take us into the world of rule bound, faith and belief based religion, which uses punishment and rewards systems to ensure its survival. This idea that if the vast majority of people believe something to be true it is, is to be frank, barking mad.

Everything within the third assignment is up for challenge. Here he is saying that the worrying aspect of physical, emotional and psychological experience can be alleviated and eventually eradicated. It is the advice of the Buddha himself and it is not about developing belief and faith. It is about developing a level of trust that is based on our own direct experience of putting his teachings into practice. If, after our own honest evaluation of any subject matter, we find that practicing it helps us to detach from the cause of our worries, then we'd be pretty stupid to ignore the result wouldn't we? Conversely, if, after honest evaluation, we found that a suggested practice did not result in lessening our worries, we'd be pretty stupid to continue doing it.

The key phrase here is '**honest evaluation.**' We human beings, as part of our conditioning process, have become masters of self-delusion. Our default status is to rationalise our behaviour and to seek to justify our unhelpful actions by pointing the finger of blame elsewhere. If we are to overcome this behaviour so that we can wholeheartedly make the journey to the experience of clarity, something has to be done. No amount of book reading will do it. No amount of debate will do it. No amount of candle or incense lighting, or praying to mysterious entities will do it. Aligning ourselves to a guru and hanging on their every word will not do it, nor will surrendering ourselves to a mystical higher power. It will not be easy. There will be high points and low points. There will be successes and disappointments. It is a very long journey but if we approach it with integrity and honesty, it will never become a burden.

Dharma practice, if based on our own efforts and our own direct experiences, will lead us in the direction of clarity. We gradually start to experience an authentic mode of living without the beliefs and beyond the worries. This is the journey of practice, the journey of transformation. It is living in action. When we fully experience and see through our attachments, the result is freedom.

It is about finding a healthy balance, our own middle way and one that works for us. It is about making just the right amount of effort. It's a bit like when we're having a bath, if you try and pick up the soap, one of two things can happen. If you try and grab at it too tightly it'll shoot half way across the room. If you try and pick it up too gently it'll slip back into the water. You have to find the balance. You have to discover the middle way.

When we see through our fears and neuroses, the result is love and compassion. When we see without filters of judgment, desire or self-interest, the result is appreciation and the quiet joy of being. Please don't believe this just because I or someone else tells you it is so. Experience it for yourself. Live it. But where do you start? How do you begin to do that? The fourth assignment that the Buddha set out was a step-by-step guide that shows us how to do that in a very practical way. This is the most active ingredient and the part that will be met with the most resistance.

The notion that there are, contained within the teachings of the Buddha, some higher, mystical, or secret hidden elements, is simply human folly. It is just the ego of man. It is the nature of institutions to become authoritarian. They create elitism, with a mass of subordinates who bolster the egos of those higher up the ladder and so the institution survives, grows and becomes dominant. In Darwinian terms, this is a prime example of the law of natural selection in action. There are no higher teachings. There are just deeper understandings. There are deeper understandings that lead to insight and insights that lead to realization. This is what the Buddha consistently told his followers. What he said may well have been taught in many different ways to suit the intellect of particular individuals or groups, but the essence of the teaching was always the same as what we have been exploring here.

Arising out of the realization of clarity, the Buddha sets out four principle assignments for his followers to engage with. He first diagnoses the problem of worrying as being a fundamental part of the unawake, self-biased mind and he encourages us to open our eyes and realize this for ourselves, from within our own direct experience. He acknowledges that this is not going to be easy, mainly because, possibly for the first time in our lives, we have to take full responsibility for our mental states. We have to undertake to eradicate the excuses that we constantly use, pointing the finger of blame at others, at life circumstances or at notions such as fate, chance, luck, coincidence, destiny etc.

Secondly, he points out clearly that the cause of our worrying is that we want things to be other than they are. He doesn't just proclaim this as something to be believed in. He says that we have to develop practices that will enable us to recognise and experience this for ourselves, in every moment of our experience, in the ever changing flow of experience. With regard to this, we find later, in the fourth assignment, that meditation practice is promoted significantly as possibly the most helpful way that we can engage with the work of the second assignment.

The third assignment is slightly different. There is a very fine line between blind faith and trust which has been formed as a result of our own direct experience. Here, the Buddha proclaims that worrying can be alleviated or eradicated. He is not asking us to believe him. He is saying that within the experience of clarity, worrying was eradicated. That was his experience. He is not even saying that it will be your experience. He is setting out a method that he considers might be the most helpful for you to arrive at the same realization of the experience of clarity. Within that suggestion he urges you to fully test and challenge what he says. After your own authentic and honest evaluation, he says that if you find it does not lead to the reduction or lessening of your worries, then throw it away.

Here lies the biggest danger for us. Because of our conditioning factors and habitual patterns of behaviour we will inevitably tell ourselves that something is not working because we are still experiencing worrying. So we quickly throw it away and reassure ourselves that we did follow the Buddha's instructions. We tend to forget the bit about 'authentic and honest evaluation'. It needs to be recognised that the Dharma journey is not a bed of roses. It is challenging to the extreme and at times can be very painful. Honest evaluation is challenging because, if we look deep enough, we will find a fear of change that arises from the pre-conscious fear of non-existence. It is only when we sit with that and experience it for what it actually is, that we will provide ourselves with the opportunity of a break through.

The Buddha used his teaching of the four principle assignments as his primary method of attempting to communicate causality. There were many others ways he later developed, but it was this one that started the ball rolling. So, we have the source realization of causality that resulted in the primary communication of the four principle assignments. Whichever direction we go within the Dharma journey, everything we tackle or engage with needs to be filtered through the primary communication and linked back to the source realization of causality. It could be said that the four assignments are divided into two parts. In the first section there is worrying and its cause and in the second there is its ending and how to end it. Simply put, it is all just arising and ceasing and this is at the heart of the realization of causality, the flow of actuality that is continually changing experience.

It is when we are in reactive mind mode that the vast majority of our wants will arise because there will be a lack of awareness that we are operating on the basis of our habitual patterns of conditioned behaviour. We are unaware that there is a pre-conscious/subconscious on-going want to find perpetual pleasure or to avoid anything unpleasant. This is not necessarily an unhelpful thing. After all, it may well have been something like this that gave rise to us seeking out a change in direction that included engaging with the teachings of the Buddha. It's really helpful to take a long hard and honest look at our wants. When we do, we will be amazed at how much wanting we actually do and until we do take that look with total integrity, how on earth do we expect to be able to do anything about it?

One of the problems is that we find it so very easy to kid ourselves. OK we get it. Worrying happens. To stop worrying we need to stop wanting. Job done. A really helpful way of checking into the actuality aspect to this is to explore what we do with our money. If we adopt a mind-set of **"do I need this or do I want this?"** to everything we spend our money on, not just the big things, everything, and then watch our motivations with integrity, we get a helpful actuality check. If we pay close attention, we might even see through to the worrying behind what we purchase and discover why we really purchase something.

Experientially, it is as if there is a void, a gap or something missing in our lives that we want to fill all the time. We find it almost impossible to be a human being and seek to be a **'human doing'** all the time. We always seem to want something to fill that void. We grab at something to eat, something to listen to, somebody to talk to, something to read, something to do, something to complete us. We eat the contents of the fridge or our hidden supply of treats because we're bored. We chase money and power because we think people will think better of us if we are rich and powerful.

By simply bringing awareness to our wants, we shift our focus from reactive mind mode to responsive mode and this is the doorway that we step through that begins our journey. What is helpful to be aware of from the start is that the Dharma journey itself might simply open up a whole new but very different set of wants. If we find ourselves buying more and more Dharma books for instance, we are wanting more knowledge, but let's face it they all contain the same knowledge. There is a school of thought that suggests that too much knowledge is actually a barrier to the realization of direct experience. It is suggested here that if you just went through your entire Dharma life with a good book about the four principle assignments and put it all into action, that's all you'll ever need by way of knowledge - apart from this book of course.

Awareness of our wants results in a gradual reduction of our habitual patterns of conditioned behaviour and in effect lessens our wants. It's helpful to bear in mind that the experience of want may not be eradicated altogether but it is the worrying aspect of the want that is reduced or eradicated. This isn't about denial or suppression. It is about seeing things as they are with awareness. The entire Dharma journey could be said to be an on-going development process of learning to see things as they are and then learning to let go of those aspects that cause us to worry, so we can realize peace of mind and maintain peace of mind. In effect we exchange an unhelpful want for worldly pleasure into a helpful want for insight into actuality.

One of the greatest myths within Buddhism is that the experience of clarity brings to an end, in the traditional language of Buddhism, all suffering. It is simply not like that. Even after awakening the Buddha continued to age, he got sick and eventually died. The only significant difference was that he saw these things for what they were with an accepting awareness, so worrying did not have an opportunity to cause so many problems by disturbing peace of mind. This is borne out in many different texts but

Buddhists tend to want to be very selective in their reading and only choose the ones that tell them about things that support their beliefs about the Dharma and of course this is very unhelpful as it tends to move you further away from actuality.

In one such text he is shown to be having a conversation with his faithful companion and he says words to the effect:

"I am now old, elderly and at the end of my life. I have reached eighty years old and just as a decrepit cart keeps going with makeshift repairs, likewise, my body seems to keep going in the same way. Only with the ending of certain experiences and not paying attention to outer signs, can I enter into concentration of mind. It is only then that this body is more comfortable."

Could that be a really good way of understanding why the Buddha continued to meditate every day of his life after his awakening right up until his death?

In another text, which is really helpful to know about, he sets out the difference by way of experience between the awakened mind and the self-biased mind. In this teaching he says words to the effect:

'That the self-biased mind when touched by unpleasant experience cries, distressed and distraught with breast beating and wailing, confusion and collapse. It experiences that pain twice, physically and emotionally.'

He likens this with being shot by an arrow and then being shot by a second arrow. The first brings physical pain and the second brings our emotional reaction to the physical pain. He then goes on to say that the awakened mind is touched by an unpleasant experience but they experience only the physical sensation that would be labeled pain, but by not reacting to it they do not get hit with the second arrow of emotional reaction. So, this is telling us that awakening does not end physical pain, it just intimates that it no longer becomes a worry because we are not reacting to it with not want, but seeing it for what it is.

In general terms the vast majority of people believe that the solution to all of their problems is getting as much of what they want that gives them pleasure or less of what they don't want because they don't like it. This is life in reactive mode and it just leads to a never ending cycle of pleasure and pain. Albert Einstein was widely recognised as the most intellectual human being of his generation. In a quote that is attributed to him, although disputed, it states:

"The religion of the future will be a cosmic religion. It should transcend personal God and avoid dogma and theology. If there is any religion that could cope with modern scientific needs it would be Buddhism".

Let's face it, we all love Buddhism. It's so nice and smiley isn't it! We buy and read book after book on it. We build up and cling to our own private collections. We sit and hang on every word uttered by the latest celebrity guru on YouTube. We put up those Buddha quotes, fake or not, on our walls, wear them on our 'T' shirts and have them as screen-savers on our computers or the latest Buddha App on our mobile phone. Yet the thing that most people seem to forget is that what the Buddha taught is of little use, unless we begin to put it into practice. What he taught is a living process of human development that is not dependent on intellectual knowledge but by direct realization.

The Dharma journey is, according to the Buddha, the most practical way in which we can make gradual changes to the way we live our everyday lives so that we will have the greatest opportunity to realize our full potential as human beings within the experience of clarity. This personal development plan has eight themes for us to work on and develop through practice. It is often represented symbolically within the Buddhist world as a golden eight spoke wheel. This wheel of practice is continually turning. We do not stop to work on just one theme at a time until we think we've got it right. We are encouraged to work on each theme collectively all the time. There may be times when we place a greater emphasis on one theme, but generally speaking we are trying to work on all aspects at the same time. This is the fourth principle assignment that was set out by the Buddha.

This is the prescriptive medication that the Buddha suggests will cure us from wanting and worrying. All I can offer you is my own personal experience of taking the medicine. That is, if you approach it with the right frame of mind, it can taste like kids medicine that is loaded with sugar. If we have understood the first two assignments, even if we haven't completed them, we will be motivated to suck it off the spoon and lick it afterwards. If you don't and just do this half heartedly, it is suggested that you make sure that your private health care insurance is up-to-date because you are going to be spending a lot of time at the doctors surgery or hospital.

Chapter Ten: The Eight-Fold Journey

The fourth assignment that was set out by the Buddha begins with a commitment to change. Irrespective of what caused you to connect with the Dharma, you make a commitment to yourself that you will engage with it by practicing it within a particular context. This is actually a very important point to remember. You are making this commitment to yourself. The Dharma journey is separated into two distinct parts. First is the realization aspect, which is then followed by the process of actualization. The realization aspect will be different for everybody. At one end of the scale you may find people who experienced that moment of clarity that changes everything they ever held true, as an instantaneous awakening. Everything they had ever believed in has been shattered by a direct experience of clarity into the nature of existence that is causality.

This was the experience of the Buddha and has been the experience of many others throughout history. Despite attempts to put this experience up there on an unachievable pedestal, it is not as uncommon as you are led to believe. Realization is not the most difficult bit. It's the actualization process that causes the greatest difficulty. At the other end of the scale there will be a realization that you are unhappy with some aspect of your life experience and you want it to be different than it is. This we call worrying.

It is called an eight-fold journey because it has no starting point and no end point. It unfolds in an ever deepening level of experience within the journey. Bear in mind that this is actually an internal journey with an external result. It is not as if you are over here and the journey is over there. With this in mind we can free ourselves of expectations that actuality is somewhere other than right here, right now, before our very eyes.

Most often our first initial moment of realization might arise as a result of personal tragedy or loss, bereavement of a loved one, the end of a long-term relationship, the loss of a job or maybe even financial ruin. It can arise at a time when someone begins to question their own existence or the meaning and purpose of life. Maybe it will happen when the children have all left home or they are looking to fill in time with something of interest. For some people this initial realization might even arise as a result of what appears to them to be an apparent spontaneous mystical experience of some kind. For others it may arise when they hear the Dharma for the first time, or whilst visiting a Buddhist temple or centre or even just meeting a Dharma practitioner who has inspired them. Something just clicks in their head as if they had found something that they had already known in the depth of their being. It's often described as a kind of coming home. Something just seems comfortable or makes sense.

Others have reported that it arose in a rare moment of bliss whilst surrounded by the beauty, peace and quiet of nature, or listening to a beautiful piece of music or exploring a work of art. It can even arise within the intellectual, or those with an analytical mind, who try to explore by reason and logic the nature of existence. It can certainly arise as a result of meditation practice when the mind lets go of any sense of **'you'** meditating within the various stages of concentration.

However this initial realization experience has arisen for you, it's important not to lose it or forget it. It needs to be cultivated, deepened and clarified to a stage where it permeates and transforms your whole being. Many who take up Dharma practice and begin the Dharma journey do lose sight of the initial realization when the level of worrying becomes manageable. Or its lost sight of when they begin to experience a bit more comfort with how things are for them, or when a particular problem appears to have been solved. It's helpful to bear in mind that the Buddha didn't teach the Dharma as a sticking plaster method of solving problems in the short term. He taught a method that potentially eradicates the entire problem for good. The approach you take in this regard is entirely up to you. If you are in the right place, nobody will be there twisting your arm. It is you who will experience directly the results of your efforts or lack of them.

One of the difficulties of the fourth assignment is it's the one we are generally not too keen on. We would much rather take a clarity pill or take a swig of an awakening elixir, or let someone else do the work for us so we can bask in their glory and hope something helpful will rub off on us. I hate to disappoint you, but no bell ringing, candle lighting or rubbing the Buddha's belly will get you there. It is you that has to do the work and the progress you make will be dependent on the amount of effort you put in. The Buddha sets out the method and points you in the direction of the journey, but it is you that has to walk the walk.

Having had our moment, several moments, or an on-going experience of the initial realization of worrying, we now turn to the eight-fold journey that is the initial actualization process. Each unfolding of this journey is governed by the overriding principle of the method, which is that each of the other seven themes accord with the development and realization of 'helpful view.' In classical Buddhism they do use the terminology of 'right and wrong' but this can give the impression that there is a right way of doing things as opposed to a wrong way. It gets itself all rule bound again and that is never helpful. In other developments some chose the term 'perfect,' but again it has unhelpful connotations for us in the west where a lack of self-worth is so prevalent.

In this approach we use the term 'helpful' because it sits well with the whole developmental approach that is set out within secular western Buddhism. Helpful view is that which is in accord with the realization of causality. This is the experience of clarity that was the realization experience of the Buddha. Because of the enormity and often mind-boggling nature of helpful view, I will leave it till last so that you can get to grips with the other seven themes first, but I will point out that it is helpful view that is the overriding and first theme of this journey. This is known as the vision aspect and the other seven themes are the transformation aspect.

The second theme of the eight-fold journey is the development of 'helpful emotion.' One of the biggest problems for those who embark on the Dharma journey is to translate what they have read and understood from an intellectual perspective into action. If we understand that the basic premise of the Dharma journey is to avoid harm wherever it is possible to do so and to learn to be kind, we can see how very simple that sounds. But how difficult is it to actually put it into practice?

Throughout theistic religion and religious Buddhism you will find people who can recite line by line great texts. They can write about it, give lectures on it, but they often seem unable to actually develop that knowledge into practice. Even the most sincere of scholars would experience a degree of worrying when they own up to the fact, that it is so difficult at times to actually do it. For many, there appears to be some obstruction within us that prevents us breaking through from intellectual knowledge, to a realization of clarity and this is where we will find perhaps the solution to the problem.

As part of our human nature we have varying levels of awareness. There is the level where we think we know something with the conscious mind, the rational part of ourselves. But there is a deeper level made up of emotion, instinct or willed actions and this is much stronger than our rational mind and it is this part of our mind that we need to tackle with practice to engage fully with our emotions in a helpful way. This is our conditioning factors, the things that drive us forward repeating habitual behaviour patterns.

One of the greatest tasks of the Dharma practitioner is to find an emotional equivalent for our intellectual understanding and until we have done this, very little progress can be made within the journey. This is possibly why we find helpful emotion as the second theme of the Dharma wheel. In many ways the remaining six themes would be very difficult to work on effectively until such a time as when we have got our emotions in check. Which is why it is emphasised how important this part of our practice is. We only have to look at our own life experience and we will know that there will have been many times where our emotions have got us into unhelpful situations, when awareness would have told us to leave the situation well alone.

Throughout the Buddhist world it is widely accepted that the most effective way to begin developing helpful emotions is to live, as best we can, within a framework of ethical principles and to undertake some form of renunciation. Now that word renunciation can sound a bit scary. It conjures up perhaps an image of a need to give everything away and going off to live in a cave or monastery or something. But this is not what it really means. We know within the context of the primary teaching of the four principal assignments, that attachment is a major contributory factor in the arising of worrying. This is why it is helpful to attempt to loosen our grip on worldly things. If we have experienced sufficient worry in relation to the unsatisfactory and impermanent nature of material things, it would bring about an encouragement to let go of stuff. If we are to make progress on the Dharma journey there is a necessity to change.

Causality shows that change is inevitable, but in relation to human beings, our conditioning factors are so powerful that we have to actually do something to kick start the opportunity to change. It is always helpful to learn to let go. We can't just continue along as we did before. If our lives are not changing in this way then we have very little chance of realizing the experience of clarity and the eradication of worrying that results in peace of mind.

There is no set pattern to renunciation and within Buddhism, if you are in the right place, there will be no one telling you what you should and should not give up. Whatever we choose to do, the resulting experience is to lead a much simpler and less cluttered life. If it doesn't, you have either let go too soon, or you haven't let go at all, or you are just kidding yourself, or are going through the motions. It is likely that most of us have far too much stuff lying around. A very useful exercise is to go around your home with a pen and paper and write down everything that you haven't used for a year. You'd be surprised how much holding on we do. It's a bit like having a just-in-case mentality. With letting go comes a positive opportunity to practice generosity. Giving what we don't need to those who may need it more than we do is always a helpful thing to do.

Generosity is recognised as the first real step onto the Dharma journey. We might not have got our ethical practice quite there yet. We might not be able to meditate regularly. But there is nothing stopping us from being generous other than our self-biased mind that lives in a world that does not fully understand the concept of authentic generosity, which is the giving just for the sake of giving, without wanting anything in return. Not even a thank you.

When you engage with the development of helpful emotions you begin to explore the origins of any emotional thoughts and experiences that arise. You observe how connected these emotional thoughts and experiences are connected to your conditioning and how many of them arise as a result of your habitual patterns of thinking, speaking and acting. If the emotional reaction is an unhelpful one, then it provides the opportunity to seek clarification from anyone you have reacted against, to see if you have read the situation correctly or not. If all else fails and you are still experiencing unhelpful thoughts or emotions you can turn your attention to helpful view and engage with it on the basis of knowing that it is not permanent and it too will pass. You do not need to hide from it, or suppress it. You see it for what it is and either wait for it to subside, or let it go.

Helpful emotion is about the complete harmonisation of the whole emotional, intellectual and habitual aspects of our being with the way things are in actuality. This is about letting go of attitudes and actions that lead to further worry for ourselves, others and the world around us and replacing them with ones that are helpful for us to move towards clarity and peace of mind.

The third theme of the Dharma journey is the development towards the ideal of **'helpful speech.'** Speech is something we engage in all the time. Our work here is to develop our speech so that it becomes not only accurate, but kindly, gentle and helpful. We develop the kind of speech that leads to harmony and unity. The problem that we have in doing this is that we tend to pad things out a bit, exaggerate a little, or want to bend the facts in the direction in which we would like them to go. How often have we heard that a little white lie wouldn't do any harm? You'd be surprised how difficult it is to be totally honest, especially when we begin to combine honesty with other ethical principles such as doing less harm. How often do we repeat what we have read or heard without knowing for ourselves how accurate it is? To learn to speak honestly we have to learn to observe our motivations, what drives us, which means we need to begin by being totally honest with ourselves yet again.

Helpful speech is not only accurate it is also gentle and caring. This does not mean just using terms of endearment. It means talking with complete awareness of the person to whom we are speaking. Perhaps you might have noticed how rarely we actually look at people when we talk to them. We look almost anywhere but at the person themselves. We like to think that we are loving and caring people, but very often in our communication with others we are simply relating to them in terms of our own emotional reactions to them. We react emotionally to others in a certain way and then we attribute that emotional reaction to them as a quality of them. For instance, if people do what we would like them to do, then we say they are good, kind and helpful and vice versa.

If we really understood ourselves and the nature of our relationships we would find that we hardly know even those who we count as being closest to us. We might have lived with someone for years, but all we have possibly been doing is recognising within each other our emotional reactions. This is why there is so much misunderstanding between people. Because we really don't know each other, we can't communicate accurately and we end up with a kind of pseudo-communication and nothing more. What we end up with is a kind of maze of projections.

According to the Buddha, we should speak that which is helpful in the sense of speaking in such a way as to promote harmony and individual growth. In the west in particular we have a serious problem with self-worth. If we are told something good about ourselves we are uncomfortable, or may even experience a sense of guilt about it.

It is helpful to learn to accept what others see in us that perhaps we have not recognised in ourselves. There may be a time for criticism, but this is a very dangerous area because, until such time as we are fully aware of our motivations, such criticism would tend to be harmful and not helpful. What we can do, is say or do something that we think would be helpful but subconsciously what we are doing is projecting our own stuff outwards.

If we can learn to communicate accurately with a concern that has an awareness of the other person's being; if we speak in a way as to promote the other's growth; if we are more concerned with their needs than about our own; if we are not projecting our own emotional states, or using or exploiting them; then the result will be, that in communicating with another person we will forget all about ourselves.

To work towards the ideal of developing helpful speech not only is it to be accurate, kind, gentle, caring and helpful it also actively promotes harmony and unity. This doesn't mean that we have to agree with everything all the time. The Buddha would say that the most helpful speech of all is when we are engaging in silence. All the while we are silent we are not lying, we're not doing any harm, we're not wasting time and effort in idol gossip. That's not to say that it is infallible, because there is still a thought process that lies behind the silence. We also have self-talk going on in our thought process and that needs to be addressed as well.

When we engage with helpful speech we can apply helpful view by looking to see if what we are saying is little more than trying to support our beliefs, or our sense of identity, or to be proved right. As an example let's look at one of the most emotive subjects in Buddhism. What we eat and the principle of kindness. What would usually happen is that both sides of this argument would start bombarding the other with all manner of rationalisations and justifications to support their beliefs and views. Quite often, if not always, it usually ends in a rage even in Buddhist circles. If we apply helpful view we will see that to survive, human beings cannot exist without doing harm, or causing suffering to other beings. We also use helpful view to realize that we are not responsible for what any other person chooses to do in this respect. That does not give us free reign but takes the heat out of what is, in effect an unhelpful view of the situation.

Speech is probably one of the most powerful tools for transformation. It gives shape to the world we live in. In naming things we give colour and expression to things around us and what we say in many ways expresses a large part of who we are and how our world is. It is really helpful to bring some silence into our daily lives and maybe even keep silent for a day or two here or there if we can. To live in this world is to speak and because our speech has such a profound effect on us, others and the world around us, we really have no option but to transform it. Helpful speech therefore is speech, which, first of all, is accurate and factual. But it also seeks to avoid creating unnecessary division between people. It is kind, caring and harmonious and never frivolous although it can be, and often is, light-hearted, ironic and humorous.

Theme four is the development towards **'helpful action.'** This brings us to the very basics of living a Dharma life. It involves adopting a set of guiding ethical principles for us to engage with fully. This is what Dharma practitioners do. Whether we like it or not, we have to act out every moment of our lives. The only question we have to resolve is how to act in a way that puts kindness above everything else. The modernist view is that there has been a general decline in moral conduct as man has turned away from mainstream religion. This is too simplistic to accept blindly.

When the institutions of religion did control the behaviour of the populace it was fear of retribution or punishment that motivated the behaviour, rather than the acceptance of personal responsibility. In the modern New Age philosophy of self-help and positive thinking, there is a mind-set that seems to have developed that **"if you do something and it seems OK then that thing is right, at least for you."** Even in an age where governments and lawmakers legislate to keep us in line, it is still a fear of punishment that keeps most in check. Eventually we will have no option but to re-think, re-examine and even re-imagine our ethical lives to survive, because all of the above are gradually losing their hold over us and it would appear, to many, that anarchy will reign supreme as a result if we don't.

Over 2,600 years ago the Buddha proposed a set of ethical guidelines that promoted personal responsibility and self regulation. These principles are not just a set of rules, although when you first come across them it may seem like that. You might even think that the Buddha is doing the same as the theistic religions creator entity, by telling us what we should and shouldn't do. In fact it is quite the opposite. The words 'should' and 'should not' have no place in the language of the Dharma practitioner. Here we are encouraged to experience for ourselves the direct correlation between everything we think say and do with what our moment by moment physical, emotional and psychological experience is. Putting to one side for one moment any belief in the concept of re-birth and the crippling and neurotic emotion of guilt that is associated with conditioning factors, it will be clear that this approach to ethics is not based on the reward and punishment systems of rules and regulations. What it allows the practitioner to do, is to develop a level of awareness that will experience directly the results of their own thoughts, speech and actions. Our actions, after all, are simply an expression of our mental states and as our practice develops we notice, on ever more subtle levels, that there is always more to do to refine those mental states.

On the Dharma journey we try to let go of terms such as 'good' and 'bad,' 'right and wrong,' 'skilful or unskilful.' Those words and how we've come to associate with them are deeply embedded in our subconscious through the western conditioning process and have far too much of an unhelpful judgmental attitude within them. For that reason they are replaced with new terms to describe our conduct as being either 'helpful or unhelpful' towards the realization of clarity or 'kind and unkind' in our everyday practice. This is very significant because these terms suggest that ethics is very much a matter of insight. You cannot act in a way that is helpful unless you can understand things, unless you can see possibilities and explore them. So it is more a matter of insight rather than one of just having good intentions. Unhelpful and unkind actions are defined as those which result in worrying in the form of want, not want and confusion. Helpful or kind actions are those that result in the practice of kindness, contentment and clear thinking. This very simple distinction places the whole question of ethics in a different light. We will be exploring the subject of ethics in depth in a later chapter.

When we engage with helpful action we can apply helpful view by observing our motivations. We can look to see what precedes what we think, say and do. We can work to lessen the protection of our self-biased mind by seeing beyond the surface of our thoughts, speech and actions. We can look, on an ever deeper level, at our ethical lifestyle and see how what we think, say and do is in accord with helpful view.

Theme five can be a bit of a problem for those of us in the west. Our society is based on materialism and consumerism and therefore we have little option but to enter the world of employment so we can pay the bills. This is no excuse to let ourselves off though, or to try and rationalise our decisions. What we do to make a living has immense ramifications for us, in relation to our psychological and emotional well-being. Here we are aiming to develop towards the ideal of finding and then working within a 'helpful livelihood.'

The occupations set out by the Buddha as those that he considered could not be reconciled with Dharma practice were stated 2,600 years ago, but are perhaps equally valid today. If you were to accept them as an initial guide, but seek to add other occupations that relate to 21st century living you would be on the same page as the Buddha. The Buddha's list consists of the following:

1. **Trafficking in living beings whether human or animals**
2. **Dealing in animals for the purpose of slaughter**
3. **Butcher or seller of meat products**
4. **Seller of poison which includes anything that has a stupefying effect on the mind**
5. **Involvement in the selling of weapons of that cause harm**
6. **Earning from palmistry, fortune-telling, spiritualism, astrology etc**

What is helpful to explore within our practice is what effect our employment is having on us, others and the wider world, even if we are employed in an occupation that is not included on the list.

Accepting that there is a requirement to earn money, we always have the opportunity to find meaningful work that helps us to develop the Dharma journey. This will often require a stepping back from the drive for more material wealth, in exchange for an existence that is much simpler, but more content and more personally rewarding and this can be quite scary for many. Within a westernised conditioned society that is wholly based on a materialistic existence and where achievement is measured by financial success and what we physically have, it may be difficult to even consider making a move that may leave us with less, because we will think we will be considered to be a failure by the rest of society. If we are serious about the Dharma journey we really have no option. If we are not letting go of any concerns about what others think of us we will be getting nowhere. The Dharma journey is about transformation of the whole being and not just the intellect. It is in the realm of what we do for a living that provides us with a real opportunity at least to make significant progress on that journey.

Within western Buddhist circles a system of employment has been adopted which is a kind of co-operative business. It is not based on profit margins but more aligned to making working lives an integral part of Dharma practice. It involves Buddhists working together. This has taken on many forms from whole-food shops, vegetarian café's, book shops, gift shops selling fair-trade products. There have also been building firms and gardening companies. Almost everything has been tried, but whatever has been undertaken, it has been done with a mind-set that is firmly based on ethical practice, thereby transforming not only those employed but providing an opportunity to be of help to those that the business came into contact with.

Nobody ever got rich doing this, but individual needs were always met and substantial amounts of money were raised to further the promotion of the Dharma by purchasing Buddhist centres and retreat centres. This kind of opportunity to extend their practice has even resulted in many people who had independent financial means and little need of earning, actually giving their time and effort for no pay at all, as they recognised the benefit of spending their time with like-minded people in an enterprise that provided such a helpful opportunity for individual development on the journey.

So what's stopping us? It is suggested here, as always, that it is fear. Fear based on the idea that we are fixed ego-identities with a future to protect. Fear of failure. Fear of the unknown. If you have understood, even the basics of what the Buddha taught, you will have already realized that the Dharma life is about stepping outside of our individual comfort zones. It is about making changes and what we do to exist financially possibly provides the most helpful opportunity to put all that we have learned to the test. What an opportunity it would be to create such a livelihood. Will we do it? Probably not and we shouldn't give ourselves too much of a hard time about that. Until that time arrives, or even if it never arrives, look to what you are doing to earn a living now and see if it can be reconciled with Dharma practice. If it's not, realistically you have a big decision to make.

When we engage with helpful livelihood we can apply helpful view by exploring, in detail, the consequences for us, others and the world around us. This can be quite uncomfortable at times, but if we are going to make progress on this journey with integrity we really have no option but to filter how we make a living through the eyes of helpful view.

The sixth theme is the development towards the ideal of '**helpful effort**.' Being a Dharma practitioner is a thing in action. It is not enough to sit back and read books, attend classes or be part of a community. There is always something for the individual practitioner to be doing to move them in the direction of reaching their full potential within the experience of clarity. No matter what stage of the Dharma journey you are on, there is always more to be done. Generally speaking, people begin with lots of enthusiasm. They want to take in more knowledge and they really get into meditation. Very often it quickly wears off. This is because our habitual patterns of behaviour are so strong that they overtake our resolve to practice, even in simple matters like getting up half an hour earlier to meditate or finding a space during the day or evening to do so. We might succeed once or twice or maybe even three times, but by the fourth morning the warm cosy bed seems more appealing, especially in the winter months.

The same problem applies to study and ethics. Other things seem to just get in the way and our Dharma life is put on the back burner for a while until we hit another patch of enthusiasm, or more often than not, when something else goes wrong with our lives and worrying comes a bit more uncomfortable than usual. Like everything else on the Dharma journey, we have to approach this with absolute honesty and integrity. If we kid ourselves we will get nowhere. There is really no point in wearing the name badge of being a Buddhist. It might make us appear cool to others, but it is helpful to be constantly aware of the deeper motivations behind the choices you make. The Buddha sets out four ways in which we need to be developing helpful effort on the path and he used the word '**exertions**' which will give you an indication as to the level of effort he is referring to in this regard.

The first effort he suggests that is helpful to explore and develop is the "**prevention of the arising of unhelpful mental states that haven't arisen yet.**" We have learned that an unhelpful mental state is one that leads to worrying in the form of want, not want and confusion, expressed as unhelpful view. In trying to locate the actual source of these unhelpful mental states we have to examine the senses. If we are walking through the shopping mall and our attention is drawn to something in a shop window and a thought pops into our head **"mmm that's nice. I'd like to have that"** what has happened is that through the physical organ of the eye, our sight sense, there arises a want to have it. The same would apply when you are walking past the curry house and get a whiff of a Madras sauce. Here the physical organ of the nose, our smell sense, allows the same want to arise in the mind. Conversely, if your not paying attention to what you're eating and you just happen to put a brussel sprout in your mouth, the physical organ of the mouth, our taste sense, allows not want to arise in the mind. After all it's an absolute truth that brussel sprouts are the work of the Devil. Well that's my story and I'm sticking to it.

So, to prevent the arising of unhelpful mental states we have to develop a greater sense of awareness and do what we can to guard our senses from opportunities where they can be overcome by unhelpful mind states. There is nothing wrong with any of these things. It is OK to buy pretty sparkly things, eat curry and even Brussel sprouts if you're that way inclined. It is just about awareness of our senses and our wanting things to be different than they are that is the basic source of all our worries.

The second effort he suggests that is helpful to explore and develop is the **"eradication of unhelpful mental states that have already arisen."** To help us with this he offers guidance based on five things that will get in our way from making progress.

1. The problem of wanting material things to make us happy

2. The problem of not want. This covers all aspects from the most gross to the most subtle; antagonism, aggressiveness, dislike, even righteous indignation, which has been a major cause of difficulties throughout religious history.

3. The problem of restlessness and worry. This is a huge problem in the west. In the western world when you observe people you don't get a sense of peacefulness about them. Their lives seem to be full of worry of some kind. We seem to live very fast paced lives. This doesn't mean that we need to slow down because we can do things quite quickly with full awareness. It means that when we find ourselves turning from one thing to another because we didn't find the first thing satisfying we are in a state of worry.

4. The problem of boredom and remorse. This is when we get a bit stiff and dry. When the head of steam we've built up for the Dharma life is beginning to wane a little. This can also be found in the mind-sets of many in the modern world who develop an attitude of why bother, what's it got to do with me. It can be a difficult thing to spot in ourselves as we may see it as being cool, calm and collected, or laid back, but again if we examine ourselves more deeply we might find that we have just stagnated.

5. The problem of doubt & indecision. This is when we are stuck in the middle, or sitting on the fence. We can't make a decision either way, when we can't make any kind of commitment. This is very common. It's called perpetual seeking. In many ways it is less unhelpful to become a believer and settle down into that comfort zone than forever wandering with uncertainty.

The Buddha compared the mind to water. In its natural state it is pure, translucent and sparkling, but it can be contaminated in many ways. In the same way, the mind, which is also pure in nature, can be defiled by these five problems. Unlike theistic religion, in Buddhism we are considered to be born as pure sensory beings and then pursue the purity that conditioning has dirtied. We are not born sinners who then have to spend their lives experiencing guilt and atone for their wrong doing.

The mind that is full of wanting things to be different than they are is said to be like a glass of clear water that someone has put their paintbrush in and wiggled it around a bit. It gets a bit cloudy. The mind overcome by not want is compared with water reaching boiling point, hissing and letting off steam. The mind that is disturbed by worry is like the surface water of a still pond being whipped up into waves by a strong wind. The mind in the grip of boredom is like a pond choked with weeds and the mind that is under the influence of doubt and indecision is like water which is full of evil smelling black mud at the bottom of the same pond, more so when that doubt has arisen as a result of third party external influence which is the hardest level of doubt to eradicate.

'Purification' is a much used word in classical Buddhism and can often be misunderstood. It has nothing to do with the wearing of hair shirts or beating ourselves up with sticks. It refers to the development of clarity. The Buddha provides us with guidance with a set of four things for us to work with.

1. Consider the consequences of the unhelpful mental state. If we get angry what is our experience? How does it affect us, others and the world around us?

2. Cultivating the opposite of the unhelpful mental state. If we have a problem with someone it's helpful to work on our relationship with them, perhaps with the awareness of kindness practice

3. Allow the unhelpful mental state to pass. Remember that nothing is fixed. Everything is in a constant state of change and our mind is no different. Paying attention, letting go and just watching the change is the key here without giving in to reaction.

4. Suppression. We grit our teeth and make an effort to push through it. This is very different from repression which can lead to all kinds of psychological problems. But, it is suggested that this is only a last ditch option if all efforts of the other three have been exhausted, as even suppression, if not processed in a helpful way, will give rise to worry later on.

The third effort he suggests that is helpful to explore is the **'development of helpful mental states."** This is not just about thinking nice thoughts or positive thinking. It means the development of higher states of awareness through meditation. Meditation is more than just about developing a concentrated mind. Its real aim, in the long term, is to transform awareness. Needless to say that without a regular meditation practice, we will always find ourselves on a merry-go-round of habitual behaviour and thought patterns. Even if we consider ourselves to be a great thinker, or contemplative by nature, or are capable of working all these things out with a mind that is not stilled by meditation, we will only be kidding ourselves to some extent. That's because without that discipline in our lives all we are doing is coming at things with the distracted self-biased mind.

The fourth effort he suggests that is helpful to explore is **'maintaining helpful mental states.'** Having prevented and eradicated unhelpful mental states and developed helpful mental states, we now have to maintain the higher states of awareness we have developed. If we stop our practice for even one moment we will find ourselves walking backwards. Consistency is therefore essential. If we give up when we reach a kind of plateau, where our level of worrying is now manageable, all that effort we have made will be devalued so quickly and you can be assured that worrying will arise again with a vengeance. When we engage with helpful effort we can apply helpful view by being totally honest with ourselves. That does not mean beating ourselves up, or doing the guilt trip thing. It is about making a moment by moment commitment to stay in a helpful mind state and the greatest aid we have for that is helpful view.

The seventh theme of the journey is the development towards the ideal of '**helpful awareness.**' For most of us our moment by moment lives consists of one distraction after another. We are rarely present with just one thing at a time. A lack of concentration is the basic problem that lies behind this activity of the mind. In many ways, because of our lack of concentration it leads to no continuity of purpose. We become a succession of different personalities as we engage with different things. We can't settle into becoming a single authentic being with the capacity for growth. Awareness is quite the opposite. In exploring the subject of awareness it can be helpful to break it down into four categories.

The first category is '**awareness of physical things.**' This relates to the whole of our material environment which is full of so many different objects. Generally speaking, we only have a vague awareness of what is around us. We probably don't even spend a nanosecond actually looking at anything specifically. What we tell ourselves is that we just don't have the time and this says a great deal about life in the modern western world. When I say stop and look I don't mean just stare at things, but actually see them fully for what they are. If you were to sit in the park and placed your attention in a sufficiently concentrated way on just one tree, it wouldn't be very long before you actually merged with the tree. In effect there would be no 'you' and no 'tree.' There would just be the experience of interconnectedness.

The second category is 'awareness of oneself.' At any given moment there are three main things that are going on within us. There is physical experience, an emotional experience and a psychological experience. To become aware of our physical experience we actually have to become fully engaged with observing our body movements and when we do this it will automatically lead to a slowing down. When we are walking, note the sensations of movements and how each body part is connected and has a role to play in even a single step. When we are sitting become aware of the physical sensation of contact between body and surface. One common misunderstanding about the slowing down process that arises when awareness is practiced is that you get less done. It's actually quite the opposite. You find the person who dashes around like a mad thing, trying to get as much done as possible, achieves very little to any real satisfaction. The person who practices within awareness, dealing with just one thing at a time, fully engaged, completes the task with a greater proficiency and in the long run actually gets more done.

You often find people talking about their feelings. It is a very common term these days. If we talk about feelings within Buddhism it is something quite different. Here, a feeling is either an awareness of a physical sensation or a thought that is connected to it, or an emotional reaction or response to something. All of our many and varied reactions or responses can be compiled into three categories.

1. Pleasant
2. Unpleasant
3. Neutral

By becoming more aware of our physical, emotional and psychological experiences, we will find that our unhelpful emotional mind states, those borne out of want, not want, or the confusion of unhelpful view, will be resolved and those borne out of helpful emotional thinking states such as kindness, contentment and clear thinking, will have the opportunity to be refined.

If we take anger as something that most people would rather do without, but find themselves engaging with at varying levels, we can perhaps see how it works. If we develop an awareness of those emotional reactions, we will first notice that we have been angry. We notice afterwards. With practice we will realize that we are actually angry in the moment. With further practice we will become aware of anger arising. With more practice the opportunity for anger to arise will subside or at the very least be brought under control.

When we turn to our thought process it is suggested that if I asked you what you were thinking right now you wouldn't know. This is because for most of the time we actually don't think at all. Thoughts drift in and out without us being aware of them. There is no directed thinking going on for much of the time. We do not decide to think about something and then actually think about it. With awareness of thought it's helpful to learn to watch, moment by moment to see where the thoughts come from and where they go. If we do this we will find the flow of thoughts slowing down and that the mental chatter, which for most people seems never ending, will slow down or come to a halt. With sufficient training and practice the mind will become, at certain points, settled and still. All discursive thoughts, ideas and concepts will be wiped out and the mind will be left in a space where insight can be encouraged, developed, or will arise quite naturally.

The third category is 'awareness of people.' Within western culture in particular we rarely make eye contact with another human being let alone actually communicate fully with them. You may have heard of something called 'Darsan' this is a very common thing within eastern culture and also apparent spiritual circles. People travel long distances just to be in the physical presence of their teacher. No actual teaching happens. The teacher just sits there and the students become fully aware of him/her as an apparent spiritual being, or as the living embodiment of an apparent spiritual ideal. Although nothing is said between them, communication is said to be taking place on a deeper level than using the spoken word. It's said to be almost telepathic at times. Make of it as you will, but it is suggested here that in actuality what is going on has nothing to do with them and all to do with what is going on with you.

The fourth category is 'awareness of the way things are.' This does not mean just thinking or contemplating about actuality. The realization of actuality as being empty of all conceptual content and beyond the reach of thought, imagination, aspiration or desire is the awakening experience. This is the world of the meditator who has traversed the different levels within the meditative process and can direct the mind to the world of non-conceptual thinking. We will discuss this in depth when we explore meditation in a later chapter. When we engage with helpful awareness we can apply helpful view by observing everything we see, hear, taste, touch, smell as it is, without the conditioned labeling of the thought process. At the same time we can work against the wanting to change any experience into something else because we find it pleasant, neutral or unpleasant. We can actually allow helpful view to just be present with the arising and subsiding of sight experience as it changes of its own accord, and with the arising and subsiding of sounds, tastes, contacts, and smells. We can just let them be as they are.

Paying close attention to what is happening, moment by moment, is essential to Dharma practice. Letting go of thoughts of the past and not fantasising about the future, but being as present as possible, moment by moment, in everything we do. Meditation and living a meditative life is the key. Human beings are a very distracted and un-integrated species. We're mostly lost in a haze of preoccupation and worrying or just numbed by sensory overload. Meditation and awareness practice is the bedrock of the Dharma life.

The eighth theme is the development of 'helpful concentration.' This is where the mind has been trained to be firmly fixed or established in one-pointed awareness. It's where the mind is settled on one thing and one thing only. It also has a much richer meaning in the sense of the whole mind/body complex being engrossed in a higher level of awareness. Quite often this second area is overlooked and the Buddha's teaching of the eight-fold journey can become based around the goal of achieving concentrated states. But the culmination of the plan represents the fruition of the whole of the journey of transformation on all levels and in every aspect of one's being. In other words it represents the transformation from a confused, self-biased mind state, to an awakened mind state. It takes us right back to the very start of the eight-fold journey where our initial realization has been transformed into the realization of the experience of clarity.

When we engage with helpful concentration we can apply helpful view by understanding that the Buddha did not teach meditation as an exercise in relaxation, or as a means to reduce anxiety or depression. He did not teach meditation as a means to make us nicer people. These may be helpful bi-products of meditation, but that is not why he taught it. That is just an example of unhelpful view. The helpful view is that he taught meditation because it was meditation that gave rise to the experience of clarity. That, in itself, is an example of causality in evidence. **'When I did this - this happened.' 'When I didn't do this - this didn't happen.'** He spent at least six years doing all manner of things and he was no nearer to the realization of clarity than the day he left home until he sat down and meditated.

On this journey towards clarity we experience three individual stages which do not necessarily go in any particular order. The first of these is **'calmness'**. In experiential terms this would be when mental activity in the sense of discursive thoughts or the clattering of the mental machinery is either minimal or not too obtrusive or bothering us. It's there, but in the background and we're OK with it. The second of these stages is the **'alertness'** phase that arises as a result of practicing concentration. Everyone who meditates regularly will experience this to some degree. The most common experience is one of lights of various kinds. These are an indication that the mind has become concentrated to a level of awareness that is raised slightly and the mind/body complex is responding accordingly. Within this experience there also arise small glimpses of insight. This is a moment where things make sense for the very first time. These experiences and others, although very transformative in themselves, are not permanent. Logic, reason, concept and intellect very quickly take over and you're almost back to where you started or you've made a little forward progress. Then we have **'tranquility'** which is a more refined level of calmness where the busyness of physical, emotional and psychological experience has finally settled down and creates the opportunity for the insight stages. Consistent meditation practice will eventually lead to levels of concentration that are experienced by only the most dedicated and skilful meditators. It can take a lifetime of practice to develop this level of concentration. This is the world of the imageless, the directionless, or no-thing-ness.

We now find ourselves back at the very start of the eight-fold journey. Here we find the overriding principle of the plan that so far we haven't explored. The reason for this is that it is so confronting at times and goes beyond intellectual concepts and everyday language that people often just give up at the first hurdle. It's the part of the plan in which our pre-conscious, biological nature aspect of being creates an inherent fear of non-existence and will encourage us to avoid engaging with it. This is where the self-biased mind will fight for supremacy. It is the classic battle between the Buddha and Mara under the Bodhi tree over 2,600 years ago. **'Helpful view'** has three very different aspects to it.

1. There is helpful view that is formed by an intellectual understanding of causality

2. There is helpful view that is formed on the basis of irreversible insight into causality

3. There is the helpful view of no view when causality is fully realized within the experience of clarity

The overriding component within the experience of clarity is the realization of causality. It is this realization that set the Buddha on his teaching ministry. It was the answer to the question that had plagued him for years and was the determining factor as to why he left home and become a wanderer. It is this experience that his entire life's communications are based on and yet it is the one that many on the journey avoid taking a good look at because it seems too difficult to comprehend even intellectually. It is this teaching that sets what has become Buddhism apart from all of the monotheistic religions and even those of the multi-deity varieties.

It is a teaching that the greatest scientific minds throughout history have failed to get close to dismissing and it was all achieved, we are told, by sitting under a tree and meditating. It is his only teaching. It is his Dharma. What followed were communications that arose within a particular context that would have included aspects that were historical, social, political, economical and religious. He used the ideas and concepts of his time, the superstitions, the rituals, the beliefs, the dogma, the language and turned all of it back on itself to communicate this new Dharma. It is vital to understand this context because it has led to so much confusion.

What the Buddha discovered within that experience was that all physical, emotional, psychological or a combination of those things, arise in response to at least one preceding cause and often an infinite web of contributory and interconnected conditioning factors. Within that experience it was realized that no first cause to any thing could ever be discovered and no end effect either. There was, in effect, just conditioned causal continuity that is no-thing-ness. He realized that all physical, emotional and psychological things have three aspects in common. They are all impermanent, i.e. they are always in a continuing process of change. Because of that impermanent nature they all contain an aspect of worry and finally that no thing is of, or by itself, existent as a thing.

In relation to human beings this is the part that we have the most difficulty with. What this realization shows is that there is no fixed or separate and enduring ego-identity, personality, individual, self, soul, spirit, essence, mind-stream, conscience, energy, vibration, inner, outer, or any other thing than can be identified, labeled or established as being you, me or I. What this teaching does not do is to deny the existence of a personality that thinks of itself as a separate ego identity or self. Of course we exist in the relative world of everyday life. But that is just the game of the conditioned, confused, self-biased mind that is the primary cause behind the experience of worrying. This aspect of the realization experience will be fully explored in depth in a later chapter.

It could be said, that the themes of the journey that relate to emotions, speech, action, livelihood, effort, awareness are the work in progress to get the mind into a state that is cleaned of all the dark and dodgy stuff that might be lurking there, so that work can begin to build concentration levels in meditation to enable insights to arise. This is in accord with his other communications such as the continuing cycle of the threefold method of **'meditation – ethics – wisdom.'** It is the skills developed in the practice of meditation and the effort put in to develop those skills that will eventually lead to different levels of concentration, each building on the previous levels.

Along the way there will be moments of insight that will make subtle changes to the way you exist in this relative world, but you are still not there. This could take a lifetime, a minute or even right now. There is no norm. What is suggested is that you apply helpful view to every aspect of your journey. Don't be concerned about goals, achievements or status. These are all the unhelpful view of the conditioned, confused, self-biased mind that is playing the game of self-delusion. The Buddha gives a guarantee. Do the work and it is inevitable. He gives that as an example of causality itself. This being – that becomes. Do the work, make the journey – clarity is realized.

At some point, helpful view moves from being an intellectual understanding to a realized understanding. This is the stage of irreversible insight. What is known cannot be unknown. What is seen cannot be unseen. What is realized cannot be unrealized. All experience is seen for what it is. No conditioned thinking required. But even then it's still not it. Finally when all of the conditions have been met we have the helpful view of no view. This is the experience of clarity that nobody is having. It is just as it is.

This eight-fold journey does not have a beginning, middle or end. It is not a case of each theme needing to be traversed once and only once. It is walked in the way of unfolding different layers each time we engage with it. With each step there is a cumulative response that moves us ever closer to clarity. The stronger our initial experience that brought us to the journey, the more impelled we are to work on transforming ourselves. Sometimes we make slow progress and at other times we can experience a significant break through. Sometimes we may experience ourselves as being a little stuck, or even find ourselves falling back a little. But as long as we keep making the effort, according to the Buddha, progress is eventually assured. In many ways it is only when we begin to notice that transformation is leading to a greater level of contentment that we encourage ourselves to walk a little faster, with awareness of course.

The purpose of the eight-fold journey is developing realization. For most there will be moments of insights into the nature of actuality, but they will be fleeting and although transformative in themselves they do not provide that break through moment that makes them irreversible. As a result we find ourselves worrying again, although to a lesser degree perhaps. But at least these insights show us where the journey points to. Perhaps at these moments we might realize that we have not really been engaged on the journey at all and sometimes it's tough to own up to that.

Maybe we will find that we have been following hunches, apparent intuition or taking on board the words we read in books or direct from our teacher a little too much, or even maybe exploring blind alleyways. It is at times like these, when no matter how strong our resolve has been there appears to be worry in there somewhere that we don't know where we are heading or why. Each step we take has a degree of hesitance and seems forced or maybe even coerced by others if you have found yourself in unhelpful practice circumstances.

As these insights with a small 'i' move towards insights with a capital 'I' our resolve gradually becomes unwavering yet entirely natural. It becomes simply who we are and what we do. There is no longer any sense of contrivance, awkwardness or hesitation. Awakening is no longer seen as something to attain in the distant future because we have realized it is not a thing but a process and this process is the journey itself. But make no mistake this experience does not make us in any way infallible. It does not create within us any sense of superiority or specialness. Until the realization of clarity we are quite capable of subverting this process to the interests of our far from extinct wants, ambitions and fears.

There is nothing particularly religious or apparently spiritual about this journey. It is accepted that there will always be those who have a need to add in those types of labels. It is simply a journey that encompasses everything we do. It is simply an authentic way of being in the world. It begins with how we understand the kind of world we inhabit and the kind of beings we are that inhabit such world. Such a quest underpins the values that inform our ideas, the choices we make, the words we speak, the actions we perform and the work we do. It provides the ethical ground for attentive and focused awareness, which in turn further deepens our understanding of the kind of world we inhabit.

As with everything else the Buddha taught these growing realizations are things not to believe in, but to be acted upon. They need to be nurtured. Just as a garden needs to be protected, tended and cared for so does our ethical integrity, awareness and understanding.

Chapter Eleven: Living in Awareness

The Buddha taught that worrying exists because old age, sickness and death are inescapable. Another way of describing worrying is that we want what we don't get and aren't satisfied with what we do get. We are separated from people and things that we like or love and have to endure people and things that we don't. When we don't get what we want, we are unhappy to some degree. What is helpful to be doing is to resolve this by paying attention. First we pay attention to the voice that asks the question. We pay attention to what it is that we want. We pay attention to the experience of unhappiness when we don't get what we want. We notice and question our beliefs, including the assumption that our problems will be solved by doing something. In that process of noticing and questioning, our attitude changes and we no longer take life so personally. In short, we shift our focus from clinging to the content of our worrying to observing the process. Already, in that shift, we have begun to lessen the level of worrying.

Soon enough, however, the worrying will be back. The Buddha's source teaching was that worrying arises from a deeply held, but mistaken idea, that each of us is a fixed, distinct self that is separate from everything else. In this approach it is referred to as the self-biased mind. The question "what do I do?" is the self-biased mind speaking. In fact, there is nothing to do because actually there is not a separate and enduring ego-identity, personality, self, soul, spirit, essence, mind-stream, conscience or any other thing that can be identified and referred to as you, me, or I. The whole idea of 'us' against 'life' is just confusion. That confusion is instilled in us from a very early age, through what we are told about the world, what we are taught about how we should be, what we observe in those around us. This is what is called conditioning, which is both the process of coming to believe those things and the internalised set of beliefs we create about them.

We are conditioned to believe in the confusion that to be acceptable, we must turn away from our own inclinations and follow socially prescribed rules. Our conditioning is so pervasive that it can be difficult to see. But that is what we do in the practice of awareness. We observe our self-biased conditioning as the only way to live free from its constraints. Here is how it all works in practice. We start to worry when we resist life. That worrying increases when we believe life should be different than it is. It gets worse when we think there is something wrong with life that needs to be changed or fixed.

Being in a position to judge in that way requires separation from what is being judged and only self-biased conditioning believes itself to be separate from life. As we see through the confusion of separation we realize that there is no separate and enduring self-biased individual and there is no alternative actuality in which life is different, our worrying falls away.

Only the self-biased mind worries. It does not want to worry, but we quickly discover that it's not that easy when we try to stop worrying. The 64 million dollar question is how do we begin to bring an end to our experience of worrying? The top five tips suggested here are:

1. **Build up a daily meditation practice**
2. **Practice awareness exercises in your everyday life**
3. **Indulge yourself in regular prolonged bouts of silence**
4. **Commit to a sitting meditation group and be around like-minded people**

5. Discover and let go of habitual patterns of unhelpful thoughts speech and behaviours

Then, just sit back and watch how resistance arises. Listen to the internal voices telling you, **"No, I don't want to do that"**. **"All I'm doing is helping you not to experience worrying"**, they explain. But you will never end the experience of worrying of the self-biased mind. The self-biased mind is the experience of worrying.

The only way to end worrying is to see through the process that keeps us believing in our separateness from all that is. Now, each time we see through a piece of that process, each time we step beyond the confused view we've been conditioned to believe in, those same voices, the voices of self-biased conditioning, will tell us we are wrong, or stupid, or worse. Having a chance to say out loud what we hear from those voices is a powerful way of disengaging from them and that is one of the great benefits that awareness practice provides. Things that seem unquestionably accurate inside our heads, become less convincing when we say them out loud to ourselves, or others who are supporting us.

Our experience of life is determined by the focus of our attention. The person whose attention is focused on what they consider is wrong, lives in a world of imperfection. Focusing on a lack of something creates a life of deprivation. Focusing on violence creates fear of danger. Understanding this is the inspiration behind the power of positive thinking, daily affirmations, and a whole host of other attempts to control the content of our minds. Having a positive attitude and looking on the bright side of life are offered as ways to address the recognition that what we pay attention to determines the quality of our lives.

The powerful forces of our conditioning are just as opposed to a positive outlook as to a negative one. We are bounced back and forth from one extreme to another, which produces constant worrying. When we're on the negative side, we want the positive; when we are in the positive, we want to keep it, but because it is the nature of life to change, we cannot and we are tossed back to the negative side. The world of duality, in which everything is either/or, good/bad, right/wrong, desirable/undesirable, provides no place for satisfaction, contentment or peace of mind

Positive and negative are both content, not process. Attending to how processes work is much more helpful than trying to change a particular piece of content. For example, rather than assume I need to change myself or the world before I can stop worrying, or being afraid, or jealous or filled with regret or whatever the form of worrying is, it is more helpful to address the process of worrying.

We begin to address the process of worrying by attending to what a worry is, how it works, where it comes from, what purpose it serves in our life, what we believe about it, how our life is with worry in it and how our life might be without worry. All we need to do is pay attention. We don't have to decide if something is good or bad, right or wrong. We don't need to have judgments about what kind of person we are simply because we have certain kinds of thoughts or emotional experiences, reactions or responses. That is just the road to more worrying. Our task here is quite different. Just notice. What is actually happening right now? We notice this, then this, then that, then that. We pay attention to all of it. Where is the worrying?

By concentrating on the process of attention, how attention works and how it is related to awareness, we can see the difference between consciously paying attention and our habitual conditioned attention. A big part of the process of worrying is the fact that before we bring conscious awareness to life, the self-biased conditioning is in control of the focus of our attention. When we attempt to wake up from confusion, to bring focus to attention, to live in conscious awareness, the self-biased mind goes into overdrive to stop us. Once we are paying close attention to our experience, we may notice fear arising. The self-biased mind does not like to be scrutinised and it has many ways of keeping us from scrutinising it. Those ways are the content of our awareness practice, the issues we work with.

We forget, fall asleep, get distracted, experience boredom, doubt ourselves, believe we are inadequate, we discover something else that needs to be done now or experience fear. These are all the games that the self-biased mind uses to keep control of the lives that would otherwise be ours to live with peace of mind. We can learn to pay attention to something like fear with a completely neutral attitude of curiosity, even fascination. We sit still and simply watch sensations arise in the body, thoughts attach to sensations, emotions attach to thoughts, beliefs attach to the emotions and behaviours attach to the beliefs.

Then an amazing thing happens. We can see that none of it means anything, an experience usually followed by a fit of the giggles or a huge belly laugh. So stay with it. Don't let fear, doubt and the rest put you off. You began this journey of non-self discovery for a reason, so see it through to the end and find out for yourself if it works. I can guarantee that if you turn back from this journey you have begun it'll be a sure sign that the self-biased mind has done its job and you'll be right back where you started in a never ending circle of searching for an answer that you don't want to hear.

This amazing thing we call mind is where all of our worries begin and end. Worrying is not a physical thing, it is discovered in this thing we call mind. The mind creates an internal voice, which we can't seem to switch off. It makes us hesitate. It confuses us with its persistent **'what if'** and **'yes but'** questioning. What we tend to do is to rely on self-biased conditioning to tell us what to do, but all the while we do that we will continue to worry. Only when we reach the stage of ignoring the **'what if'** and **'yes but'** moments, will we have the opportunity to be free from our conditioning.

Awareness practice helps us to stay present in each moment as it arises and falls away and all we have to do is pay attention. What will inevitably happen for quite some time is that the self-biased mind will react like a child with attention deficit hyperactivity disorder. It will be screaming at you **"I can't do this"**, **"I'm too tired"**, **"this is boring"**. Let's face it, the self-biased mind does not want to give up its control over you.

In Buddhism, if there were such a thing as original sin, (which there isn't) it would be assumption. Assumption is the veil of confusion that keeps us from seeing what is. Failure to see what is leads us to worry. We don't pay attention to what we assume to be so, and we don't even notice that we are not paying attention. Our most basic assumption is that we are the way we see ourselves and the world is the way we see it. We are taught to believe life should be a certain way and that we should be a certain way. When it isn't and we aren't, we assume there's something wrong and something should be done to fix things. Worrying will always surface when we want life to be other than the way it is.

This belief in life as it should be, often leads to self-judgment and attempts at self-improvement. Neither of these activities are particularly helpful. In awareness practice we turn away from assuming that something is wrong with us or with life and from the self-criticism that results, and we begin to dismantle the processes that keep these unhelpful views in place. Worrying is a habit of thought, emotional reaction, perception and interpretation. We continue to see the same things as long as we look to the same assumptions in the same way. But we can learn to recognise and question our assumptions, explore what we habitually attend to and ignore and see our beliefs as the conditioned opinions they are, rather than how we have been taught to believe them to be.

Most important of all, we will come to understand that none of this is our fault. We are not to blame for life. No one needs to be blamed, because in fact there is nothing wrong with life or us. When we see through our unhelpful views, we will realize that, exactly as it is, life is perfect. We might not like it. We might actually hate it. But it can't be anything other than what it is, so it is always perfect.

Awareness practice is the moment by moment recognition of assumptions and a good way to recognise an assumption is to ask yourself how do I know that? Ask yourself that question whenever you find yourself speaking or acting from a place of knowing or certainty. Remember, this is awareness practice. You can't do it wrong. Just pay attention to every thought, emotional reaction and conditioned assumption throughout the day. Everything you notice, even judgment, informs you.

Doing, is the lifeblood of the self-biased conditioned mind. Every time we have an apparent profound awareness moment, every time we get close to seeing through a process of our conditioning that keeps us stuck where we are, the voices are going to come up with some form of doing. **"What should I do?" "How do I deal with this?" "How can I get rid of this?"** There is nothing to do. Just sit, breathe and relax. Awareness expands to include everything. Attention rests in awareness and when you are paying attention, the little ah ha moments will inspire you and worrying will begin to fall away. The Buddha taught of the existence of worrying, what causes it, that it can be ended and the way to end it. With awareness practice we are learning the way to end worrying. If we remain focused on the existence of worrying itself, it will never end.

Conditioning is always going to try to pull you up into your head, into your conditioned un-awakened self-biased subjective reality, as a way to take you out of this ever changing moment, away from the flow of presence within actuality. Just notice that and try not to fall for it. Be aware of how easy it is to get lost in the story. The quality of our life is determined by the focus of our attention. The lightning fast movement of attention from one thing to another thing makes it appear that it can multi-task, but that is not so. Attention is strictly on one thing at a time. It is not possible to have full attention on more than one thing at a time.

Awareness practice in everyday life provides us with an amazing opportunity to bring focused attention on things such as assumptions. We can spend all day just noticing assumptions as they surface in the mind. We can do the same with habits. Habits are another area that gives rise to a great deal of our worrying. When we act out of habit and are not aware we are doing so, worrying is often the result. Deception is another good one to keep a watch on. It's one of the little tricks that the self-biased mind plays to keep us from awareness of what conditioning is doing with our lives. Control is another issue we can shine the light of awareness on. In fact, we can use awareness practice to open our eyes to any aspect of our life, if we simply stay present and pay attention to each moment of experience as it arises and subsides without judgment. Remember that self-biased conditioning has its life in the past and in the future and cannot exist in the flow of presence unless you let it.

The Buddha taught us to live in awareness of the sensations in the physical body and the emotional experiences that arise. He taught this because all those things keeps us trapped in a cycle of worrying. The way to release ourselves from worrying is to see this clearly and to let go. We talk about our conditioned state as confusion, because the whole process of worrying and how we experience it remains unavailable to us, hidden behind habits and assumptions. We learn to focus on our attention, to be aware of it, because this is the process for opening up and shedding light on these hidden areas. By practicing awareness you won't be happy because of getting what you want. You will be content because of the accepting, kind, trusting, open attitude of mind you bring to each transitory moment. Life is a process. If we are accepting and compassionate in our process, the content will become irrelevant.

As for positive thinking and affirmations, if we focus on what is so in each moment, rather than derailing into the self-hating judgment and criticism of conditioning, we'll do just fine. If we walk around all day saying things to ourselves like, "I'll **never get a decent job,"** or **"no one is ever going to want to be with me,"** that is bound to have an impact on our lives. However, the alternative doesn't need to be an obsessive focus on how the self-biased mind thinks life has to be for it to be happy. It is suggested that the most helpful alternative is to be in the moment we are in, being open as possible, noticing everything, realizing as much gratitude as we can muster for how amazing this opportunity of life is.

The first step to the realization of peace of mind is to pay attention to everything. Bringing an end to worrying requires us to see how worrying happens. If we are willing to be quiet and pay attention to the process of worrying, every moment of life becomes an opportunity to step beyond confusion into freedom. Let the person who gets the intellectual understanding have it. It's of little use to them, but of course assumption, habit and the control of self-biased conditioning will not let them see that. All you need to do is take a long deep breath, look at this moment you're in, remind yourself that this moment is utterly new and that you know nothing. You know nothing because there is nothing to know about what has not yet happened, so smile and get on with your life. It is simple but exceedingly threatening to the self-biased mind and therefore very challenging to practice.

Awareness practice is born from formal meditation practice. It is the way we can bring formal sitting meditation practice into our moment by moment daily lives. If you have been practicing meditation for a while you will have experienced, to some extent, the calmness of mind that arises with practice. Imagine for one moment what it would be like if you could do this outside of sitting meditation. In this process we call life, in each and every moment of existence there are always three things present. There is always a physical sensation or other sense experience happening. There is always a pre-conscious unaware response of it being pleasant, unpleasant or neutral and an emotional reaction that is driven by the thought process about it. When you can realize that a sense experience is not pleasant or painful and definitely not a permanent state it is much easier to just accept it in that moment. When you can realize that our emotional reactions are born out of our habitual conditioned responses and belief systems, we provide ourselves with an opportunity to drop them. When we can realize that our thought process is not us, we can become the silent and unaffected observer.

The second step to realizing peace of mind is to believe nothing. This goes to the very centre of the Buddha's approach to teaching causality. If you memorize just one thing it needs to be this: **"Test, challenge, realize the actuality of anything against your own direct experience."** When you think, say or do something, does it lead you in the direction of worrying or does it lead you in the direction of peace of mind? We believe as a way of not facing the very uncomfortable fact that we don't know. Life never repeats itself. Each split second, everything in the universe is different. Each moment is brand new. Not having a guarantee about what is coming next, we imagine what will happen, we project the past into the future and cling to a belief that our imaginings are accurate. Believing is supposed to make us have a sense of greater security, but if we believe something we don't know to be fact and possibly may suspect is not fact, worrying, not security, is the result.

As a culture we operate out of the assumption that if enough people believe something it must be true. The process of group assuming and believing seems to work, because when people believe something is true, they experience whatever it is as true. If I told you that I was going to bring a speaker along next week to a class who is one of the wisest, clearest, most awakened masters living today, you would hear what that person had to say as wise, clear and awake. If I told you the speaker was an intellectual, masquerading as an awakened master you would hear what he had to say very differently.

In each example you would filter what you heard through the influence of a third party and put to one side, to some extent, your own un-biased direct experience. Put another way you wouldn't dream of criticising anything the Dalai Llama had to say but there will be many times when you are likely to get angry with your own teacher and in effect they are telling you the same thing. It's just that you will have pre-conceived ideas of who you believe these two people are and more often than not, those ideas will have had contributions from a third party and very rarely match their actuality.

The Buddha encourages us not to believe in anything. He asks us to challenge everything, including his own teachings. Not in such a way as we give it a cursory glance but with a fierceness of a flame that will melt gold. If we are ever going to make a start in breaking down our lifetimes worth of social conditioning so that we can be free from worrying, this will involve examining, in detail, what we think say and do. All of our assumptions and our beliefs are examined in minute detail and that is not always comfortable.

By way of example let's take a common statement such as "I love my family". Because I know that, believe that, assume that, I don't need to spend much time or energy exploring what that actually means to me and whether or not my life is in keeping with that meaning. I can do what I do and say what I say without scrutiny, because I know **"I love my family."** What I need to do in this situation may not make them happy, but if it seems unloving to them, well, they're wrong, because **"I know I love them."** I may not always be considerate, or sensitive or available, but that's not a problem, because **"I do love them."** In other words, without a great deal of observation, this thing we call love can give us permission to kid ourselves and do whatever, because whatever we do happens within a context of what we define as love.

There is a very useful communication practice that you might find helpful to begin breaking down your beliefs and assumptions in this particular area. Ask your partner or child what makes them experience being loved. Ask what it is that you do that makes them experience being loved. Ask them what it is you do that makes them experience being unloved. Ask them what habits they would like you to change. What assumptions they would like you to drop. How they need to be listened to. Doing this you will very soon notice if the focus of your love is on you or them.

Dharma practice is quite often described as a continual process of letting go. If we are to make progress along the journey to clarity, it is helpful to accept, from the outset, that we actually know nothing other than what we have been conditioned to believe. It's helpful to be moving in the direction of momentary experience. If we are to assist in the end of worrying it is helpful to let go of all that we cling to that is worrying, regardless of how right we think we are, or how wrong we think someone else is, or even how we might be judged by others. For example, we might think it very noble, or at least understandable to get upset when people abuse children or animals or minorities or the environment.

If we didn't get upset nothing would ever change would it? But that upset that we are experiencing is a form of anger, which in turn is a form of hatred, yet we find in the ancient texts words to the effect:

'Not by hatred are hatreds ever pacified. They are pacified by love. This is the eternal law'.

Makes sense doesn't it? How is the world a better place if we become cruel in response to our worrying over the cruelty of others? How is it helpful to kill others as a way of showing others that killing is unhelpful?

Awareness practice is about not believing what our self-biased conditioning tells us is true. It is the perfect antidote to help us not to pass on our unhelpful conditioning to the next generation. It goes against the views of some modern therapists that concludes that we will automatically screw up our kids so just do it in a way that is most comfortable for you. This assumption or belief follows the familiar pattern of **'this is how it's always been and always will be'.** The Dharma challenges that. It offers an alternative approach and that is we can, with awareness and effort, pass along to the next generation a model of adults who continue to grow in awareness, take responsibility and let go in an effort to be the most authentic human beings they can be.

"Yes but." We couldn't survive if we didn't believe in anything. Believing in something won't make the slightest difference. It will be what it will be whether you believe it or not. For example, you could say I have to believe that the local coffee shop will be where it has been every other day I've gone there or I wouldn't bother going to where it usually is. The actuality is that the coffee shop will either be there or not whether you believe it or not. One day it might not be there, after all, no thing is permanent. An attitude of not knowing is just realistic. We don't know. The thing that makes us so worried and insecure is that rather than face not knowing, we choose to believe as some kind of comfort blanket. Children tend not to get worried until they get information that there is something to worry about. It seems that all creatures have a built-in survival response that enables them to be alert to danger but human conditioning tends to turn that into fear, which then controls our lives even when nothing fearful is going on. It is a fact that anything could happen in any moment, but that just makes life an exciting adventure, not a fearful thing from which we need to cringe and hide.

You will find many paradoxes within the teachings of the Buddha. Consider this:

'If you never had another thought in your head for the rest of your life you'd be more insightful than you could ever imagine.'

That's because insight is present moment clarity, which is greater than the sum total of all that has come before, all that is now and all that ever could be. It is all there ever is. If you are living fully in the present moment you know nothing. So, there is no need to have a thought in your head. Since there's nothing you should know, there is no possibility that you should have known better. If you believe nothing, everything is possible. If anything is possible you are not holding onto anything, so you're available for the anything that can happen. You become present, open and spontaneous, able to go with any twist or turn of life. The mind becomes fresh and creative and is not limited by any preconceptions. Living this way, you will find that worry falls away and is replaced with a heightened sense of aliveness and joy.

There is a story within the legend of Jesus when he sends out his disciples to preach his message. Naturally they were scared as they were rocking the boat a bit and it could be very dangerous. They wanted to know what they should say if they were caught and thrown in jail. Basically, he told them to take no thought of what they would say, because when the time came, what they needed would be given to them. There is a great message for all of us in that teaching and it is true today as it was back then and is true for Buddhists and Christians alike. If we come into the present moment with nothing, the helpful response will arise in that moment. If we come in with what we think is a better idea about what the moment will require, we end up with only what we thought would be best. It never is.

Of course there is a difference between approaches. Christians will be taught to simply have faith and as the majority of world population follows the faith patterns of religions in one form or another, one could assume or believe there must be something in it and take great comfort in that. That is not the way of the Buddha. He suggests that we should stand in front of whomever or whatever without a thought in our heads and wait for whatever the helpful response to arise. To begin with this could seem like an agonisingly long and scary time but after a while it becomes supremely restful. There is another great teaching of the Buddha that goes some way to highlight the approach to life it is helpful to be doing.

"In the seen, only the seen. In the heard, only the heard."

Experiencing life as it is in each moment, without adding in any content from our self-biased conditioning. In those moments we will find there is no worrying.

One of the biggest problems there has always been within Buddhism is that nobody, including the Buddha himself, has been able to communicate adequately the experience of clarity, awakening or even insight. Have you ever tried to communicate an experience of anything? Try it. It's very hard, if not impossible. That's because it is your experience and it will be different for each individual. There might be some similarities, but there will be many more differences. What seems to happen is that individuals look to the historical story of the Buddha and assume that to be awakened means being the same as the Buddha was reported to be. As he is historically portrayed as ultimately infallible in every detail, it therefore follows that the awakening experience is beyond us because we are clearly not. It perpetuates the myth of unworthiness that is so prevalent in the west and is the feeding ground of the doctrinal religion that much of classical Buddhism has become.

It is suggested that what really lies at the heart of the historical story of the Buddha is that he was born a human just as we were. His conditioning factors would have been different but he broke through those by his own efforts and we have the exact same opportunity as he did. One of the main reasons we find it so difficult is because we continue to believe. What is seen in a moment of seeing is irrelevant. The seeing is all there is. In a moment of insight you see. You know. But there is no one to know and no thing to know. There is no knowledge. Nothing of the content of the seeing can leave the moment because it is irrelevant. Anything could have been the content for that process. In a moment of clarity you could read a box of corn flakes and realize causality.

Out there in the world of the reportedly awakened beings and celebrity guru's you will find all manner of suggestions as to how to become awakened. I call it the 'Orange School of Awakening.' A person is eating an orange and has an awakening experience. The person concludes that the awakening experience is connected to eating the orange and sets out spreading the news that all you have to do is eat oranges and you too will become awakened. There's one guy who has thousands of followers eagerly buying up his books and DVD's and he tells them that they don't need to do anything at all as it happened to him just walking through the park. Another sells books in the millions and fills large venues on the basis that there is no distinction between mental break-through and mental breakdown as that is what happened to him. Another gives a moment by moment description of his journey through the vertically expansive meditational states to the moment of his awakening. Of course you are free to buy into any of these things, but to simply believe without testing and challenging what they say would be doing yourself a great disservice. An awakened mind is of no use to you other than as a pointer to a way that you might realize it. None of the above provides that. It is all just about them and you being inspired by them. The Buddha suggests that the threefold path of meditation ethics and wisdom is the way forward. Of course there will always be someone who will then say **"well of course he would, that's how he did it."**

The point being made here is that insight experience is just that. It is just an experience. It might be subtle or it might change everything and nothing at the same time, but it is just a realization experience. Either way it still needs to be actualized.

168

It needs to be processed and that is what the Dharma journey is all about. To some degree or other insights are nothing more than moments of expansive clear thinking and there is nothing within them that we can drag around to use later. **It'** is gone and **I'** is back. The only significance is if the **'I'** that returns is filtered through the self-biased mind or the awakened mind. If it is filtered through the self-biased mind, the only way we can hold on to the experience is to turn it into a belief and then we're back where we started. It is suggested that much of the worrying that we experience on the Dharma journey has been created by religious Buddhism because it was created by people who had not realized or actualized causality, but had only grasped at it intellectually. They, in effect, became the orange sellers of classical Buddhism.

Picture the scene: The awakened divine master, bathed in a soft golden light, with a smile on his face that is so serene, utters the following words in a soft, gentle voice **"Love is all"**. Those in the audience are not experiencing what the master is experiencing so they look at each other to see if anyone else is. One person says to the person beside him **"I get it. What he means is that all we need to do is love"**. On the other side of the hall another person turns to the person beside him and says **"I get it. What he means is that we are love already and don't need to do anything"**. It doesn't take too long before two factions are formed, both with sub-groups and disgruntled cliques in each faction. Hatred, competition, antagonism and violence grow. **"Ours is the one true way. No, ours is the one true way. All of you must die it's what the master wanted. No, all of you must die; the master has spoken to me."** Welcome to the world of institutionalized religious belief that can often include aspects of religious Buddhism.

169

Bringing an end to our own worry, according to the Buddha, requires us to be quiet long enough to see how worrying arises. Quiet is necessary because the clamour of modern life and the endless chatter in our heads detracts from our ability to discern the automatic conditioned patterns of behaviour we mistake for who we are. This daily deluge of images and information literally rips our attention away from our internal process. Completely unaware, we adopt beliefs, make assumptions, accept and reject and generally speaking, many people seem to make a dog's dinner of life. In fact, if we were to be completely honest with ourselves, even for a moment, we would realize that within western culture we could be considered to be addicted to distraction and information.

Try it for yourself during the week. Turn your attention to the information that comes to you via the media including TV, radio, internet, newspapers, magazines, even what arrives in the post. Notice what relationship you have to the information and believing. How much that passes before you do you see as true? How much do you accept? What do you believe? What do you not believe? Are there certain people you automatically believe and others you automatically disbelieve? Who do you tend to accept as an authority on any subject? If you don't believe something, is it because the person is mistaken or are they lying? Do you ever wonder if the facts are accurate? It's a really interesting eye-opening practice to pay attention to things in your life.

With awareness practice you are encouraged to just notice. No right. No wrong. Just notice. What happens when this? What happens when that? We're so conditioned to believe that we have to figure something out so that we will have the correct information and then and only then we'll be OK. If we practice noticing for a while, we see that getting the correct information does not make us OK. Perceiving ourselves to be OK makes us think we're OK. Ironically, having more information can often leave us thinking we're not OK at all. Would we really be any less caring or compassionate beings if we were unaware of the catastrophes going on at any given moment somewhere on the planet? Again, if we were honest with ourselves, most of the time we probably don't give much thought to anyone outside of our immediate circle of family and friends unless it is thrust in our faces. There seems to be an actuality aspect in the saying **"Today's news – tomorrows fish & chip wrapper"**.

We hear so much nowadays about how jaded, cynical and resigned we are as a society. We hear things like **"People don't vote because they don't believe there's any choice". "All politicians are, after all, self-serving crooks"**. It's a difficult balancing act we find ourselves in. On the one hand my own personal perception of quite a few people is that they would just about do or say anything to earn a crust, yet I choose to keep a high level of trust in and respect for my fellow human beings. I don't want to believe that everyone is pulling a fast one, but each time I turn on the TV or pick up a newspaper or magazine, it sure seems that there's growing evidence that honesty and integrity might be a thing of the past. But then I drop my wallet in the supermarket and a young kid goes to great lengths to track me down and hand it back to me and isn't the slightest bit interested in any reward for doing so and my trust in human nature is again restored until the next unhelpful intrusion.

Dharma practice is about looking after our mental states. The Buddha urges us to guard our senses. First we work to get our mind into a helpful state of awareness and then we work to maintain those helpful states in an on-going moment by moment way. The world that opens up for us when we bring our attention back from all of the distractions in our life is so much more fascinating, exciting, interesting, compelling and yes, you could even say newsworthy, than anything you'll ever see on TV or read in a newspaper.

The third step to realizing peace of mind is not to take anything personally. As human beings we have the ability to perceive ourselves as separate. Our minds are able to remember and discriminate. We can recall ourselves in situation after situation over time, thinking, emoting, moving and interacting. It seems reasonable and logical that there is a constant and enduring **'someone'** who is the actor who experiences life. Even as we age and admit there is nothing about us that is exactly the same as in our youth, we cling to the belief that there is a constant 'I' who has this awareness. That self-biased mind which believes itself to be separate, produces a desperate battle to maintain itself against the perceived threat that life becomes. For the self-biased mind each moment of life is a threat to its survival. The self-biased mind does not experience being at home. It believes itself to be separate from life, in opposition to life, attempting to get what it wants and needs in spite of life. The self-biased mind takes everything in life very personally.

When we exist in the world of the separate self-biased mind, we can't help but take life personally and that causes us to worry. It is suggested, that from the first moment that we are able to understand language we were taught to take it personally. Childhood social conditioning relies heavily on reward and punishment as a means of eliciting **'acceptable behaviour'**. If you don't eat vegetables, you can't have desert. If you don't do your chores, you can't ride your bike. When you get a little older, you are grounded. Freedom of movement, communication and friendship are taken away if you 'misbehave'. Not getting what you want is punishment and losing what you have is punishment, while getting what you want is proof that you are good and deserve reward. We conclude that it is all very, very personal. I am good when I... I am bad when I.... I should experience this.... I should experience that.... I shouldn't experience that.... I am this... I am not that.

I've often referred to human existence as being the greatest situation comedy ever written. It is the cosmic joke. We're born, we age, we get sick and we die. We spend so much time worrying about the inevitable that we forget to actually live the bit in the middle. With this situation as an expression of actuality how can we possibly take ourselves so seriously? This is a very individual thing, but my own experience of coming in contact with the Dharma has evolved into an on-going comedy show where I find myself laughing with and at myself all the time. I can respond as is helpful to the worrying of others without having to get caught up in their dramas and still retain a sense of joyous existence. This could be viewed or experienced as being cold, unemotional and detached but I don't experience it as such. All that's happened is that I've allowed the helpful response to arise and what is always helpful is compassion.

All things are processed by this thing we call mind. Self-talk insists that we exist separate from everything and everyone else and should take things very personally. Self-talk is the voice of self-biased conditioning. The voices say this, the voices say that. OK, voices all over the world are saying all sorts of nonsense all the time. It seems to be a big part of what voices do. Do I really need to take these voices personally? Do I really need to worry when a voice has an opinion about what I'm doing? Who is that voice? Why do I prioritise that voice? Why do I believe that voice is more helpful, meaningful, or important than the voice of someone who loves me? It is fun to watch all of this going on if you don't take it all so personally.

We live in a world of infinite possibility. As humans we have the ability to experience ourselves as separate from that and then cling to that separation, all the while decrying our loneliness and isolation and experience worry in the process. We search every-where for relief, but we fail to notice that the confusion of separation is actually conducting the search and it has no interest in realizing causality as to do so would destroy it.

When we begin to work on letting go of our fixed beliefs, as-sumptions and living a Dharma life that is not driven by our conditioned self-biased mind, we will discover openness, a spaciousness that was previously filled with confusion and misinformation. There are a number of common words used within classical Buddhism to describe this such as 'voidness' 'sunyata' or more commonly 'emptiness' or promoted here as 'no-thing-ness.' This can sound like a lack or a loss of something. It can sound cold and unemotional. But all that has been lost is the control over our lives that the conditioned self-biased mind clings to at all costs. It's not a loss of anything. It's a no-thing-ness that is actually fullness, abundance, all that is, a world of limitless possibility. Another name for that spaciousness is joy. That's why the Buddha says that joy is what is there when you stop doing everything else. By everything else he means assuming, acting out of habit, trying to control, judging, knowing, believing and all the other aspects of our conditioned reaction to life, including trying to be joyful.

The Buddha's very simple and clear message is that all confused human beings are subject to worry. He prescribes the medicine and encourages you to take it. The biggest tragedy of all is that in our conditioned westernised society, human beings do not appear to be prepared to take the medicine according to the instructions. They want someone to take the pain away for them, but haven't heard the message that only they can do it. No guru, teacher, apparent spiritual advisor or mentor of any description can. They are nothing but the finger pointing at the moon. The more you look to them to solve the problem for you, the more you will worry. That worrying will then be blamed on them because the nature of worry is that it arises when you don't get what you want or get what you don't want and you have to blame someone and it's not going to be you that cops it.

He also tells you that this worrying aspect of life can be eradicated within the realization of causality. Consider this:

If it is realized that there is no separate and enduring ego-identity, personality, self, soul, spirit, essence, mind-stream, conscience or any other thing that can be identified and referred to as you, me, or I, then who is this you, me or I that is capable of worrying? Where is this you, me or I that is capable of worrying? Where is this you, me or I who was ever born in the first place? Where is this you, me or I who is going to die?

Chapter Twelve: Instant Karma

In an ancient Buddhist text we find a teaching that actually sets out what karma is not. It says, words to the effect:

'**Saying whatever a person experiences, pleasant, unpleasant or neutral, all this is caused by what was done in the past, they exceed what is known by oneself, they exceed what is considered true in the world; therefore I say that those ascetics and Brahmins are wrong,**"

What he is saying here is that this is simply belief in something that can't possibly be known. He is saying that although all experiences arise as a result of previous causes and conditions it is not always as a result of karma. A bucket falling on your head when you walk under a ladder is probably not as a result of karma. It has its own causes and conditions, none of which are based in superstitious twaddle.

When exploring the subject of karma it is not helpful to maintain that it is a teaching of the Buddha. It is more helpful to understand it was used by the Buddha as a teaching method to explain causality to a population who believed in a number of different versions of the pre-existent concept of karma. In this period and in this region there were at least two different version of karma that taught it in an entirely different way. What the Buddha did here, just as he did with the medical formulation of the four principal assignments, was to take something that people already understood and then communicated it in a way that was in accord with his realization of actuality. He did this so he could show them that it could be a helpful and very practical development tool for growth, rather than a superstitious belief system.

So, let's be vey clear about this, the way the Buddha communicated karma is not meant to explain our aches and pains, your coughs and splutters, or why some people get cancer and some don't etc. Also, it's sad to say, it wasn't meant to be used as a way to justify why, in some classical Buddhist countries they treat abandoned children or those with any form of disability in ways that a western person would not consider kind, or compassionate. This view of karma and its responsibilities within classical Buddhism seems so out of step with the core principle of compassion and kindness that I struggle at times to understand how it came be to be so misunderstood.

If we take the view that the Buddha used the idea of karma for the specific purpose of communicating just one aspect of causality, it will help us to understand that this source experience that led to everything the Buddha ever taught has many other different aspects to it. He also drew on existing systems and concepts to try and communicate it in many different ways because of its complexity. Although the essence of the teaching of causality is that all things exist as a result of preceding causes and conditions, karma is just one aspect of that arising existence. We also have the **physical aspect** such as the world of atoms, molecules, quarks, quantum mechanics, space etc as explored by science, physics, mathematics and chemistry. We have the **organic aspect** such as the world of living beings from microbes to man following an evolutionary process as explored by biology, ecology etc. We have the **subjective aspect** such as the world of the mind, the conscious, subconscious and pre-conscious processes of perception, memory, imagination and dreams, all explored by the world of the physiological collective. We also have the 'Dharma aspect' itself; the journey to awakening. It unfolds step by step as a developmental journey towards our own realization of actuality.

Karma is, as we can see, just one of the ways that our current experience comes into existence. For instance, we may be being treated for a mental illness such as depression. What caused it? It could be simply a lack of serotonin, a naturally produced chemical in the body. It may have resulted in response to a psychological trauma in our early life. It may have lifestyle conditioning factors. It could be a combination of all manner of things that have nothing to do with karma.

This is why the Buddha moved the pre-existent understanding of karma towards being aware of the motivational intent behind what we think, say and do in each moment. He did that so you can experience directly, there and then, the karmic consequences in your next moment of existence, rather than being caught up in searching for some unexplainable reason that could then be used as a rationalisation or justification to continue in the same way. This is in-line with his whole approach to the Dharma journey being an experiential, developmental journey rather than a belief based system.

The Brahmins were not that concerned with ethics because of their belief in rituals as a means of dealing with things. It could be said that they were at one end of the extreme spectrum of promoting karma their way. The Jains, with their unrealistic attempt to do absolutely no harm could be said to be at the other end of the extreme spectrum. Within their belief system, even eating a root vegetable would apparently be considered doing harm. There is an idea there that by brushing the path in front of you, it ensures that you don't step on insects. Let's be honest, if you were an ant, quietly minding your own business and a great big broom wacked you round the back of the head, I'm sure that just as much damage gets done. So, again what we see, is that the Buddha in his proposition of karma, sets out a middle path that avoids the extremes of behaviour of the prevailing religions of his day who also taught karma but very differently.

For the Buddha, karma is all about motivational intent. He teaches us that the primary focus for our practice is the intention that lies behind our thoughts, speech and actions. This is made very clear in many ancient texts such as:

"Friends, I say that karma is intention; having intended, one does an action with the body, through speech, or with the mind."

Having established clearly that it is all about our motivational intent, he then moves on to teach how we are to recognise those motivations and what would be considered helpful or unhelpful in developing an ethical lifestyle on the basis of this understanding of karma as cause and effect and as an expression of causality.

Let's take for example an act of giving money to charity. On the face of it we can say that giving to charity is always a helpful thing to do. It helps others and also helps us to be generous. When we do give to charity freely, if we observe the reaction, I am sure you will have experienced a helpful state of mind follows. But if you take a look at what happens when you give to charity with an unhelpful motivational intent, the experience will be very different. I'm thinking of situations where we find those people who stand outside shops rattling their tins and we go to great lengths to avoid making eye contact with them. Or when we think we are obliged to give because people are looking at us and we don't want to be judged as being stingy and so we rummage around in our purse or wallet to try and find something to give, although we are allowing ourselves to be pressurised into doing so.

There are other situations where we may see someone begging on the street and we start telling ourselves all manner of different stories to prevent us from having to give. There is also the media hard sell disaster type emotional blackmail that manipulates us into giving. So, in these kind of circumstances, although our giving has been helpful for someone else, it has actually been unhelpful for us because our motivational intent was based in our own selfish greed and a need to be well thought of by others and we are left in a state of worrying.

The concept of karma is a helpful tool to assist us to engage with an ethical lifestyle that is not based on externally imposed rules and regulations. It is about the observation of our mind states and attempting to keep them in a helpful state and free from worrying. As we develop those helpful mind states, they in turn become the encouragement to move us deeper into our ethical lifestyle and move the mind into a greater degree of contentment with itself, others and the world around us. For the Buddha, this thing we call mind is primary and this is why meditation is promoted as an integral part of his developmental method. In what I consider to be one of the most important teachings that is ascribed to the Buddha and actually the very first text I ever read he says words to the effect:

'All experience is preceded by mind, led by mind, made by mind. Think, speak or act with an unhelpful mind and worrying follows as the wagon wheel follows the hoof of an ox. Think, speak or act with a helpful mind and happiness follows like a never departing shadow.'

In some schools of classical Buddhism this teaching is often taken to mean that the existence of the world itself is mind made and on one level, that of subjective reality, that could be justified. But that view does move away from what is the actual point of this teaching. It is saying that our experience of the world is based on how the mind interprets the raw sensory data and by changing the way we think and respond we can, in effect, change our world.

By teaching karma very differently from the pre-existent ways of the prevailing religious systems, the Buddha is setting out how, with the development of awareness practices, at the point of contact and the pre-conscious response within the twelve link chain of causality, (which we will be exploring in the next chapter) we have the opportunity to develop creative responses and develop contentment, even when we are being driven by our raw emotions in response to sensory data input. By observation of our mind state we can move from being reactive to responsive.

By exploring the teaching of karma as an expression of causality, we can see that it is just one of a complex and often open-ended system of ways in which we experience things. No matter what we have done in the past, we can always change our minds in each current moment and free ourselves from the kind of neurotic guilt that can often weigh us down about our past. This is highlighted by the story of the mass murderer 'Anguilimala' who used to cut off the fingers of his victims to wear as a necklace.

It is said within the story that when he met the Buddha he was so impressed by his calmness, kindness and lack of judgment he became a follower and went for refuge and through his efforts on the Dharma journey transformed himself. There lies the importance of this aspect of the Buddha's teaching of karma. It is all about transformation.

Since our on-going next moment of mind experience is defined by karma, by developing more helpful ways to observe our motivational intent we can redefine the world we exist in. Generally speaking, there are motivational intentions that are based subconsciously on the three poisons of want, not want and confusion. Thoughts, speech or actions arising from any of these mind states will result in our next moment of experience being one of worrying. So this is unhelpful in developing or maintaining peace of mind. Motivational intent that is based on non-greed, kindness and insight will result in peace of mind.

In classical Buddhism these three poisons are also known as 'defilements.' In essence what it means is that peace of mind has been disturbed and has given rise to worrying. In classical Buddhism this state is also known as an 'affliction.' In this context, want represents all of our efforts to try and own something, get something, cling to something, grasp something, attach ourselves to something, or simply just wanting our current experience to be other than it is. It could be said that the other two poisons of not want and confusion are the smokescreen that prevents us from seeing how things really are, or what is actually happening.

Want, not want and confusion are the engine driver of the conditioned self-biased reactive mind. But by developing their opposites with the on-going practice of kindness, generosity and insight, we move in the direction of eliminating the reactive mind into the world of creative responses that assist the development and maintenance of peace of mind. Our reactive lifestyles are born from our conditioned habitual and repetitive patterns of behaviour that is, more often than not, an expression of group think and behaviour.

In classical Buddhism it is often said that it is karma that is the basis of Buddhist ethical conduct. But that is tied in very much with the belief systems of religious Buddhism and can be somewhat of a diversion. It is suggested here that karma is being taught as an expression of causality. It is a developmental tool for the observation of our mind states. Buddhist ethics are simply guidelines around a central principle of non-harm and kindness. But even that is just a somewhat idealistic principle, as it is actually impossible to survive as a human being without doing any harm.

In a well know Buddhist text we find a verse that sets out the guiding principle as:

'All living beings are terrified of violence; all of them fear death. Comparing oneself with others, one should not do harm or incite it.'

This appears to sit quite comfortably with other ethical systems, the **'do unto others'** or **'golden rule'** kind of thing. But as far as I am aware all other forms of religious belief systems have the rules and regulations imposed by an external entity or authority that is based on a system of punishment and reward. The Buddha went in the complete opposite direction. He offers you the steering wheel. He teaches you to drive. He slaps on the learner plates and then sends you on your way to take responsibility for not crashing your own car. It is suggested here that he also offers a money back guarantee insurance policy, or at least a really helpful no claims bonus.

Causality shows that all actions have consequences for us, others and the world around us. It shows us that nothing is random. There is no fate, destiny, luck within the teaching of karma. Everything that arises does so as the karmic consequences of the conditions that previously existed. Seeds give rise to shoots, which give rise to plants, which give rise to flowers, which gives rise to seeds. You buy a lottery ticket and the result will depend on what numbers get drawn and not because your numbers were lucky, or you were wearing your special shirt/dress, or you were carrying a rabbit's foot or rubbed the Buddha's belly.

Karma, as taught by the Buddha, governs the way in which one's voluntary actions in this moment of existence shape the quality of our mind state in our next moment of existence. This primary aspect of karma only deals with willed action. These are actions that are predetermined by our motivational factors. Ones where we think before we speak or act. Acts that are not premeditated or have unaware motivational factors behind them will still have an effect for us and others but that would be a secondary aspect of karma. We tend to call these kind of things accidents. We may have already realized that in our 21st century culture of blame seeking and litigation even an accident is the effect of a preceding cause and conditions where we can find someone else responsible for.

For example, one evening, years ago, when I was driving home from work on my 50cc motorcycle along an unlit country road, I suddenly found myself flying through the air and crashing to the ground without my bike, which was now damaged beyond repair and caught up in a tangled mass of tree. At the precise moment I reached this spot, a roadside tree decided to fall over on top of me. Was it an accident? One would think so. But there I was with my pride and joy and method of transport totally wrecked through no fault of my own. This got me thinking. That tree must belong to somebody? Somebody must have planted it by the roadside which means somebody must have some responsibility for its upkeep and safety. After some research I found that the tree actually belonged to the local council, who each year collected money from every household in the district, a portion of which was meant to be spent on maintaining roadside furniture. A little more digging revealed that for the past five years they had carried on collecting the money, but had cancelled the contracts to maintain the trees to save money. They basically took a chance that trees just don't fall over that often and if they did nobody would complain or come chasing them for money. After an exchange of a few letters and an understanding that I was prepared to take the matter to a civil court, I received full compensation for my written off motorcycle. It would have been a very interesting scenario had I gone to court and made my case on the basis of causality and karma.

Early Buddhist scholars divided causality in relation to karma into five different categories:

1. **Physical**
2. **Biological**
3. **Psychological**
4. **Ethical**
5. **Transcendental**

Scientists in the west concentrate their efforts on a physical and biological exploration to arrive at their theories in relation to human existence. Religious Buddhism, can at times, be in conflict with science. Secular western Buddhism cannot be in conflict with science. It places its emphasis on the psychological and ethical dimensions of karma, in order to support the changes in thought and associated behaviour patterns that are the basis of the integration of the pre-conscious and the subconscious into the experience of clarity. This, in effect, would be the transcendental aspect, as what has been transcended is the idea of a separate self-biased mind.

If you hit your thumb with a hammer when banging a nail into a piece of wood, it will have a physical dimension to it. You will experience a physical sensation that you do not like, that you will label pain. It will be accompanied with a biological dimension. The area where you hit will begin to swell up and bruise. It will have a psychological/emotional dimension. You will probably take a huge intake of breath, stick the thumb in your mouth and suck it whilst possibly uttering a few expletives at those around you laughing. Let's be very clear about this, awakening is not going to stop any of those things happening. Maybe the Buddha might have been inclined to respond a little differently, but he would still have experienced the physical and biological aspects of the incident, but might have left out the expletives, but that relies on believing the myths around the awakening experience as projected by classical Buddhism. Although hitting your thumb with a hammer would be construed by most to be an unpleasant experience, it will not have affected you ethically to any tangible effect. There has been no substantial change in the nature of your character as a result of the incident. Intentionally striking someone else with the hammer would have entirely different karmic consequences.

The karmic, or ethical outcome of any act depends on the intention behind it. According to the Buddha what makes a thought, spoken word or act helpful or unhelpful is the motivational factors that underpin them. He says that actions based in kindness will result in a helpful state of mind and actions not based in kindness will result in unhelpful mind states. This does not mean that if you are out there being kind to everybody that you will be rewarded materialistically. It doesn't mean that just because you are being kind that others are going to be kind to you. This idea of what comes round goes around is something from the hand book of **'New Age woo wooists'** and has nothing to do with the way the Buddha set out karma. Another feature of the way karma is now misinterpreted is by these apparent quotes of the Buddha you see on the internet that say things like **"You are what you think"** or **"What you think you become."** It all sounds so deep and profound doesn't it? Well, start thinking abut pink unicorns and see if you become one.

Let's take a look at an everyday scenario that we can play over and again and explore from different perspectives, the way the Buddha used it as a learning tool for development of awareness. You go to the local deli to buy a sandwich. You only have a $50 note which you hand over to make the purchase. Unknown to you, one of the $20 notes you get back in your change is counterfeit. It's a very good copy and only really close inspection would give you even the slightest indication that it was a dud. On your way home you stop off at a supermarket to do some shopping and give the counterfeit $20 note as part payment. In this scenario, the act of handing over the fake $20 has **'neutral karma.'** There are no karmic consequences for you or the person you handed it over to as you are both unaware of it being a fake. But the karma aspect doesn't stop there because the fake note is still in existence and at some point it will be noticed by somebody and then it will result in the consequences which will no longer be directly linked back to you.

If we now re-run the story with a small change in circumstances, we begin to unravel how karma works. This time, at the point when you received your change from the $50, you noticed something unusual about the texture of one of the $20 notes you were given. It was a very subtle sensation but it was there. You were in a hurry, so you allowed that little niggle to drop down into the subconscious and got on with your day. On your way out of the door you notice a sign saying '**Please check your change. Counterfeit $20 notes are in circulation locally.**' Despite experiencing the subtle difference in texture and noticing the sign, somehow you have still not put two and two together, possibly because your focus was on getting to the supermarket before it closed. By the time you arrive at the check-out at the super market, those memories have long gone from your mind and you hand over the dud $20 as part payment for your shopping. Although at no stage was there any intention to defraud the shop assistant your actions have been carried out through a lack of awareness. You ignored both your initial instinct and the visible warning. As a result, the karmic consequence would move from neutral to being '**slightly uhelpful.**'

In the third scenario you see the notice on your way out of the door and link it to the sensation you had when you originally touched the $20. Outside you take a look at it and realize it is a fake. You are a bit embarrassed about going back into the deli in case the owner thinks you're trying it on. You weigh up the odds and decide you'd easily be able to shift it at the supermarket. It's a good copy and the young kids on the check-out always seem to be on almost zombie like auto-pilot. Here the physical act of handing over the dud $20 is the same as before, but the motivation behind the act is very different. Now, we have an unhelpful willed action and the level of karma increases accordingly.

If however, having realized the $20 is fake, you handed it in at the police station on your way home, although you lost out financially, the karmic consequence of your act is very helpful.

Chapter Thirteen: Re-becoming

We now head into a territory that has classical Buddhism very much divided. But it is even more at odds with its secular western reformation. It seems clear that throughout Buddhist history, much of its development headed in the direction of religious belief. It is suggested here, this is the opposite of what the Buddha was trying to communicate. This difficulty is highlighted most noticeable whenever the subject of **'rebirth'** arises. In the early texts, the Buddha is clearly showing people a way of trying to understand the process of rebirth in relation to worrying on a moment by moment basis. This is not only supported by a number of texts, but also within his life story as presented to us. His only concern from day one was to find a solution to worrying and a way to end it. He had no interest in the questions about the origin of the universe, or life after death. It appears that from the point of the first reformation period, when the religion of Buddhism was created, there was an agenda that would not have been supported by the Buddha. During this period and in later reformations, this same teaching seems to get expanded to relate to things like past and future lives, because of the way some have chosen to interpret the wordings in the texts and taken them as literal and at face value, without testing and challenging them.

As far as I am aware there is not a single scrap of credible, plausible or verifiable evidence that has been conducted under controlled test conditions that suggests that you or I will be entitled to another life at the end of this one. According to current neurological studies, it is now suggested that human consciousness, which is simply another name for aliveness is 100% dependent on a living human brain and cannot exist independently of it. All living things are consciousness. They do not have consciousness. Human consciousness/aliveness evolved to be an ability to be aware, of being aware, of being human. The current scientific data suggests that at the moment the human brain dies so then does human consciousness/aliveness. As there has never been a single recorded case of a human being surviving brain death we are left with a dilemma. Do we simply believe something because it is stated in an ancient book that was written under somewhat dubious circumstances and with its own agenda, or do we look for the actuality aspects within those teachings that do accord 100% with what can be established as current theory today, using technology and knowledge that would not have been available 2,600 years ago? This is the line in the sand that is being drawn by classical Buddhism who will resist this fourth reformation at all costs and there really is no need to do that.

The teaching that we are going to explore now will take a look at the moment by moment interpretation of this teaching, as the secular western approach is based on non-belief and the practical application of the Buddha's teaching. It is pointed out though that there is no denial here in any way that in Buddhist texts there are many references that appear to suggest that an **'apparent you'** may have had **'apparent past lives'** or will have **'apparent future lives.'** It is clear that probably the majority of Buddhists believe this to be true. It is also pointed out before we get underway that whenever this matter is usually discussed within Buddhist circles people tend to produce only the texts that support their belief and ignore the ones that say the opposite and that also applies with much that goes on by way of classical Buddhist discourse.

Soon after the realization of clarity, the Buddha began to actualize that realization experience by exploring ways in which to attempt to communicate it to others. One of these methods came much later to be known as the wheel of life. It was first set out as the twelve linked chain of causality and originally only related to how worrying arises as a process so it could be explored experientially, worked on, reduced and eradicated. It always needs to be hammered home that this was the sole purpose of why the Buddha communicated.

In an early Buddhist text this process was set out in words to the effect of:

Because of confusion, formations arise; because of formations, consciousness (the ability to be aware of being aware, of being human) arises; because of consciousness, mind/body complex arises; because of mind/body complex, the six senses arise; because of the six senses, contact arises; because of contact a pre-conscious response arises; because of pre-conscious response, want arises; because of want, attachment arises; because of attachment, the process of becoming arises; because of that process of becoming, birth arises; because of birth, death arises.

This is the on-going process of worrying that operates in a circular movement for every self-biased mind. This is the repetitive process of birth and death that has two very different interpretations. The first is belief based and opposes the Buddha's realization experience. The second is experiential based and supports his developmental learning approach set out in the eight-fold journey.

Within the same text he points out the same process but in relation to the reduction or ending of that worry words to the effect:

'By reducing or ending confusion, formations decrease or end; by reducing or ending formations, consciousness decreases or ends; by reducing or ending consciousness, Mind/Body complex reduces or ends; by reducing or ending Mind/Body complex, the six senses reduce or end; by reducing or ending the six senses, contact reduces or ends; by reducing or ending contact, the pre-conscious response reduces or ends; by reducing or ending the pre-conscious response, want reduces or ends; by reducing or ending want, attachment reduces or ends; by reducing or ending attachment, the process of becoming reduces or ends; by reducing or ending the process of becoming, birth reduces or ends; by reducing or ending birth, death reduces or ends.'

At first when we look at this reverse order, it doesn't make much sense. How can you reduce death? The answer is that this entire teaching is that death, in this context, means the end of some thing and here that some thing is going to be observed happening within the thought process that we call mind.

Much later in the development of Buddhism, this teaching came to be represented in pictures and although much of the iconography lends itself more to the superstitions and beliefs of classical Tibetanism, it can be helpful to use it as a visual guide to help us understand it experientially. In essence the whole of the pictorial representation is an amalgamation of a number of the Buddha's teaching and it is said to be like a mirror being held up in front of your face. It's a mirror that reflects back at you the actuality of your moment by moment experience.

In this mirror we will find that the central image, which contains four separate but interconnected wheels, is held by a grotesque and scary figure called Yama, the Lord of death. Why? Because physical death is inescapable. It can happen in any moment and it will be the driving factor behind settling down into a life of engaging in any belief that will try and help you avoid that fact. But, it also goes much deeper than that and points to the pre-conscious fear of non-existence which is vastly different from a fear of death. We are so terrified of not existing that we create a range of fantasies about what happens to us after we die. We create moralistic rules and regulations geared towards making us behave or conform now, so that we can benefit in the speculated possibility of some kind of future life. We enter the world of belief and blind faith to keep ourselves oblivious to the actuality of causality because of that very terror. We want security for the known and never want to lose the pleasant things or experiences that we have and as a result we worry now.

In the circle in the centre of the central image we find images of three animals. The pig represents the primary confusion of the self-biased mind. It has nothing to do with stupidity or a lack of intelligence or intellect. Nor is it to do with anything mystical or magical. The pig represents our lack of insight into the actuality that there is no fixed or separate and enduring ego-identity, personality, self, soul, spirit, essence, mind-stream, conscience, energy or any other thing that can be identified and referred to as you, me, or I. It is the driving force behind every thought, speech and action that we engage in. In pig mode everything we think, say and do arises from the confusion that we are separate, that there is 'us' and other things that are 'not us.'

The cockerel represents the unsatisfactory nature of human existence. Because of the confusion of the pig, we continually think, speak and act in ways that give rise to worrying. We worry in the form of wanting things to be different than they really are. We find ourselves in this never ending search for perpetual pleasure and avoidance of pain. We chase after that which we like and run away from things we don't like, but continue to worry because we have failed to recognise the transitory nature of all things.

Dissatisfied with our current state of boredom, we switch on the TV and mindlessly take in a few moments of soap opera or the latest unreality TV show. Bored with that, we wander into the kitchen to put on a bit of surplus weight for the sake of some fleeting sense experience of pleasure, despite not even being hungry in the first place. We drift back to the other room to make a phone call to a friend where we speak sarcastically of a mutual acquaintance that irritates us, or we moan and groan about anything under the sun. We follow that with a bit more channel hopping, trying to find something to keep us entertained and when that doesn't work either, I guess we can always open a bottle of wine to try and take our minds off being in that constant underlying state of worrying. The symbolism of the cockerel was well chosen. If you get a chance take a good look at one. They never stop for a moment.

The snake represents of all the unhelpful aspects that arise in relationship to the confusion of the pig. All of our relationships with other living beings now become conditional and transactional. We justify and rationalise our thoughts, speech and actions on a set of beliefs that have arisen as a direct result of our conditioned lives to date. This allows us to manipulate the living world around us to feed our pre-conscious drive for survival. Anything that is recognised as a threat to us is dealt with by some degree of unhelpful reaction. Everything that we find useful for our survival we cling to. We know that to survive we need to eat and drink. We know that in order to do that something else has to die.

We begin to create a kind of hierarchy of living beings in our minds which is formed by our conditioned lifestyle. At the top of the list is us, followed by (not necessarily in this order) our partner, our family, our friends, pets, our work colleagues. These we have a personal investment in. We create a catch-all word called '**love**' to describe our relationship with things that are useful to us, but '**love**' is such a misunderstood and overused word. In our confused world of the snake this kind of '**love**' is always conditional and transactional. From the perspective of actuality '**love**' is neither of those things. It is a word to describe the way things are. For instance, we say we '**love**' someone, but the mere fact that we are recognising them as separate from us, is the opposite of what '**love**' is in actuality.

Our hierarchical list then divides into two columns. On the left we put all the things that we don't like and on the right we put all of the things we do like. The snake also represents the poison of '**not want**' which can arise as aversion, or ill-will in all its different forms from mass genocide right down to mild irritability. This sets up the conditions of the '**like, don't like**' patterns of conditioned thoughts and resultant behaviour that give rise to our worries that arise from confusion.

These three animals are seen chasing each other's tails in a never ending cycle and so it is with us. We want to be happy. We want to have a sense of purpose. But we look in the wrong direction. We look outwards and not inwards. We look for the security of permanence in an impermanent world and it drives us around the wheel again. Like everything else in the known universe we are constantly changing from one moment to the next. Our hopeless attempts to resist change by leading our lives in safe, familiar ruts, or by pursuing neurotic habits like comfort eating and retail therapy, generates a life of worries for ourselves and then we project them onto others. Even if we have the latest car and always drink cappuccino on the coffee strip, as long as we depend on these experiences for our sense of worth and psychological security, our position will remain fundamentally untenable. Even those who spend a fortune on designer clothing, cosmetics, surgery and a life of luxury will one day get old, get sick and die.

This confused sense of ourselves as somehow fixed, separate and complete, separate from the rest of life, that we constantly try to achieve, is impossible to attain in the face of the actuality of causality. We can never be separate. On a moment by moment basis we affect and are affected by everything else in our environment. From the air we breathe, to the food we eat, the impressions and ideas that we take in, all come from outside of ourselves. There is nothing within us that is not affected by the continual process of exchange between ourselves and our environment. The world we move in is a constantly swirling mass of change. But, having constructed ourselves in a fixed sense of the world where we, as more or less bound and unchanging things, interact with a stable world of other things, we experience a constant friction between things as they are and the world of our confusion. Bumping up against actuality, but unwilling to face up to it and break free into it, we experience worrying time and time again.

Only by letting go of our confused clinging will we ever be free. The pig, cockerel and snake of want, not want and confusion are the drives within us that keeps the wheel of life turning and will keep it turning until we decide to apply the brakes a bit to either slow down the process or jump off altogether. This process begins by understanding the symbolism of the second circle within the wheel. This part of the wheel is directly linked with the way the Buddha used the pre-existent idea of karma as a learning tool for development.

It gives us a very early indication of a way in which we can move away from our worries towards the realization of peace of mind. In effect, it describes the Buddha's approach to ethics as not being rule-bound and also how karma and its resultant consequences originates in the thought process at the moment of motivational intent. We see a white section and a black section. In the white section we see beings, or possibly lotus flowers, which represents human potential for growth, ascending or developing higher states of conscious awareness and in the black section we see beings or lotus flowers, falling into unhelpful mind states. The experiential aspect of this image is to observe your own direct experience. When you think, say and do anything that is helpful, in that it leads you away from worrying towards peace of mind, you will notice that within the helpful state of your mind. When you think, say and do anything that is unhelpful, in that it actually creates worry or reduces peace of mind, you will notice that within the unhelpful state of mind.

This second circle indicates that at any given moment there is the opportunity at least, to be consciously aware of the choices we make. Unlike theistic religions (and to a lesser extent religious classical Buddhism) that underpins the traditional ethical systems of the west, secular western Buddhism does not talk in terms of **'good and bad.'** No thought, word spoken or resultant action is either good or bad in itself. In the same way no individual is inherently good or bad. Buddhism focuses instead on the intention behind the thought, word or action. What matters is the quality of the motivational factors that precede our thoughts, speech and actions. This is not to say that those things we do unintentionally have no consequences. If I slip in the kitchen and spill scalding hot tea on my partner it will certainly have consequences for her and me. But those consequences are of a completely different nature to what they would be had I emptied the teapot over her head deliberately.

We know from within our own life experience how what we think, say and do has an effect on us. But for the most part we ignore this experience and repeat habitual patterns of behaviour. By bringing some clear thinking, some awareness to our thought process, primarily through the practice of formal meditation and daily awareness, we can begin to discover and experience the consequences of our actions more clearly. As the average human being wants to be content we can learn very quickly how unhelpful thoughts, speech and actions prevent us from being that which we seek. The practicalities of the Dharma journey provide a real opportunity for us to take 100% responsibility for the consequences of our thoughts, speech and actions without recourse to the punishment and reward system of theistic religion and rule-bound Buddhist ethics.

There is nobody to forgive you and nobody to promise you a more delightful apparent future life. This is a huge responsibility, but it is also very liberating. The irrational and neurotic guilt that is symptomatic of theistic religion and the coercion and manipulation of the rules and regulations of classical Buddhism are extremely damaging and unhelpful to human development. It is helpful to abandon that kind of mind-set in favour of one where we recognise we are not infallible and that there is always room for improvement. This way we can learn from our experiences and grow, rather than beating ourselves up for having them so others might think well of us or so we can fit in somewhere.

Next we find six segments, each of which, in this context, represent a particular psychological mind state. In classical Buddhism they are often seen by many as actual places where people are reborn into as a result of their karma and although reference will be made to their traditional names, it is their secular psychological counterpart that is being pointed out here within this context.

The first is the realm of the gods or deva's. This is the mind state of '**Pleasure and Contentment.**' This is when life is going well for us. Our basic needs are met and we think we're relatively happy or we're managing to avoid things we don't like too much. For Dharma practitioners, this is possibly the most dangerous mind state to be in as it can often lead to a slacking off of meditation, study and ethical practice and very quickly we slide down the ladder and land on a snake. This is those moments when everything seems to be effortless and things around us seem to fall into place very easily.

We remain in this state only as long as this amazing thing we call the mind is being activated from the basis of that which is helpful. A continuation of helpful thoughts, words and actions will determine how long we remain in this mind state. The moment we think, say or do anything that has an element of unhelpful motivational factors, we enter into a different mind state. If we were to understand this clearly, bearing in mind we seek to be content, we can begin to see how, even on a selfish basis, living a life in a way that is helpful to the realization of clarity, is the only thing that will provide us with that contentment. If we acknowledge, that by being content ourselves our actions then have a direct helpful effect on everything else around us, we can see directly how we can affect the way the world actually is.

Next is the realm of the titans. A titan is a kind of competitive demon. This is the mind state of **'Jealousy and Power.'** It's when, dependent on the consequences of our thoughts, speech and actions we engage in competitiveness. We try and create hierarchical structures based in getting our own way. We strive to be the best, the richest, the strongest, the fastest etc. Typically, you find people who spend a great deal of time in this frame of mind working in the worlds of politics, business, sport, entertainment, the military and the criminal underworld to name but a few. This mind state relates to others on the basis of dominance and submission and never one of equality. Males in this mind state are said to use brute force and cunning to get what they want. Females in this mind state are said to use their femininity or sexuality in much the same way. We enter this mind state the moment we are experiencing jealousy or envy of others who seem to be a lot happier than us, but are not prepared to do the work that needs to be done ourselves and keep putting it off for the future. In this state we often turn to external materialism rather than introspection.

Next is the realm of the hungry ghost. This is the mind state of **'Unsatisfied Want.'** This is us in worry mode. It is us engaging with the world on the basis of our confused self-biased mind. We seek permanence in things that can never be permanent. We place unrealistic expectations on things we buy and do, to try and make ourselves happy. Within western culture we are conditioned to seek happiness externally. Advertising conditions us towards materialism and consumerism. Careers are built upon the attachment to status. We look down on alcoholism and drug addiction, yet in actuality they are all cut from the same cloth. We seek stability, security, lasting pleasure and the end of our worries in ways that are incapable of providing them.

In this mind state we are in a constant state of wanting our current experience to be other than it is. We linger in the past trying to re-live the happy bits, or more often than not clinging to the bits that hurt us as we haven't yet found a way to let go. And of course there is absolutely nothing we can do about the past, as it no longer exists other than as a memory and most, if not all of them, will be seriously flawed. In this mind state we are restless and try to fill all of the gaps in our life with unsustainable pleasure which inevitably results in more worry.

Next is the hell realm. This is the mind state of '**Physical Pain, Emotional Turmoil and Psychological Imbalance.**' This is when the mind is blinded by not want, ill-will and anger in all its various forms. This is also where we are experiencing guilt associated with things we have thought, said and done that we know are unhelpful and have resulted in worrying. In this mind state we tend to beat ourselves up for not being infallible. We even start to hate hating and that causes us to worry and then we hate worrying which just causes more worrying.

In this mind state we are disconnected with the way things actually are. Although it arises in the same way as the others there is a subtle difference here. This mind state throws up a sense that something is not right. Something is wrong with us. Something is missing, that somehow we are not whole or complete. It is this aspect of confusion that gives rise to depression, stress and anxiety disorders because we can't seem to find an answer to the problem and are forever looking in the wrong direction. This is the mind state that is, more than most, representative of that fundamental human dilemma of worrying.

Next is the animal realm. This is the mind state of **'Ignorance and Unawareness.'** This is us on auto-pilot, stumbling through life being led by our habitual patterns of thinking and behaviour without even given them a second thought. We settle down into group think and group behaviour, questioning and challenging nothing. Just like animals, all we are concerned about on an everyday level is to satisfy our physical needs and our survival, such as (in no particular order) eating, drinking, urinating, defecating, sleeping and sex. This is the mind state of repetitive habitual patterns where we are not even looking to change. This can create an ever present fear of attack, so we are ever alert to a predator who we automatically think is a wolf in sheep's clothing and cannot recognise their compassionate nature.

Finally, we come to the human realm. This is the mind state of **'Potential and Awareness.'** This is when we are fully present with our moment by moment experience. We are not dwelling in the memories of the past or projecting into the fantasies of the future. The opportunity to be born a human being is, by any stretch of the imagination, an amazing experience. People seem to spend so much time attached to things from the past and concern themselves about what might come next when all they can ever actually know is that they are going to age, get sick and die. Everything else is mere speculation. This is that amazing opportunity of the next breath and the transitory now moment where, with awareness, we can actually make informed choices, arrived at as a result of our Dharma practice. This will lead us away from worrying towards peace of mind. It is only in this mind state that the realization of clarity can arise and liberate us from our worries.

By exploring and understanding these six mind states intellectually and experientially we can begin to develop an awareness of how our mind operates and why. At any moment we can turn our attention to what is going on in the mind. We can observe what state it is in. Because we have the ability to make conscious decisions that will affect our states of mind, it provides us with a realistic opportunity to engage head on with our habitual patterns of behaviour. We can recognise them for what they are and experience directly how much worrying arises as a result of them. Although change is inevitable, by developing this level of awareness we can point that change in the direction of things that are helpful and ease the tensions of worrying. How we work within this mind state is by observing the moment by moment twelve links of the chain of causality.

Our current moment by moment psychological mind states are determined by our thoughts, speech and actions in the preceding moment of experience and are, according to the Buddha, dependent on whether or not those thoughts are kind or unkind or helpful or unhelpful to move us away from our worries towards peace of mind. The twelve links of causality, in this context, is a cyclic and interconnected process of continual becoming and ending, arising and subsiding, birth and death of each moment of experience within our world of the confused self-biased mind of conditioned existence.

The first link in this chain is 'Confusion.' It is illustrated with a picture of a blind person trying to make their way through life, symbolically at least, of never having the opportunity to see how things are in actuality. This is the confusion of there being a fixed or separate and enduring ego-identity, personality, self, soul, spirit, essence, mind-stream, conscience, energy or any other thing that can be identified and referred to as you, me, or I. It is only ever fully destroyed within the realization experience of causality, which means, until that moment of realization we are going to go round and round in circles living the twelve links of causality until we find a way out.

This confusion has nothing to do with ignorance or lack of intelligence. One may have an enormous capacity for intellectual and conceptual thinking. But because we retain a sense of being separate we remain blinded to actuality and we are confused by that blindness. Its roots are as much emotional and reactionary as intellectual. For example, the deeply held belief that we can be happy by just getting enough of what we want is a profound instance of confusion. Even if we won $10 Million on the lottery, our acute sense of incompleteness would not go away. According to some research amongst big lottery winners, a significant number actually report that they are now unhappier than they were before the win. Maybe we tend to believe that somehow things can be permanent, our friends and lovers will always love us, our home will always be there to return to. Maybe we believe that somewhere we can find our own true self nature, that is somehow us in essence, which others must accept and rely on. Failing all of those we can always fall back on the old favourite such as a belief in a creator entity that can provide us with what we need and who must be appeased at all costs.

In the ancient texts, confusion is also noted as being a lack of insight into the four principle assignments that the Buddha set out in his first public teaching, words to the effect:

1. A lack of insight into the actuality of worrying being a fundamental part of the self-biased mind
2. A lack of insight into its root cause, namely wanting any current experience to be other than it is
3. A lack of insight into the actuality that worrying can be alleviated and eradicated
4. A lack of insight into the proposed developmental method that leads to that alleviation or eradication of worry

This was his first attempt to communicate his realization of causality in relation to worrying. Here we can see that he was trying to show us that all experiences arise because of a preceding primary cause and an infinite number of interconnected conditions. He is encouraging us to explore our inner world, primarily through meditation, to integrate our pre-conscious and sub-conscious habitual patterns of thinking, speaking and behaving so that we can take effective action to change.

We need to explore and discover directly how much of what we think, say and do is based on fixed beliefs or views that we cling to that are not based in the actuality of causality. Ideas such as fate, destiny, luck and superstition are examples of confusion. Turning towards the magical and mystical world of conditioned beliefs and personal truths is an expression of confusion. All of these things provide the building blocks of a wall that becomes so high we will never be able to climb over it. Our only way through is to smash our way through at the ground level of conscious awareness. In dependence on confusion arise our formations.

The second link in the chain represents our 'formations' and is illustrated with a picture of a potter throwing lumps of clay onto a wheel and making pots. Formations come into being because of the preceding link to our confusion. Formations are our expressed thoughts, speech and actions that arise as a result of our habitual patterns of conditioned existence, which is our basic level of the unawareness of actuality. A helpful way of thinking about this is to consider confusion as being a bit like when you are drunk and the formations are the kind of things you say and do when you are drunk. Even if you've never been drunk yourself, I'm sure that you have witnessed, at some time in your life, the violent extremes and also pure comedy at times of drunken behaviour.

So, the primary cause of formations is our preceding confusion and they are acted out because of the conditioning we have been subject to from that first moment when we thought of ourselves as being a separate personality that we call 'I.' Of course, not all habitual patterns of thinking and behaviour are unhelpful. We also have helpful patterns, but as they are born from confusion they will tend to be reactive rather than responsive. They will become part of our survival strategy to get us through the day until such time as we can find the next distraction from our on-going worries. In dependence on formations, arises consciousness.

The third link of the chain is **'consciousness'** and is illustrated with a picture of a monkey in a fruit bearing tree. The monkey is seen constantly swinging from branch to branch in search of the one piece of fruit that will bring him lasting satisfaction. Because of confusion, formations come into existence. Because of confusion and formations, consciousness comes into existence. Consciousness is another word for **'aliveness.'** In our case we have human consciousness which gives us an ability to be aware of being aware of being human.

All living things are consciousness and what we tend to do is to judge what we see, hear etc, of other living things against what we can know about human consciousness and then make assumptions that we know what is going on. Maybe some of that is plausible or even accurate, but in actuality, until such time as we develop a two-way communication method for a different species, we cannot actually know. So the question that we can answer is that all living things are consciousness, but we can only make assumptions about their level of awareness or ability to be aware.

These actions of body, speech and mind are now being carried out by somebody who thinks of themselves as being a separate individual. Consciousness now becomes a source of our on-going worry because we now believe that there is a separate personality that is present experiencing things via its senses.

In this link of the chain, consciousness is seen to be a re-linking one. It links this moment to the next moment in the continuity aspect of causality. The monkey swings from branch to branch and consciousness passes from moment to moment. But we need to be aware not to take this image too literally. The consciousness which moves from moment to moment is not unchanged in the process. What comes next is neither exactly the same as, nor entirely different from what went before, but arises in dependence upon it.

When considering this, it is helpful to bear in mind that prior to the Buddha it was universally accepted that there was some element of a permanent essence of 'you' that moved literally from life to life. He recognised that this religious assumption of his time led people down blind alleyways of faith and belief and reliance on rites, rituals and superstition that moved them further and further away from actuality and the very liberation they sought. In communicating causality, he attempts to bring people into the present moment as a means for their liberation from worrying now, rather than being overly concerned about a no longer existent past and a yet to come possible future as a means of liberation. In dependence on formations arises the mind/body complex.

The fourth link of the chain is the '**mind/body complex**' which makes up the whole human psychophysical organism that we call us. It is illustrated by a picture of a boat with four passengers who are often depicted as rowing. The boat here is representative of our physical body and the rowers or passengers represent the mind aspects of '**emotional experience, perception, motivations and awareness**' and it is awareness that is steering the boat. These five aspects of becoming are a collection of interdependent shifting processes that when, combined together, create the human being that we now believe is us. They are what we, with all our changing experiences, in the end come down to.

Our physical body is the thing we use to engage with our sense experiences. We see with the eyes, hear with the ears, smell with the nose, taste with the mouth and touch with the hands. When we engage with any of the sense experiences we are doing so on the basis that the pre-conscious signaling of pleasant, neutral and unpleasant will set up an '**emotional experience**' that we will become aware of. '**Perception**' consists of the process of recognizing and assimilating the sensations that are presented to us so we can begin to make some sense of them.

Although we do use two terms such as mind and body in everyday language, in actuality it is a single connected process. Mind we can say is this thing we experience as an active thinking process. It is our labeling system for all experiences. It creates our ideas, concepts and beliefs about things. Body is considered to be the elements that are said to make up the physical body that include the big four of earth, water, air and fire and possibly many more. The mind/body complex will always be a source for worrying all the while we believe that our minds and bodies are who we are in actuality.

After the evaluation and labeling process of perception our **'motivations'** kick in. Mostly they will be habitual and we will be unaware of them. When we experience something as pleasant we will want more of it, or seek to repeat the experience. If we experience something as unpleasant we will try and push it away, avoid it, remove it or replace it with something pleasant.

The final aspect of becoming is **'awareness'** which here is discriminating because of the existence of the self-biased mind within the experience. This creates the dualistic sense of separateness. We see things as ultimately separate from ourselves, separate from the world and we imagine that somehow it is fixed and unchanging. We do not see that things exist only as a changing pattern in the constantly moving flow of life and that, along with every other thing they just play a part in a vast web of interconnected aliveness.

There is a school of thought within classical Buddhism that suggests that we are really just pure awareness that is witness to experience. It is suggested here that this view is just as extreme as thinking that we are just our physical bodies which would be the opposite extreme. It is suggested that the middle way, as set out by the Buddha, shows us that consciousness and the mind/body complex are co-dependent and cannot exist without each other. This middle way approach, is also set out in an ancient text where two of the Buddha's disciples are discussing this subject. In that text one disciple says to the other words to the effect:

"It is like having two sheaves of reeds leaning against each other. If you take away the sheave on the left, then the right sheave would automatically fall over. If you took away the sheave on the right, then the sheave on the left would automatically fall over.'

What this text is saying is that consciousness/aliveness exists because it has the mind/body complex as its conditioning factor and the mind/body complex exists because it has consciousness/aliveness as its conditioning factor. It is saying that you can't have one without the other. Therefore, the extreme view of there simply being pure consciousness is a kind of idealism that is not in accord with actuality. And the extreme view of there just being a physical body is also not in accord with actuality. In classical Buddhist language they would both be considered as **'unhelpful views.'**

The first four links in the chain of causality set up the conditions for our everyday experience in the world of self-biased conditioned and subjective reality. We find ourselves in a world where we can never find lasting satisfaction with any thing. We experience this sense of incompleteness, this on-going worry, that somehow, something is missing and we need to go and find it out there somewhere so we can be complete. We ride the ocean of life on our leaking yacht that is being driven by the eight worldly winds of **'pleasure and pain, praise and blame, loss and gain, and fame and disrepute.'** At the helm is captain **'us.'** The captain is busy looking to the stars for guidance instead of relying on the satellite navigation system of the Dharma. The captain is looking out for rocks through his ancient telescope instead of following the charts that have been shown to be accurate. And the biggest mistake of all is that the captain has decided he is a captain in the first place because he bought himself a captain's hat from a market stall instead of learning how to sail in the first place. In dependence on the mind/body complex arises the six senses.

The fifth link in the chain is the **'six senses'** and this is illustrated with a picture of a house that has one door and five windows. The house represents the mind/body complex we call us and it is engaging with the world around it via the windows of the five senses, namely the eyes (sight experience), the ears (sound experience), the mouth (taste experience), the nose (smell experience) and physicality (touch experience). They are all being filtered through the doorway to the thought processor that we call mind, which in Buddhism is considered a sixth sense (thought experience.) The six senses can only arise because of the preceding conditioning factors of the mind/body complex combined with consciousness. It is accepted that some people do not understand how the mind can be a sense and wonder why Buddhism added it into the usual list of five that is found everywhere else. This has much to do with the practice of awareness. As this practice develops it is possible to be aware of what is going on in this thing we call mind without having to locate it somewhere.

Our thoughts and memories can be observed clearly without an apparent need to get caught up in the drama of attaching ourselves to those memories or thoughts. If we pay attention enough we will come to see that all that is happening is thoughts arising and subsiding and with practice, we can learn not to judge them as good or bad or seek to change them in any way. We also learn that we don't have to believe them either. Also, it is helpful to bear in mind that memory is such a flawed system to be dependent on. Much of what we think of as our memories are, or have been, implanted by external third parties and not our memory at all. It is said that much of the time we are simply remembering the last time we remembered the same thing and not remembering the actual experience at all.

For most of my life I had a vivid memory of childhood. It had become a significant part of my life story. I was very young and in hospital having my tonsils and adenoids out and my mum bought me a brand new toy to console me. Considering my early life was one of abject poverty in London's notorious East End, it is no wonder that such an incident lodged itself into my subconscious. This amazing gift was a toy car being driven by Enid Blyton's character Noddy, who was resplendent in his red jumper, spotted neck-tie and blue hat with a bell on. It was so vibrantly coloured red and yellow and was designed a bit like a cool version of an open top VW Beetle. It was such a joy to play with how could it not be anything other than the truth? It never happened.

Years later, well into my fifties, during a conversation with my elder brother whilst doing the whole family nostalgia thing, he told this story about the time he was in hospital having his tonsils out and how our mother had given him this toy car. After further investigation, which included talking this out with my mother, it transpired that I had never even been in hospital as I'd never had any operation on anything. I didn't even go to the hospital to visit my brother and had no connection to this toy whatsoever. We traced the switch to a time when my mother was telling the story to a relative and got us both mixed up and I had then taken on the memory as mine. This is such a great Dharma teaching. Nothing is ever as it seems. Test and challenge everything. To this day none of us know what the actual factual version of this story is. In dependence on the six senses arises contact.

The sixth link in the chain is **'contact'** and is illustrated by a picture of a couple kissing. It has nothing to do with sex or romance. It simply represents contact between an external thing and one or more of the senses and like everything else is dependent on the preceding conditioning factors. The external thing could be anything. There isn't a moment in our life when we are not in contact with some thing via at least one of our senses. The reality of gravity means that we are inevitably in contact physically with some thing. Even if we jumped in the air there would still be a physical sensation that we are in contact with. Unless we are blind or we walk around with our eyes closed or asleep, seeing is going on all the time. Unless we are deaf there will always be sound going on. How much we notice or pay attention to the senses is another thing, but they are always active. Contact is that now moment when the external thing and sense experience combine together to create a reaction or a response. In dependence on contact arises the pre-conscious reaction.

The seventh link of the chain is the **'pre-conscious reaction'** of the contact being pleasant or unpleasant and it is illustrated by a picture of a person with an arrow in their eye. Whether we realize it or not this happens each time we make contact through any of the senses. It's not so much that first there is contact and then the pre-conscious reaction follows. It's more a case of it is just one experience, but has been separated here to express two different aspects namely the reception of the experience and the pre-conscious reaction to it. By way of example, if you were to take a bite of your favourite banana muffin, there is contact between your taste sense and the muffin and the pre-conscious reaction arises at the point of contact. It's not that you take a bite and then have to wait until you start enjoying it.

This is a crucial junction point in the wheel so it is worth having a quick recap. At the start of this process we had confusion which gave rise to formations. These two links make up the cause process of the past. As a consequence of these, next to arise is the linking process to the current moment that is consciousness which then leads to the mind/body complex followed by the six senses which now determine our interaction with the world. This interaction may please us or it may not, but there is nothing we can actually do about it. We cannot go back and change the past, but we can do something about a possible future. The past is closed and there really is no use crying over the milk we have already spilled. It's more helpful just to clean it up there and then so we don't slip on it later. What we need to do is turn our attention to the present moment as it will define what is to come, because the future is completely open.

Having exhausted the result process of the present, we are about to embark on the cause process of the future. We are about to begin the process of bringing a new self and a new world into being. If, as we usually do, we give way at this point to want or not want, we will find ourselves back in the central circle of the pig, cockerel and snake and will follow the rest of the links of the chain of causality until we start again with confusion and this will be an on-going process. If, on the other hand, we reflect on the actuality of the situation with an understanding based on our previous experiences that our wants are endless and never provide lasting satisfaction, we give ourselves the opportunity to bring some degree of conscious awareness to the situation that will lead us away from the automatic pilot mode. In dependence of the pre-conscious reaction arises want.

The eighth link of the chain is **'want'** and it is illustrated by a picture of a man who is seated at a table being offered a drink by a woman. Here, the term want is aligned to other words in use within the vocabulary of Buddhism like craving and desire but we avoid them here because of their associations that are not helpful. This want, seeks the pleasure and rejects the pain that is dependent on that pre-conscious reaction. It is also this same want that drives us to be somebody, to find ourselves as we used to say in the hippy era. Or conversely it can drive us to be a nobody, the loner, Billy no mates, we just don't want to be noticed as being distinct from anybody else at all.

As we will discover later, it is being aware of the gap between the pre-conscious reaction and want that provide us with the opportunity of stepping outside of the chain of causality even for a moment. Without that awareness we will just be on auto-pilot, reacting to a pleasant experience with wanting more, or reacting to an unpleasant experience by trying to get rid of it and the really sad bit is that we will not even notice it. It is what happens in the gap between these two links that is a main contributory factor in the creation of our worries. When we learn to bring conscious awareness to our moment by moment experience, it will become possible to simply observe the pre-conscious reactions as they arise and as they are, without a need to react to them. This is the only part of the chain that has a weak link and the gap that causes the weakness is barely visible unless full attention is being given to the observation.

There is nothing wrong with these experiences. They arise automatically as a result of contact and to add in an element of judgment would be counter-productive. Simply becoming aware of the experience provides us with the opportunity to make informed decisions. We can respond in a helpful way rather than react from habit. The third pre-conscious reaction of neutrality, or not being concerned either way can be very confusing. On one level it seems like the ideal position or middle way between pleasure and pain, but on another level the uncertainty of the experience can actually create a stronger sense of worry when it becomes unsustainable and the urge for continuous pleasure kicks in.

When engaged with, on the basis of conscious awareness, this teaching becomes a really practical guide to lessen our worries on a moment by moment basis and if we manage to squeeze through the gap and stay on the other side for good, eradicate them all together. For example, if, with practice, we become aware that we seem to react in an unhelpful way whenever we engage with a particular person and we don't know why, (and it is suggested here that we rarely do) it provides us with the opportunity to respond in a helpful way by making a conscious decision not to engage with them for a while so we can explore those reactions and the reasons why they arise.

This can be very effective when we combine this response by including this person within a structured awareness of kindness meditation practice. With practice we might become aware that we tend to eat sweet or fatty foods, or turn to the bottle when we are worrying and make ourselves a little sick, or at least over indulged. We can choose a more helpful response by choosing to fill that gap with something a little more healthy, so we can explore how that works for us. In dependence on want arises clinging.

The ninth link of the chain is 'clinging' and it is illustrated by a picture of someone picking fruit from a tree. This is all about ownership, or holding on to things. It could be our sense experiences, our beliefs, views or opinions, even our habitual patterns of thinking, speaking and doing. It's about being attached to all the things that we try and define ourselves by to make ourselves seem safe and secure with the way we want the world to be. On one level this seems to make sense, as some kind of survival strategy against worrying but it's seriously flawed. I'm sure that if you're honest with yourselves, you will have experienced directly how difficult people can seem when they become closed down to any other point of view. You may have even found within your own experience how being so rigid actually causes you to worry. It's actually OK and far less stressful, not to have a view about anything or to cling lightly to just having transitional views dependent on currently available information. This is called the 'current theory of everything' approach. In dependence on clinging arises becoming.

The tenth link of the chain is 'becoming,' or about to become and is illustrated by a picture of a pregnant woman. Within the context of this approach to the teaching, this picture represents the next moment of experience that is about to arise from the previous moment of experience. This is the moment by moment continuity aspect that provides us with the opportunity to experience for ourselves the consequences of what we just thought, said or did and learn from it, once that moment has actually come into being. This is the continuity process of what we think of as us. We bring from a past that is just about to expire and vanish forever, our memories, our conditioned habits of thinking, speaking and behaving, our personality and the very thing that causes all of our worrying. We bring the idea that we are, yet again, about to become a fixed or separate and enduring ego-identity, personality, self, soul, spirit, essence, mind-stream, conscience, energy or any other thing that can be identified and referred to as you, me, or I.

It can be viewed from two different perspectives within Buddhism. Some see this as representing the completion of the causal process of the present moment and others see it as representing the first link in the result process of the future moment. In any event, what it represents, in its most helpful understanding, is that it is the arising of a new situation. When we give way to our fantasies of winning the lottery, we become mildly obsessed with unfulfilled wants and start to worry. When we give way to our anger we enter the mind state of jealousy and power and start to worry. It is our mental state that will define the quality of the next moment of psychological experience. When we are happy in that mind state of pleasure and contentment, people smile back at us and the world we live in is a happier place for a while. The subjective self-biased mind and the world arise together. As a result of becoming arises birth.

The eleventh link of the chain is 'birth' and it is illustrated, unsurprisingly perhaps, with a picture of a woman giving birth in full and glorious technicolour. Within the context of this approach to the teaching, birth represents the arrival of the next moment of existence that, for a moment, we engage with in accord with our habitual patterns of conditioned thinking, speaking and behaving before it comes to an end almost instantly. In dependence on birth death arises.

The twelfth link in the chain is **'death'** and is illustrated by a dead body, usually seen being carried off to the funeral pyre. In classical Buddhism this represents ageing, sickness and death, but within the context of this approach to the teaching, death represents the end of the current moment of existence. Dependent on the end of this moment arises confusion and the whole wheel starts its next rotation within the blink of an eye, a breath or a heartbeat.

After the death of the Buddha, his followers split into several different groups and went their own way and began to explore what the Buddha taught in different ways. One of these groups were focused on meditation and the connection with this thing we call mind and were responsible for the creation of a body of work known as the **'Abhidharma,'** which is very philosophical by nature. It is a systematic description of how, according to them, the mind works and within that system they give an explanation of the twelve link chain that supports the idea that is common within classical Buddhism of previous and future lives.

It is helpful to bear in mind this took place over 2000 years ago and we have moved forward considerably with the use of science, technology and in particular neuroscience. But, considering this was as a result of human introspection and contemplation, what they arrived at is pretty amazing stuff and does not make for light reading I can tell you. In this belief system the twelve links come to represent various stages of a human life rather than the on-going momentary experience model we have explored so far.

In their system, we are born into this life in confusion as a result of our actions in our previous life which is our formations and it is consciousness that becomes the linking factor in bridging the gap between that previous life and this. It is consciousness that is said to move on after physical death in this life that then finds an opportunity to enter the womb of the next mother when the time is helpful for the conditions of those actions in a previous life are due to ripen as a result of the law of karma. The mind/body complex becomes the body and mind of the embryo which begins to develop the six senses whilst waiting to be born. After birth, when the conditioning begins on contact with the external world and the pre-conscious reaction that arise as a result of that contact a new being is created. Up until this moment all of this has occurred, it is said, as a direct result of a previous existence in a previous life.

Having arrived in this new birth and having experienced contact and pre-conscious reaction, this new life comes into its own as we then begin the on-going journey of wanting things to be other than they are, becoming attached to things we like and rejecting things we don't and live our lives on auto-pilot of conditioned and habitual patterns of thinking speaking and behaving as we age, get sick and die. We then start the whole process again, dragging all this rubbish with us into our next life and so on and so on.

In the primary teaching of the four assignments, the Buddha highlights that it is the want for things to be other than they are, that is the cause of worrying. In this later communication, possibly after he had reflected some more in the search for different ways to communicate causality, we find him expanding that original teaching and showing us that there is not just one cause of our worries but a whole web of interconnected conditions that have no discernable first cause but is cyclic in nature and follows a set pattern which never alters.

This twelve link chain drives the human process, from moment to moment, round and round in circles, and is assisted by the conditioned factors of want, not want and confusion that results in our actions. This in turn creates our mind state that is the twelve link chain. It is an amazing learning opportunity when approached on the basis of its practical application, but to simply believe it on the basis of blind faith seems to do an injustice to the communication that the Buddha gave for the benefit of all beings.

The difficulty is that the pre-conscious, biological nature aspect of being is hard-wired for survival. This in turn sets up the conditions for the fear of non-existence. This then sets up the conditions to believe in anything of an irrational nature that may bring some comfort or relief from that fear. This is where the religion of Buddhism set itself up as an ally of every other religion that offers a similar comfort blanket that is subject to an adherence to religious beliefs and the rules of the controlling institutions.

All the while we remain in a state of confusion there will be present a sense of there being a fixed or separate self. Because of that separation you experience the world around you as being separate from you. That is how you perceive it to be through the senses, because, let's face it, it looks pretty real doesn't it? Once perceived and then believed to be separate from you, you begin to react automatically whether you realize it or not, with this auto-response of I like it, I don't like it and from that arises this reaction of trying to grab onto it because you like it or push it away if you don't. This is where the conditioned self-biased and reactive mind is born. It develops an identity, a personality, that it spends the rest of its life promoting or protecting.

It is only when this enormous iceberg of confusion begins to be chipped away at with the small ice pick of Dharma practice can our worries begin to lesson. By our own effort, we create the right conditions and as a result of our practice we might even find the one spot that when we tap on it, the whole iceberg crumbles into the sea and is destroyed in an instant and we are free of worrying. This, in secular western Buddhism, is known as awakening. It is that breakthrough moment of clarity into the way things are in actuality. It is the birth of the responsive and creative mind, or the deathless state. Once the confusion of the self-biased mind is seen through who is there to be reborn? Who is there to worry?

This subject is a huge point of contention even within the different schools of classical Buddhism. As hard as I tried to explore this subject within those schools, all I could ever get for an answer is that it is true because it says so in a book, or somebody had a memory, or even experienced it directly. Now, I am not one to refute or deny the experiences of any other person. I've had quite enough weird and whacky ones myself and I know how real and convincing they are. But to say that I base my life on what is written in a book is, to be frank, barking mad. In the Bible it says that Jesus was born of a virgin. Really? In Harry Potter it says if you run into the wall at platform 9 $\frac{3}{4}$ you get to Hogwarts. Are we really going to base our practice in the 21st century on story books?

I too have had the whole near death and out of body experience thing, and yes there was a bright white light and yes there was a sense of looking down at myself being bounced around the garden like a Tom and Jerry cartoon, whilst being electrocuted to death. And all because I had wired up the cable on the lawnmower the wrong way and decided to mow the lawn in bare feet on a very dewy morning. It was just an experience. It wasn't real. Nor were the very vivid and detailed previous life experiences I have had in meditation when I explored them in detail. Why believe in this kind of thing? How does it help you right now other than give you a false sense of security and make you lazy? This is a very practical teaching, with practical implications for the one life you know you have.

In one of his teachings, the Buddha used an image of a house being built as the basis of trying to convey what it is we do within our world of conditioned habitual patterns of behaviour. Although a house gives us a sense of security and a boundary fence surrounding the garden where we can seem safe, we can get stuck behind those four walls and never have the opportunity to go out for a walk on the beach and smell the ozone. The house represents the self-biased mind that is trapped in confusion and it is want that is the builder of our worries and it features a lot in texts from the second period of Buddhism known as the Mahayana such as the White Lotus Sutra.

In an early Buddhist text that many suggest is the closest we can ever get to the actual words spoken by the Buddha, we find the following to the effect:

"Through many a birth in samsara, (conditioned existence/daily life) have I wandered in vain, seeking the builder of this house (of life). Repeated birth is indeed worrying! O housebuilder, you are seen! You will not build this house again. For your rafters are broken and your ridgepole shattered. My mind has reached the unconditioned; I have attained the destruction of want."

224

Using the image of the house and the house builder we can see how our everyday world (samsara) has come into being because of our confusion and our want for independent existence. The house we have built is that sense of personality that we call 'I' and we worry because we think it is safe and sound to believe in it as a self-existent and separate and permanent or enduring thing. But, like any house, it is subject to subsidence, damp, dry rot or even worse if you live in Australia, the ravage of white ants. Owning a house, as we know, is very high maintenance and so it is with us. We have to maintain the personality we have created for ourselves. We have to wear a variety of different masks in different areas of our life. We struggle to find that authentic us or go off in search of ourselves. When we finally do, someone comes along and tells us we've been wasting our time as it's all just confusion and we tend not to like that.

The Dharma journey and the practice of conscious awareness means that we can rip up our building permit, hang up the bricklayer's trowel and stop mixing the cement that keeps us stuck and begin to live our life out in the open space under the stars. It allows helpful, creative energy to flow and carry us all the way to the end of the rainbow that is the end of our worries. But first we have to find that gap again so we can squeeze through it.

Within classical Buddhism much is made of the apparent recollections of previous lives of the Buddha. These stories are used as a major selling point for the religious belief system that is now Buddhism. They appear to go almost into panic mode if anyone even begins to challenge those beliefs. They seem to see it as some kind of threat to Buddhism and think the entire system will fall down if we begin to view these stories on the basis of known facts rather than ancient fantasy.

What they seem to miss is that these things arose within the meditative process. All manner of things arise within that process. I could probably write a separate book detailing a number of past life experiences that I have had over the years. The major difference is, that not being a blind faith believer I have gone off and done the detective work to discover the actuality aspect of them. Just as an example of how believable this all becomes I'll tell you about just one of those false memories. Years ago I went through a phase in meditation where very detailed images arose with entire stories attached to them. Interestingly enough, in my case I was never a Red Indian chief or an Egyptian Princess in the memories but more often than not I would be something like an insurance salesman from Bradford. In this particular one I had a name and a story that related to Singapore, a country I had never ever visited, at a time during the outbreak of world war two.

Years later, on my first ever visit to Singapore, I was walking around town and came across the Raffles Hotel which I had never seen before. What happened next wasn't like a déjà vu experience. It actually stopped me in my tracks because the thought arose that it was simply in the wrong place. I recognised the building but it wasn't supposed to be in the middle of town. It was meant to be out in the open with beautiful gardens with sweeping majestic views. Over the course of the next couple of days I experienced a number of similar things and really began to explore those memories I had years earlier in meditation that told me that I was this person with the connection to Singapore but could get nowhere.

Years later again, long after I had more or less put this to bed as the science was more or less in on this, I watched a re-run of the BBC series Tenko that was a particular favourite of my wife the first time it ran years earlier. I wasn't that interested at the time but now I had this thing about Singapore and the war going on in this memory in meditation so I got into the series. By the third episode I had cracked the final piece of the puzzle. The name of this person who I was supposed to have been in a previous life flashed up on the screen in the final credits as a sound recorder on the film crew. I later discovered that he died after I was born. It was clear to me then that the most probable reason for the false memory was me taking in brief images and a name that connected into the subconscious and like all memories each time we recall them they get embellished and grow.

The thing that I find most amazing about this whole re-birth/reincarnation thing is that when you explore, even the Pali Canon, I have yet to find anything where the Buddha actually and literally says it is 'you' or 'anything to do with you' that is going to be reborn. Yet the pre-conscious fear of non-existence is so strong it will make us believe even the most ludicrous of stories. The thing is I know first-hand what those stories are like. The details are amazing. But that, it is suggested here, is all they are. In actuality there is no reason for classical Buddhism to fear this new approach as it aligns itself to what can be known now and in the future and actually accords with the original texts when you stop adding in the stories.

The institutions of classical Buddhism are secure because of the human need to believe. But this secular western approach to Buddhism need not be suppressed or put down by the ancient institutions of classical Buddhism just because it has found a way to communicate the Dharma that actually accords not only with original Buddhist texts, despite their suspect origins, but more importantly it actually accords with what can be known now and in the future. It is still capable of being considered authentic Buddhism but without the belief element.

Of course, institutions are institutions and the primary objective of all institutions is to protect the institution at all costs. So, as with all of the previous reformation periods of Buddhism there will be resistance, outrage, ridicule and undermining by those who cling to the holy scripture of the deity Buddha they created.

There will be hostility and attempted humiliation by those who have been stuck within those institutions treading water for years and have been too afraid to step outside of their comfort zones in favour of the easy life, prestige and status. Also there will be the historic and continual one-upmanship of the varying groups of followers whose approach to the Dharma creates a kind of Jehovah's Buddhist mentality. It pretends to the outside world that all is well within Buddhism but continues to play the **'my dad's bigger than your dad'** game by those on some kind of spiritual ego-trip. All secular western Buddhists can do is get on with it and say watch this space and not collude with that. Collusion is never compassion.

Chapter Fourteen: The Middle Way

Conditioned causal continuity that is no-thing-ness is not a doctrine. It is not something to believe in. It is something to explore within your own direct experience on a moment by moment basis. It could be said that it is the perfect example of the Buddha's philosophy of the middle way between determinism, which is the idea that everything that is currently happening now is the result of previous karmic influences, or nihilism which in this context means that nothing that we do actually matters. Although, by and large, the conditioned self-biased mind operates on the basis of habitual patterns of thought and behaviour, there is always the opportunity at least, when awareness is established, to make conscious choices and therefore provide us with the opportunity to move away from our worries towards the development of peace of mind.

From his very early communications and throughout his teaching life, the Buddha sets out this middle way philosophy as a practical means of living a life that is not bounced back and forth between extremes. This same middle way philosophy was the initial insight that helped him see through the futility of living within the extremes of hedonism and self-mortification. It is also the same principal that can even be applied to the controversial subject of death and suggests a middle path between ideas of a permanent existence and complete non-existence.

This initial insight that gave rise to his middle way philosophy came at a bit of a cost to the Buddha as his companions who were fully engaged in the process of self-mortification at the time are said to have abandoned him when he took the decision to eat food and not starve himself to death. Despite that rejection, we are told in the traditional story of the Buddha, that the moment he had realized the awakening experience and after struggling for a while as to whether he should, or was even capable of communicating it to others, it was to this same group of ex companions he turned to, to use as guinea pigs for his first attempt at communication, possibly because he knew that they would be the toughest audience of all.

According to classical Buddhism what follows here is a representation of that very first communication after the awakening experience of the Buddha. The Buddha is purported to have said words to the effect:

"There are two extremes not to be followed by one who has gone forth. The first is that which is devoted to happiness and pleasure in sensory wants, which is common, vulgar, ordinary, ignoble and not helpful in making progress towards the realization of clarity. The second is that which is devoted to self-mortification, which is painful, ignoble and unhelpful in making progress towards the realization of clarity. Avoiding both of these extremes is the middle way which has been realized and makes for knowledge and vision for peace, realization, awakening and is that which is set out in the eight-fold journey which is the fourth principle assignment."

It is interesting to note here that his first communication was about his middle way philosophy. He didn't begin by setting out the principles of causality, which was the realization experience of awakening, or by setting out his four principal assignments, which he had devised as his first attempt to set out his approach for others. It seems clear that he had to set the scene first to prepare his friends so they could drop their attachment to one of those extremes and open themselves up to what he had to say.

So, in a nutshell, this middle way philosophy which runs throughout his communication from the outset, although not directly connected to the realization of causality, it is by understanding the middle way philosophy that we can begin our exploration of the entirety of his teachings.

We know very little about the actuality of the Buddha's life. All we have is a traditionally handed down story that no longer stands up to much scrutiny. But it is still very valid as the story itself is an expression of the Dharma and can be used as a teaching aid in a very practical way, which is why it's important to continue to engage with it, but not accept it as infallible in the same way that you are encouraged not to accept anything else the Buddha taught as infallible. In the ancient texts we find many examples of the Buddha talking about the extremes of his early life and in one of them he is purported to have said words to the effect:

"My life was refined, utterly refined, extremely delicate. My father even had lotus ponds made in our house. We had one which had blue lotus's, one that had red lotus's and one that had white lotus's. I used no sandalwood that was not from Benares and my garments were also made of the finest Benares cloth. A white parasol was held over me day and night so that I could avoid the heat, dust, dirt and dew. We had three palaces. We had one for the winter, one for the summer and one for the rainy season. For the whole of that four month rainy season I would be entertained by all female musicians and never left the palace."

According to what we now think we know about that particular period of history it is unlikely that any of the above is actually factual, but that does not detract from the message it is conveying in Dharmic terms. If we were to relate that part of the story to our situation today, perhaps we could imagine ourselves living in a massive canal home that faces the sun for most of the day and looks out onto our own private jetty where the luxurious motor boat sits moored up for 11 $\frac{1}{2}$ months of the year. Maybe there would be a house with huge walk-in wardrobes filled to the brim with all the latest designer gear and a state of the art surround sound 3D theatre room. Maybe there will be a young nubile Asian housekeeper and the in-house chef. Maybe even the odd holiday home here and there in exotic locations so we can escape the very mild winters here for sunnier climates. It's going to take a lot of persuasion to give all that up isn't it?

Later on in the traditional story the Buddha tells how such a pampered and self-obsessed person would react with horror when confronted with the actuality of sickness, ageing and death. This is why he suggests that this kind of hedonistic lifestyle is actually an avoidance of actuality and one that keeps us stuck in the cycle of pleasure and pain, which then hinders our understanding of the nature and reason for our worries and prevents us from making progress towards the realization of peace of mind. Check this out for yourself. What is the first thing you do when faced with any kind of difficulty? It is suggested here, that if we are being honest, you would already know that what we tend to do is try to avoid facing that difficulty, whatever it is, as it is and instead choose to divert our attention as best as we can to something that will indulge our senses.

Never let it be said that the Dharma journey is about not engaging in pleasurable pursuits. It is more about seeking ways to engage with pleasure in ways that are going to be helpful in the development of ourselves and the way we live the Dharma life. For instance pleasure can be experienced in meditation, in ethical actions, in generosity. Pleasure can be experienced in even just knowing that we have found the right context or method for us and are making progress as we notice how we have changed. Maybe the Dharma journey could be considered a more refined version of hedonism, where we are actively encouraged to pursue these higher states of awareness that lead to a greater depth of inner contentment and peace of mind.

At the other end of the spectrum the extreme of self-mortification has been used by many different versions of apparent spirituality as a means to conquer the raw passions of human nature in an effort to subdue them and find freedom. We can find in these belief systems expressions of will-power and self-denial and once again the Buddha gives a very graphic account of his own experience of the pursuit of such activities in the early texts as a way of highlighting the futility of such an approach. In one text he says words to the effect:

"My body became extraordinarily emaciated. It was like knotted joints of grass or bamboo stems, so likewise were my limbs, just from eating so little. My backside was like a camel's hoof, just from eating so little. My ridged and furrowed back-bone was like strung balls. My gaunt, wasted ribs were like the gaunt, wasted beams of an old barn. My eyes shone from deep in their sockets like the sparkle of water, way down deep in a well. Like the skin of an uncooked gourd, shriveled and with-ered in the heat and wind, my scalp was shriveled and with-ered. Thinking to rub my belly, I reached my backbone too. In fact my belly was stuck to my backbone from eating so little. Thinking to urinate or defecate I fell headlong into it, just from eating so little. To soothe my body, I stroked my limbs with my hands, but in stroking my limbs with my hands my body hair fell out, its roots rotted, because of eating so little."

As I was writing this what came to mind is those black and white harrowing films of Nazi concentration camps and much later the films of the famines in Africa and other places around the world. If starvation was ever the answer then there would be a plethora of Buddha's alive today wouldn't there? If we relate this back to our world today, even on a much lesser scale, how often do we think that subjecting ourselves to a strict diet and rigorous exercise regime we will become happier and healthier people? That's not to suggest that diet and exercise are not important, but do we push those limits a little too far at times?

How often do we sit in meditation willing ourselves with all our might to be quiet and just cause ourselves even more problems? What the Buddha is suggesting in this middle way philosophy is to set up the inner conditions such as kindness and awareness, which assist integration and helpfulness but with a flexible responsiveness to areas where we recognize that improvement can be made without the need to beat ourselves up or give ourselves a hard time about it. What we are looking for, according to the Buddha, is finding the balance that always sits in the middle of extreme thinking or extreme views based on the intelligent application of what we understand causality is within each current experience as it arises.

A significant part of the Buddha's approach is often about the way we live our life. He promotes ethics, meditation and a simplistic lifestyle as part of his overall strategy that leads to the end of our worries and the realization of peace of mind. We also see something of a philosophical approach with his communication of the middle way. It is clear within the ancient texts that the Buddha was reluctant to talk about things that required a speculative belief within them. This is because such things were irrelevant to the basic premise of his teaching which was to show people a way to move the mind from worrying towards peace of mind. Because of this, some people suggest that it is therefore pointless to think about intellectually, or contemplatively, within the meditative process the nature of actuality because the Buddha didn't seem to go there and answer direct questions about it.

It is suggested here that this is an unhelpful approach as it seems clear that the first theme within the eight-fold journey, namely helpful view, is all about that set of ideas about the nature of actuality that lends support to our ethical and meditation practice. So, if we avoid exploring such things because it is difficult to understand, we would be actually doing a disservice to the Buddha and our own development, as it is this insight that sets everything else into motion.

The Buddha himself defines helpful view as a middle way as it consists of seeing things as they are. It is seeing that things, be they physical, emotional, psychological or a combination of those things, within the external world or within our own direct experience neither really exist as things in themselves nor are they completely non-existent. This goes to the very heart of what it was he realized within that moment of awakening. All things are conditioned. All things come into existence as a result of causal factors. As no first cause of any thing can be found or no end effect of any thing can be found there is just an on-going continuity. In one ancient text the Buddha explains something like this:

"This world mostly relies on the confusion about real existence and complete non-existence. But when one sees the origin of the world as it really is through helpful view, one does not have the idea of complete non-existence in relation to the

world. Seeing the cessation of the world as it really is through helpful view, one does not have the idea of real existence in relation to the world. While this world is mostly bound up with attachment, clinging and inclinations, if one does not embrace or cling to attachments, mental fixations, inclinations and tendencies and one is not fixated on thinking about 'my self', then one will not doubt that it is just worrying arising and just worrying ceasing. In this one's knowledge is not dependent on others. To this extent this is helpful view. Everything exists is one extreme, everything does not exist is the other extreme. Avoiding both of these extremes is my teaching."

When you unpack the text a bit you can see how easy it can be for us to make assumptions about existence and non-existence so that we can make everything fit in with our personal view of the world. This is just us in self-serving, conditioned habitual mode which is what is meant by the terms attachments, mental fixations, inclinations and tendencies in the text. This is our comfort zone reaction that prevents us from breaking through into actuality time and time again. By sticking to what seems to make sense on a subjective and relative level of reality we actually set up the conditions for further worry.

Worrying is a word and an experienced thing. It is a word that exists independently and is separate from other words such as tiredness or guilt, but they are actually interconnected. Because our thinking process revolves around words, we can come to believe that somehow the words are independent and stand alone. When we are in that frame of mind that is saying **"I don't like this worrying and I want it to go away,"** it can lead us to think that this worrying is a kind of thing that now exists in a fixed and unchanging way and all we really want to do is get rid of it. But it won't go away and often gets worse the more we try to get rid of it. This is us bouncing back and forth from one extreme of seeing it as self-existing and the other of not wanting it to exist at all so trying to make it non-existent which is the other extreme.

In actuality, worrying, like everything else, arises in dependence on conditions and ceases when those conditions cease. It clearly isn't a thing that exists in itself because it depends on so many other things. Is there anything within our experience that we can actually point to and say **"there it is?"** There is this worrying thing? No, of course we can't, because what we call worrying is an amalgamation of many different things. There is a physical element, an emotional element and a psychological element. Learning to see that worrying is a co-arising as opposed to a single arising thing we can begin to explore each symptom separately and thereby changing the conditioning factors bit by bit until it becomes less and less of a problem. Simply wanting it to not exist or to be other than it is, is just about the worst strategy that we could have taken but how often is that our chosen or more often than not our habitual strategy?

The helpful view that the Buddha sets out as the middle way could be said to be a process without a fixed existence element to it. In effect, seen in this light, we are actually a human becoming rather than a human being. When we are on auto-pilot and just existing on the basis of our conditioned habitual patterns of thinking and behaving we tend to superimpose ideas of existence and non-existence on things that we are experiencing. As a result our judgment will always be clouded because we are not acting on the basis of the helpful view of actuality. This again then sets up the conditions for the arising of our worries. In the workplace, when we have a deadline to meet for instance, our worrying is in its element because we are seeing it as real, yet when we take a step back and see that it is just part of an interconnected process it becomes manageable.

Think of all the excitement there is running around in your head at the thought of getting hold of the latest must have gadget, the new car or the next holiday. Yet within a couple of days the gadget is stuck in a drawer, the car is dirty and has a dent in the bumper and the flight to Bali was cancelled due to another volcano eruption. When we keep in mind the principle of causality and bring it into our everyday thinking and activities we can begin to lessen our worries by not siding with either extreme view. Helpful view helps us to avoid our tendency to try and fix things.

As we make our way on the eight-fold journey, taking our ethical conduct and meditation practice into ever deeper levels of engagement, we begin to chip away at some of our conditioned beliefs about the nature of actuality. Because of the pre-conscious fear of non-existence, the primary concern for many is about trying to solve an apparent mystery surrounding the two extreme views in relation to what happens after physical death in this life.

Eternalism is the view that some aspect of what we think of as us has an opportunity for some kind of future existence and nihilism is the view that there isn't. So, within this context we have the extreme view that there is real existence and the extreme view that there is non-existence after physical death in this life. One of the difficulties we have today around this subject is that we have ancient texts, written in an ancient language that took into account the pre-existent beliefs and superstitions of the people it was communicated to and often many people select the text that best suits their own personal belief. So we need to take a much closer look and align what we read with what can be known and plausibly verified today and that will often be resisted by those who are engaged in classical Buddhism.

We regularly find that the Buddha was very reluctant to answer questions about metaphysics and would often just point people back to the application of causality. He simply points out that human consciousness, which is defined as the aliveness process having an ability of being aware of being aware of being human, is dependent on many other things, one of which, according to current neurological science is a living human brain. By exploring this subject in this way, it will become clear eventually, that human consciousness is not some fixed thing that continues or transmigrates after death which would be the extreme view of eternalism. But it also doesn't means that what we think say and do in this life will not continue and result in consequences after we have died which would be nihilism. What the Buddha was setting out here, was a clear indication that he saw causality as an on-going process that provides both meaning and purpose, but no externally imposed divine or mystical influence. This ties in perfectly with the way he describes the process of karma as being a way of taking responsibility for the quality of our mind states in each moment of existence by being aware of the motivational intent behind what we think say and do.

This will, for many of those that have been conditioned by western culture, usually bring up the vexed question of the existence or non-existence of some kind of creator entity. In the Buddha's day the comparison with the western idea of a creator entity would have been Brahma. The Buddha, rather than possibly wasting time and effort trying to convince a blind faith believer that no such thing could exist, because such a thing is incompatible with a universe where all things arise in dependence on preceding causes and conditions with no discernible first cause or end effect, he rarely answered. But there are texts where he can, some suggest, seem to mock these blind faith beliefs.

In one of these stories he is heard telling a group of followers a story in which Brahma is a powerful but deluded creator who thinks he has created other beings, even though they really just appeared to him as a result of their own past karma. It seems clear that in many western countries the idea of a creator entity is gradually losing its hold, which is possibly due to the expansion of scientific materialism that started sometime around the 1700's with the proposals around the evolutionary process which has no need for any kind of divine intervention. It also seems clear that there is a significant counter-revolution going on within the two main apparent opposing sides of creator entity believers who are willing to continue the mass slaughter of human beings who choose the wrong creator entity. Even that, it is suggested, is just a convenient cover story for something more materialistic.

If we are going to make progress along the Dharma journey, it is not helpful to cling to ancient knowledge and make it holy and unchallengeable. This approach seems to be the exact opposite of what the Buddha originally set out and is the domain of classical religious Buddhism. We have the basis of everything he ever communicated within that primary realization of causality that is defined by no-thing-ness. Each new piece of information that comes to light or new development in the fields of science and technology needs to be tested against this current theory of actuality that the Buddha set out 2,600 years ago.

The world of neuroscience and the various psychological therapeutic models that we now have are in a constant process of developmental change. Our practice of the Dharma journey needs to align itself to those changes or we just become yet another blind faith religious believer. It seems that current theory within the area of neuroscience is that this thing we call human consciousness is entirely dependent on the complexity of a living human brain, which eventually, if it keeps moving in that direction, is going to have serious implications for the blind faith believer in relation to such ideas about a creator entity, death and the beliefs about a continuance after death.

A possible downside to this approach for some, is that it will tend to dissolve the romanticism of mysticism, apparent spirituality, higher meaning and purpose and replace it with an unhealthy balancing act between the superficial and short-lived happiness of materialistic consumerism, traded against an acceptance that we will need to experience worrying as a result. If we apply causality within our secular western Buddhist context, we would see that we are not created by some kind of external creator entity or being, nor are we just an uncontrolled mish-mash of blibs and blobs of atoms, molecules or quantum bits and pieces etc. Both of these views would fall into the category of extreme views. The middle way view could be said to be one that recognises that we are the bi-product of millions of years of an evolutionary process that we can not find an initial cause for and that this thing we call human consciousness is simply the ability to be aware of being aware of being human and more.

Causality has no need of a creator entity as it sets out the overriding principle of the universe that everything can be tested against. Human consciousness that has developed as a result of the evolutionary process is still in an on-going process of change. Like everything else, as we can find no first cause of this process we will never find an end effect of it either. Although neuroscience has made great inroads into discovering how the process of the brain functions, it is still in its infancy in evolutionary terms. Nothing that has been discovered to date implies that human consciousness can be reduced down to something as simple as brain activity. To be in a state of conscious awareness is to know the subject matter of experience. With this in mind we could say that our worries are not simply a product of brain activity. Our worries arise as a result of our thinking process and it is that thinking process that we seek to develop within the meditation practices of awareness of the breath and awareness of kindness and within our ethical lifestyles.

Chapter Fifteen: Going for Refuge

As Buddhism spread from Northern India to almost all parts of the globe it absorbed on its journey, rites, rituals, traditions, beliefs, superstitions and cultural aspects. It did so to the extent that today we are left in a state of confusion, when trying to establish what Buddhists have in common. The differences are clearly evident. This Buddhist wears maroon robes, this one wears saffron robes and this one wears black robes. This one doesn't wear robes at all. This one has his head shaved and this one has long hair. This one eats meat, this one doesn't. This one smokes cigarettes, this one doesn't. This one drinks wine, this one doesn't. This one chants for world peace, this one chants for a BMW.

This one undertakes five training principles, this one takes eight, this one ten. This one lives by a set of 200+ rules. Some understand Buddhism to be a religion, some a philosophy, some a way of life. This one lives in a monastery and is celibate but this one has a wife and child, a house and a mortgage. This one is ordained but this one isn't. This one prostrates 100,000 times towards an image of the Buddha, this one bows three times, this one just sits and smiles. This one meditates every day, this one hardly, if ever, meditates at all.

This one calls himself a Tibetan Buddhist, this one a Zen Buddhist, this one a Theravadin Buddhist, this one a Shingon Buddhist and this one a western Buddhist. This one is a monk, this one a lama, this one a geshe, this one a venerable sir, this one a priest, this one a dharmachari, this one a lay practitioner. The list of differences is never ending to the extent that the casual observer is left wondering what exactly defines what a Buddhist is.

Anyone can call themselves a Buddhist. In the west many do because it's kind of cool to have that label. If you tell someone you're a Jehovah's Witness, the likelihood is you'll have the door slammed in your face, be verbally abused, or have a bucket of water thrown over you. If you tell someone you're a Christian you'll possibly notice a glazed look suddenly appearing on their face and they'll try and move away from you. If you tell them you're a Muslim they might have some kind of conditioned fear of you. If you tell them you're a Buddhist, they go all gooey eyed and think you must be some kind of special person. All of these gross generalizations are of course based on maybe media influenced or culturally conditioned fixed impressions that people have about religions, but I'm sure you get the picture.

Throughout all of the many and varied Buddhist schools and traditions there is one thing that is common to all. It is called **'Going for Refuge'** to the **'Three Jewels'** - The Buddha, the Dharma and the Sangha. It is helpful to understand from the outset that becoming a Dharma practitioner is entirely voluntary and that being a Dharma practitioner is not about what you choose to believe in, but what you actually do. It is about how you try your best to act with body speech and mind in your moment by moment everyday life. It is a thing in action, hence the term **'going'** as in moving towards something in a forward movement. Its **'for'** aspect is its intended purpose which is the realization of clarity within the awakening experience.

As a Dharma practitioner you are making a continual effort to move forward towards that ideal. It should also be understood that you don't need to declare yourself a Buddhist or a Dharma practitioner to reap the benefits from what Dharma practices and teachings have to offer you. The decision to formalise your commitment to the Dharma journey can have profound and far-reaching personal significance of a helpful nature. Many people have found that at some stage in their involvement with the Dharma, this act of formally declaring themselves a Dharma practitioner and receiving the refuges and precepts is a major turning point in their lives.

This primary act of going for refuge marks the moment when you begin to take your first faltering steps on a journey to realize your full potential as a human being within the experience of clarity. It is also helpful to bear in mind that just as becoming a Dharma practitioner is voluntary, you are also free to leave behind anything within Buddhism that you find, having tried and tested it fully and with integrity, is not helpful to your own development including that of being a Buddhist itself.

For the newcomer to Buddhism the term going for refuge can be a bit problematic because we can associate the word 'refuge' with taking shelter, or hiding, or something akin to some kind of escapism from the realities of life. Within the context of the three jewels it is in fact the opposite. To take refuge in the Buddha means to take refuge in the nature of existence. In how things actually are and not how we perceive them to be within the self-biased mind.

So, let's begin to try and understand something of what, from a Buddhist perspective, a refuge actually is and perhaps then we can see, from within our own experience, how we are continually going for refuge to something. We can then begin to understand what it means to commit ourselves to going for refuge to the three jewels.

The Buddha taught that every thing is in a constant state of change, that every thing is impermanent and insubstantial. As humans, we respond to this actuality with a fear that drives us round and round in circles, forever trying to pretend it isn't how it is. We try to bring order and stability to our lives, but no sooner have we got one area of our lives under apparent control, another begins to change and so it goes on. Everything we try and grasp hold of slips in the end from our fingers. In the face of this it is only natural to try and find something to rely on and organize our lives around. Something to give us our bearings amidst the dilemmas and confusion of daily life and this is where we try and take refuge.

For most, one of the first refuges is the physical body. In the midst of the actuality of change, it at least seems somewhat solid and permanent. To be alive is to have a body and from the way our senses work, we get the impression that our mind is somehow firmly located within it. Our bodies give us a sense of having a 'me'. We preen, pamper and adorn our bodies making sure they are comfortable and by whatever means possible, we try and forget, that like everything else, our bodies are impermanent. Eventually the body will age, sicken and will die and if we realized that fact we would begin to understand that the physical body is not something we can actually take refuge in.

Some people go for refuge to their careers, putting their job ahead of all other considerations. We take refuge in our lovers, husbands, wives, our families, in the things we own, in the things we do. All these things give us a sense of meaning and identity. We go to almost any lengths to try and battle against the actuality of change, because somewhere within us we seem to have an apparent intuition about the terrifying nature of no-thing-ness.

246

Because we fear this open dimension we try and shut it out of our lives so we can settle down to a warm and cosy predictability. Here we would know who we are what we should do and we would be safe. That in Buddhist terms is the very nub of our confusion

Whenever this open dimension begins to make itself known, even a little, we run for cover. We do something, to distract ourselves, to turn our attention away from the uncomfortable facts of impermanence and insubstantiality. Without knowing it, we are doing it all the time. We are in a constant state of going for refuge to something. Whatever it is we are doing, at some point there will be an experience, perhaps just a sense, that something is wrong, something is missing from our lives, there is something unsatisfied, something we're not getting, something we want to change. Then, at some point we find what we think will be the solution and we go for refuge to it in the vain hope that it will fill this void in our lives. A bar of chocolate perhaps, another glass of wine, a new pair of jeans, the latest mobile phone, a new job, a new partner. It could be anything, but whatever it is, we have a sense that if only we had this one thing, we would be able to put an end to this experience of worrying.

It's helpful to understand that there isn't anything wrong with these refuges. They are a very normal part of human existence. It is just helpful to understand that they are unhelpful refuges. They cannot deliver what it is we are searching for, the end of our worries. Yet we have to order our lives somehow or else we would be swept away by the chaotic whirl of events. Consciously or subconsciously, we work to shape our lives somehow or other all the time. The pattern and shape of our lives, our behaviour, our values, all these indicate what we take refuge in. Rather than try and hide from the way things are, Dharma practitioners take refuge in the way things are.

They take refuge in the Buddha, which is represented by the colour of his jewel that is yellow. He discovered and embodies the highest potential of human existence. They go for refuge to the Dharma, his teaching of causality and the various methods he set out to assist in its realization which is represented by the colour of the Dharma jewel that is blue and they go for refuge to the Sangha, which in this context, means all those men and women who make an effort to live in accordance with this teaching which is represented by the Sangha jewel that is red. Having now reached perhaps a provisional understanding of what in Buddhist terms the words going for refuge means, we can begin to explore the deeper aspects of the one thing that defines exactly what a Buddhist is, by exploring each of those three jewels separately.

In some parts of the East, taking refuge in the Buddha has come to mean seeking his help by way of prayer. Students might pray to the Buddha for help with their exams, women might pray for the birth of a son, others a good career and so on. Whatever the value of such practices, it seems clear from Buddhist texts, that going for refuge has little, if anything, to do with this type of activity. It's really about authentic commitment. The early texts often describe someone meeting the Buddha for the first time. They enter into a discussion and that person is so over- whelmed by the Buddha's presence, his understanding and insight, that their whole world is rearranged and they commit themselves to begin the journey that the Buddha's teaching opens up for them. Sadly, once the Buddha's teachings became a religious belief system, the essence of going for refuge to the Buddha got lost along the way and became just another symbolic institutional add-on, or even worse became almost deity-like to be worshipped from afar. Both of these options take us away from the real meaning of going for refuge to the Buddha.

To go for refuge to the Buddha, is to aspire to awaken. All human beings have the potential for awakening deep within them in the same way that acorns have the potential to become oak trees deep within them. Of course, not every acorn becomes an oak tree and likewise not all humans become a Buddha. Both outcomes are entirely dependent on causes and conditions. In going for refuge to the Buddha, one commits oneself to becoming more than you are right now by developing the conditions which will help you to unfold more of your potential for creativity and understanding. One sets out on a journey of self-transcendence that has no limit. If we're honest, we hardly know who we are now let alone who, with the most helpful kind of effort we might become.

To go for refuge to the Buddha is to commit oneself to leave behind all of one's fixed views of oneself. One tries to let go of the false security of the self-biased mind and to align oneself instead, towards the open dimension of awakening. Given that we engage in effort that is helpful, one thing is assured. You can become more than you are now. Every one of us has the capacity to experience some degree of transformative insight. To go for refuge to the Buddha effectively you would possibly first have to arrive at a conclusion that such a character as Sidhartha Gautama actually existed at some point in history and that by his own efforts he realized clarity. There is no way you can actually be sure of this. But even at the lowest rate of the balance of probabilities you shouldn't have too much difficulty in accepting, even on a provisional basis at first, that he did exist. Was he awakened? Let's face it we have no idea what that means. Again, you can't actually know for sure, but when you look at the influence this man and his teachings have had in history and on the world around you, I don't see that anyone would have too much difficulty in accepting that he was, at least, a very unique human being and worthy of taking seriously.

To go for refuge to the Buddha, we need to know something of his life and work. We have to make our way through the minefield of trying to work out what is fact, what is legend and what is symbolic and come to our conclusions based on our own direct experience, intelligence and insight. We need to study his teachings on our own and with like-minded individuals. We need to put them into practice in our daily lives and experience for ourselves if they are helpful, the Buddha once said, words to the effect:

"If you can be sure, that a teaching leads to calm, not to agitation; to freedom, not to attachment; to moderation, not to covetousness; to contentment, not to discontent; to delight in kindness, not depravity; to energy, not to indolence – then you be sure that it is the Dharma"

This is our own litmus test. Even if we cannot resolve any issues about the authenticity of any part of the story it doesn't really matter.

It's important to understand that in going for refuge to the Buddha we are, in effect, going for refuge to our own potential for the realization of clarity. If we choose to pay homage, either physically, verbally or mentally to a Buddha figure or shrine, we are acknowledging his achievements as a human being and the legacy his teachings have left us with. We are recognising and acknowledging that, just like him, by our own efforts, we too can reach our full potential as human beings. It seems clear that some westerners find it difficult to let go of their deep-rooted conditioning factors against this kind of activity, but to go for refuge to the Buddha effectively it is something we have to overcome because until such time as we can truly recognize our own potential for authentic growth that is represented by the life and teachings of the Buddha we will always remain treading water and uncommitted.

Just as we have discovered that there are many differences between individual Buddhists and Buddhism itself, it will probably come as no surprise to see, even within the central act of going for refuge, the very thing that defines what a Buddhist is, there are also differences. There are, it is suggested here, four different levels of gong for refuge and it will be helpful to have something of an understanding of these so we can perhaps work out where we are in relation to our own involvement with the Dharma journey or our own commitment to the three jewels.

'Nominal Going for Refuge' is best described as when one is born a Buddhist in a traditional Buddhist country like Thailand, Myanmar, Sri Lanka, Tibet, Japan and others. It has long been a tradition in some of these countries that at least one male child from each family becomes a monk and enters the monastery whether they want to or not. It's understood that this tradition arose as a means of ensuring the survival of at least one family member in countries where to die from hunger was a very common experience. Although those extremes of poverty may no longer exist, the tradition continues in some form or other. In some traditional Buddhist countries the monasteries replace mainstream education and in others they are a kind of right of passage. Sadly, this has led to a situation now where some monks get up to all manner of unhelpful things that are not conducive to an authentic Dharma life, because they are not there through choice and this causes difficulties for western observers who automatically relate the wearing of robes and shaven heads to signify at least some higher ideals.

What we find within nominal going for refuge are a populace, that in general terms, are people who perhaps support the monks by supplying them with food in exchange for blessings in the hope that it will bring them good luck or a better apparent re-birth. Little effort, if any, seems to be made toward their personal development or Dharma journey. They will attend the temple on a regular basis, light candles and incense and make offerings and donate money, but it is purely a cultural or traditional habit. To some extent you can witness the same kind of thing going on within Christianity, Catholicism and Islam and all of the other mainstream theistic religions. Included in the concept of nominal going for refuge would be the person who reads endless books on Buddhism without acting upon what they read or someone who attends Buddhism courses purely out of curiosity or to feed a thirst for knowledge.

The next level of going for refuge arises when that nominal element moves in the direction of becoming provisional. 'Provisional going for refuge' is the point when one decides to try and put the teachings into practice in your daily life. Perhaps we have no intention to formalise any kind of commitment to the Dharma journey, but we recognise that by changing our habitual patterns of behaviour towards something more helpful, it might just make our lives a little easier. It also includes people who may have been practicing Buddhism for many years and have considered themselves Buddhists for just as long, but still have other preoccupations and commitments to which they accord greater priority. At the upper end of the scale of provisional going for refuge it would also include those people who formalise their commitment to the Dharma journey in a particular context by ceremoniously receiving the refuges and precepts from an Ordained Buddhist within that context. They might still have lots of other priorities going on in their everyday lives that take poll position, but their motivational factors have significantly changed.

Provisional going for refuge becomes **'effective going for refuge'** when the commitment to the three jewels has become the central, defining characteristic of their lives. All of their other priorities now form an integral part of their Dharma practice. Quite often this is marked by a person seeking Ordination. They might still have jobs, families, hobbies, but their commitment to the realization of clarity is at the heart of who they are and what they do.

The fourth level of gong for refuge is described as the no going back position. This is defined as **'authentic going for refuge.'** It may take place over a period of time, as in the journey model of practice, or it may arise in a single moment of irreversible insight that appears to come from nowhere. In some schools of Buddhism this is synonymous with the concept of the Bodhisattva ideal. Awakening has taken place but full enlightenment (whatever that is supposed to mean) is put on hold for the benefit of all beings. This is the breakthrough moment, the point of no return. What has been seen can't be unseen. What is known can't be unknown. What has been realized can't be unrealized. Now begins the actualization process. This is also known as entering the stream or stream entry.

We now turn to the second refuge jewel that of going for refuge to the Dharma. Dharma is a complex word. It can mean actuality, law, mental event, doctrine or path but in the context of going for refuge it means the Buddha's teachings and all those other communications of the awakened mind which point the way to the experience of clarity. In an ancient text there is a story of a group of blind men and an elephant. They are asked to touch the body of an elephant and then describe it. Those who touched the head said it seemed like a pot, those who touched the ear said it was like a winnowing basket, those that touched the tusk thought it was part of a plough and so on. Eventually, each one vehemently maintained their own opinion as being the truth and so they began to quarrel and fight. The story illustrates not only the one-sidedness of the sectarian teachers of the Buddha's own time, in connection with whom the story was originally told, but also the wide divergences that can be noticed between the different classical Buddhist approaches that exist today.

Broadly speaking there are three basic approaches to Buddhism. These are referred to as:
1. **The sectarian approach**
2, **The fundamentalist approach**
3. **The encyclopedic approach**

Quite early on in the history of Buddhism, following the Buddha's death, a number of different schools began to emerge. Although they differed on points of doctrine and discipline they shared a common tradition which united them. As Buddhism spread to different lands and different cultures the gap began to widen and as a result there came into being a number of different versions of Buddhism. These were, in effect, laid side by side and overlapped to some degree. But they were also distinctively different in many ways. To identify Buddhism with one particular version on whatever grounds is really unhelpful and those who do fail to understand that the teachings of the Buddha, conceived in its full breadth and width comprises all those teachings which are linked to the original teaching by historical continuity or by content.

'**The sectarian approach**' quite often bases its approach on highly selective reading and understanding of a particular branch of literature and presents itself as the whole tree of wisdom. It is within the sectarian approach that even today we find one tradition putting down another or attempting to claim the high ground.

'**The fundamentalist approach**' is concerned with what the Buddha '**actually**' said. It has two basic forms. The first, to some extent, coincides with the sectarian approach in that they maintain, even in the face of abundant evidence to the contrary, that the Pali Cannon is the actual words of the Buddha. The second, the intellectually respectable form, is a product of modern scholarship, largely non-Buddhist, who by means of textual criticism, comparison with archaeological evidence etc, endeavours to work out what of the original utterances of the Buddha have possibly survived. This approach takes into account the serious misgivings with accepting the infallibility of the human capacity for memory as nothing was apparently written down for many years. This area, more than any other, has been the most helpful in the development of understanding because its agenda is open and honest and serves to be of benefit to the sincere Dharma practitioner, rather than being restricted by the other side of the coin.

To a lesser extent this approach also misses the point as it's unlikely that any known Buddhist text contains a line which preserves the Dharma in the same language or dialect in which it was originally taught by the Buddha. The other factor that is often overlooked is that the Buddha taught on the basis of the experience of clarity. Those that eventually wrote down the texts have filtered what they have written through the memories of many who had not realized the experience for themselves, so were setting down their self-biased understanding of what the Buddha taught. It would appear that the greater the scrutiny, scientific or otherwise, undertaken by the fundamentalists the greater the likelihood that all they will be left with is the Buddha's noble silence.

The third approach is **'the encyclopedic approach.'** It emphasizes breadth rather than depth of knowledge. It tends to confuse knowledge about Buddhism with insight. It is more concerned with the facts than with principles and tries to see them from without instead of experiencing them from within. This approach has serious limitations for the authentic Dharma practitioner. It aims to achieve complete factual knowledge about Buddhism and from this inferring its nature and this seems unachievable considering the vast extent of Buddhist literature. Once again we find in this approach that someone may have an amazing and extensive library of Buddhist books, all of which they may have read many times but they have still to realize that you actually have to live it and the best way of doing this is to start with the source teaching of causality and begin living it.

The approach of secular western Buddhism that is set out in this book, promotes incorporating elements from all three approaches, but with their perceived imperfections filtered out as best as they can. In this approach it provides an opportunity for insight into the Dharma derived from the actual practice within the journey that is supported by the practical aspects of teachings from within all of the major traditions of Buddhism so that the richness of views and beliefs can be tested and challenged directly by experience. This seems to be the most helpful option for authentic Dharma practice for those born or living within a westernised society.

Many students of Buddhism are at first staggered by the vastness of the field before them and bewildered by the abundance of material. Like Christianity and Islam, Buddhism is not only a teaching but a culture, a civilization, a movement in history, a social order. In fact it is a whole world in itself. Classical religious Buddhism, like other religions comprises of systems of philosophy, methods of meditation, contemplation and reflection, rites, rituals, manners and customs, clothes, languages, sacred literature, pagodas, temples, monasteries, poems, paintings, plays, stories and a thousand other things. Despite all of this the six million dollar question will always be: **What is the essence of the Dharma?** The only way you are ever going to find the answer to that question for yourself is to practice what it teaches and work it out for yourselves from your own direct experience.

Going for refuge to the Dharma therefore is to put into practice that which you learn through study and spending time with like-minded individuals and especially those who perhaps may have travelled a little further into the journey than you. Just bear in mind that length of service is not always a good indication of progress. Coming to trust and rely on the teachings without any element of blind faith or blind belief is the way forward. This develops when you can experience for yourself the helpful difference Dharma practice makes in your daily life. You may hear claims such as **'This or that is a higher teaching,'** but in actuality the Buddha taught nothing but the existence of worrying, its cause, that it can be eradicated or alleviated and the journey to the realization of this. The endless lists, formulations, stories, legends, texts etc are all tools to help you come to an understanding that goes beyond the intellectual mind into the realm of irreversible insight into the nature of existence. In actuality, there is no higher teaching, there are just deeper understandings and as with everything else on the Dharma journey you only make progress by commitment and effort.

It has to be understood right from the start that this is not a race. As best as we can, we need to put to one side our westernised conditioned response to wanting an immediate result or giving up at the first hurdle. Dharma practice can sometimes be described as like a car mechanics manual. You have some basic skills in mechanics that you've learnt over the years, but to do a proper job you have to keep going back to the manual. If you follow the instructions, the car will run like a dream. If you try and cut corners to get a quick fix it's going to stall at the precise moment when you're furthest away from home, with no mobile phone, no public transport, its pouring with rain and you left your wallet at home.

We now come to the Sangha jewel. In our westernised society we have developed a heightened sense of individualism and as a result we have become more and more isolated from each other. The Sangha jewel is possibly the one aspect that is most often missing amongst western practitioners. The Sangha jewel is such a vital element that even from a classical point of view, without being engaged with one you could not authentically consider yourself to be a Buddhist. Context is everything. Without a context for practice you will be lost. Without regular and ready access to like-minded individuals who share that same context you will be lost.

In classical Buddhism the word Sangha is defined very differently. It's used to create a divide which sets up an institutional hierarchical structure that is designed to protect and maintain the status quo of the institutions. On paper at least, it falls into three different levels. The first level is that of the Arya or Noble Sangha. This is supposed to be for those who have realized the experience of clarity. In some schools of classical Buddhism this also includes non-human, archetypal beings that manifest within the apparent higher states of awareness, often depicted in Buddhist art as representing different aspects of awakening.

The next level is that of the ordained Sangha who in real terms often consider and declare that they are now the Arya Sangha if they are monastics, but also includes ordained practitioners outside of the monastic system. Often non-monastics are not recognized by the monastic community, but realistically that is just institutionalized self-interest popping up again. The third level is that of the lay practitioner within the terms of the monastic system and a non-ordained Dharma practitioner in terms of non-monastic Sangha's.

The secular western approach to Sangha is attempting to re-define the boundaries of Sangha, placing an emphasis back, as it was in the Buddha's day, on the question of commitment as primary but now seeing the lifestyle through which one lives out that commitment as secondary. Sangha, in this sense therefore refers to any Dharma community whose members are effectively going for refuge to the three jewels. Such a community is not a group in the ordinary sense of the word. One of the characteristics of a group is that it seeks to preserve itself, if necessary at the cost of its individual members. It tends to enforce conformity and to require unquestioning allegiance from its members. The effective Dharma community, on the other hand, encourages its members not to conform, but to become increasingly more authentic individuals themselves, unfolding more and more of their unique, creative potential.

The effective Dharma community actively encourages its members to seek out the open dimension. The group always tries to erect high walls against it. The group, whether it be a family, clan, tribe, nation, club, race, team, squadron, church, regiment or political party, comes down, in the final analysis, to a frail conspiracy against the winds of change that are blowing from the open dimension whereas the effective Dharma community embraces that open dimension.

Whilst it is acknowledged that it is possible to live as a Buddhist and be a lone practitioner, to be able to go for refuge effectively, bearing in mind all that has been said, there needs to be all three jewels placed at the centre of your practice. Each jewel, although separate in themselves are simply facets of a single jewel called the Cintamani jewel which represents the arising of the will to realize clarity. So, in effect, you may go for refuge to the Buddha and the Dharma but if you have no contact with a Sangha to provide a context, that which is the only thing that binds all practitioners together throughout history, culture and tradition crumbles away. The very thing that actually defines what a Buddhist is cannot exist unless all three refuges are in place.

To join a Sangha is to engage with a particular presentation context of the Dharma that is usually based on the insights of one individual, usually referred to or recognised as the teacher. Or a traditional lineage system where what is being taught may be doctrinal rather than insightful. You will find that many of these teachers have formal qualifications but that is something very different from insight. If at any stage you decide, for whatever reason, that the context is not for you, the most helpful thing to do is simply leave that Sangha and look elsewhere. It would be absolutely pointless, counter-productive and it is suggested, ethically unhelpful to stay within a Sangha if you are not intending to practice within its context. Sadly, both of these systems within classical Buddhism and modern western versions have a very long and involved history of scandals, coercion and manipulation.

The secular western approach, as you will by now come to have seen, seeks to do things very differently, having had the opportunity of observing the development of Buddhism in the west and recognised its unhelpful aspects. It chooses not to have a hierarchical structure, even if it is based on the insight of one individual. The communicator of secular western Buddhism does not have disciples, students or followers. They do not sit on a high pedestal looking down, or lead from a position of power or privilege. They are there to walk beside you on an even and level playing field simply sharing, pointing and supporting on the basis of Dharma friendship.

There is no point in joining a Sangha if you are not intending to engage with its activities. It's not a social club, although it clearly has social elements as it is based in friendship. At its heart it is all about practice and providing a support network for practice. If you are not studying the context or discussing the context with other Sangha members or making time available to meet up with Sangha members to develop a deeper level of friendship within the Sangha it also becomes pointless, counter-productive and unhelpful to stay.

It is there for you to take what you need at any given moment. You are not obligated to it or anyone in it. The only commitment you ever make is to yourself. Within secular western Buddhism not only are you free to explore the work of any other teacher, you are actually encouraged to do so. All that is asked of you as a Sangha member is that you filter all of those things through the context of the journey you have undertaken to see how they fit or don't fit with your chosen context of the Dharma.

Fundamentally, it isn't about what we like or don't like. The Buddha never taught people what they wanted to hear. He taught the Dharma because he realized that was what would be most helpful to hear to be free from worrying. It was never about just listening to what he had to say and deciding if we liked it or not or whether it fitted in with our existing beliefs, views or opinions. To go for refuge to the Sangha is to engage not to avoid.

If you travel to traditional Buddhist countries today you will find, in many ways that effective Dharma practice has more or less disappeared. Not only within the lay population but also within the monastic system itself. There will of course be exceptions such as those who engage fully with the forest tradition in Thailand or its approach that has grown elsewhere. But, in the main, Buddhism is not the healthiest of things in many of these countries. In some, Buddhism is used by the various government agencies as a means to control the population in similar ways as the early Christian church did in the west. As a visitor or outsider you will undoubtedly be impressed by the outward appearance of classical Buddhism. As an initial point of inspiration this has played a significant role in people choosing to explore Buddhism further. But when you begin to scratch away at the surface, nothing is ever as it seems. But there is no point in colluding with what goes on behind the scenes away from the public eye. When it comes to the point when we have Buddhist monks advocating ethnic cleansing in Myanmar, monks stirring up racial hatred in Thailand and Sri Lanka and monks oppressing religious freedom within large sections of their communities within Tibetanism, maybe it's time for a collective awakening to a recognition that the world of Buddhism has gone astray from its roots and seems beyond recovery if no significant changes are made.

There is just one more thing for us to consider now and that is the implications of the secular western approach to the Dharma and its move to bring an ancient and institutionalised communication in-line with what is known now with the benefit of advances in science and technology and maintaining that link in the future. It is the move to let go of the magic, the mystery and the romanticism of the past in favour of what can be established, verified or refuted within direct experience so that the original communication of the Buddha, that set out to show people a very simple and practical way to develop opportunities to move this thing we call mind away from a state of worrying towards a state of peace of mind.

There is no doubt that this will lead to some difficulties in the relationship between classical Buddhism and its secular version. We have seen when we explored the history of Buddhist development there have been several times when the communication got stuck in a cultural time warp. When it became a dogmatic belief system that others then attempted to un-stick but then found later that it too had become stuck. To the extent that we now have so many variants of this thing that is called Buddhism, that has been mixed and matched with so many other cultural influences that have formed vast institutions of faithful believers that it is inevitable that the institutions of religious Buddhism will seek to resist their reformation with modernity because that is the nature of institutions.

'**All things are subject to change.**' Six words that basically sum up everything the Buddha ever communicated. As yet, as far as I am aware, nobody has ever come even close to refuting that actuality but classical Buddhism sure gives it a '**fair go**' as we say in Australia.

That does not mean that it is true. It just means that it is a current theory to be continually tested and challenged. It is clear that this model of actuality was based on what could be known back then by observation and reflection. It gave rise to a model of actuality that is based on a one way version of cause and effect. This being, that becomes. This model has served us well in explaining how things worked in the past and by and large is still relevant in relation to most things still. But recent scientific discoveries are already chipping away at that linear idea, especially in the field of quantum physics where they are discovering unpredictable results that do not conform to the linear model. The field of neuroscience is throwing light on things that couldn't possibly have been known 2,600 years ago and this is why we have to view what the Buddha communicated in light of these new discoveries and with any future discoveries and there is nothing to fear within that.

264

The Buddha never set out to be a scientist. He never set out to discover the origins of the universe or the origins of man. He never set out to do anything but find an answer as to why he couldn't find lasting satisfaction with any experience. He set out to find if he could find a solution to his worries and be at peace. He found that within the realization experience of causality. What has changed in relation to that communication? According to modern science things are still conditioned. Things are still causal. There is still continuity. All things still have no self-essence. The only thing that has changed or is in the process of changing is a new understanding of the causal process, so in effect science is still operating on the same on-going current theory that the Buddha originally set out, but has simply expanded it further just as it was at other times in history. The only major difference now is that with this new secular western approach to Buddhism it cannot get stuck again as it will develop in tandem with it.

This does mean that some of the original texts or their interpretations will need to be reviewed and that in itself is a helpful thing. Otherwise we end up with a kind of Holy Bible of Buddhism which again goes against the charter of free-thinking inquiry the Buddha is purported to have championed from the start. Huge chunks of classical Buddhism, including the big guns and holiest of holies of karma and rebirth have to now be explored in light of new evidence that does not make the practical application of the communication any less valid. Modernity and secularism may be seen to be a threat to classical Buddhism but it is not a threat to the Dharma. It provides a real opportunity to get back to what was the Buddha's original intent prior to its institutionalisation.

It provides a real opportunity to eradicate the blind faith aspect that crept in over the years. It provides a real opportunity to let go of the magic, the mystery and romanticism so that the very down-to-earth, very simply and practical developmental model that formed the original communication can once again be put into practice in our daily lives in an effort to reduce or eradicate our worries. The Dharma was always meant to be a thing in action and the world of the Dharma practitioner itself has always been an expression of that primary communication. The Buddha only points the way and no matter how amazing and profound or practical and simple that communication is, it only works when you do it. How do you do it? He provides you with four principal assignments that include an eight-fold themed journey. The rest is down to you.

Chapter Sixteen: The Three-Fold Method
1. Ethics

In classical Buddhism, there are set of five ethical principles that are adopted by those that formalise their commitment to the Dharma journey by going for refuge to the three jewels. Later on, additional principles may be voluntary undertaken by some as part of an ordination process. Others take on a number of vows and others also take on a substantial number of actual rules and regulations should they wish to live a monastic life. The wording of these five basic ethical principles do vary within different schools or systems of classical Buddhism. So, as a comparison I will set out each in terms of classical Buddhism and the secular western version that is promoted within this context. First we need to explore the background to the origins of this very novel approach to ethics that provides us with the opportunity for taking responsibility for our own mind states.

Generally speaking, views about the intrinsic nature of human beings basically fall into two camps. There are those who believe that we are all born either pure, or at that the very least blank screens and that it is our conditioning factors that create our resultant personalities and behaviour patterns. The opposing view is that we are pre-disposed to behave in a certain way by either some supernatural force or some kind of genetic code. It is suggested here that the actuality is more than likely to be found somewhere in the middle ground.

It seems clear that we are born with a survival instinct of some kind and history shows us that even mild mannered individuals can be responsible for horrific acts when their own survival, or well being is threatened. Conversely we also discover those with horrific life conditioning factors that are capable of acts of great kindness. If we examine our own society, it seems apparent that the vast majority of people appear to be, on the surface at least, what we would conditionally describe as good and that the bad people are in the minority.

This is where a basic study of ethics and particularly Buddhist ethics begins. How on earth do we define what is good and what is bad and on what basis do we make those decisions? In some societies multiple marriages is the norm. In others you'd be sent to prison. In some societies it has been perfectly acceptable to kill and eat your grandparents. In others you'd either abandon them in the bush, or put them in an aged care centre. In almost all societies it is acceptable to kill other human beings if they control anything that is vital to the economic well being of your country, but you'd be punished if you took anything out of desperation that will ensure the survival of yourself or your family.

Within Western culture it seems fair to assume that we have arrived today at a basic set of moralistic rules that have been passed down through the generations, based originally on a set of commandments, purportedly given to Moses by an apparent creator entity. It seems that at no time in our history can we find that human beings have voluntarily stuck to those rules. They have always needed to be enforced by a threat of punishment for breaking them or with a reward for abiding by them. This tends to support the notion that if we were left to our own devices, we would swiftly return to the natural, evolutionist law of the survival of the fittest or natural selection. Others suggest that we are by nature co-operative.

This handed down set of moralistic rules brings with it added complications. It seems apparent that this same apparent creator entity gave a different set of rules to others. Either that, or we have to own up to the fact that we are just incapable of knowing what was meant by them, because there is so much religious conflict that has arisen and continues to arise as a result. Other aspects of theistic religion has tried to sort this out by creating the golden rule approach to moral behaviour ie always treat others as you would like them to treat you. But even this approach gets watered down as the teachings themselves also suggest that you should actively do good deeds to those who have done you harm and that you should turn the other cheek etc.

What we are left with today is a kind of social contract that changes over time as views change. This contract is legislated by an apparently democratically elected representative body of our society. We are led to believe that they apparently put to one side self-interest to act for the welfare of the majority. They in turn hand over responsibility for the enforcement of those laws to an apparent neutral third party like the police or in some cases the military. What we actually experience is something very different, so it doesn't take long before we begin to search for ways that we can get round some of these imposed rules and avoid punishment at the same time. Just as we did with the religious ones, when we are told in black and white **'Thou Shalt Not Kill'** we search for ways around it and add in some get out clauses such as **'unless I want your oil,'** or **'unless you had sex with my wife,'** etc

What is missing in all of these systems of rules, regulations and controls is the development of individual human conscience. We see it developing slowly over time within our legislative process. It wasn't that long ago that it was legal and therefore considered OK in this country and others to kill people who committed certain crimes. Now it's not. That pattern of change spread throughout western culture in what we might call the development of a kind of collective conscience. It has to be said that in some countries in the west, capitol punishment has been re-introduced due to public demand as the ultimate deterrent or ultimate retribution. You can see clear evidence in Europe that some effort is being made to ensure that human rights are considered a fundamental aspect of doing economic trade with other non-European countries who want to join the Euro-club. But only as long as they are small and pose no threat, otherwise a blind eye approach is clearly adopted.

The secular western Buddhist approach to this is very different. It is very much about the development of individual conscience on a voluntary basis for the benefit of all beings, which includes you. It is helpful to bear this in mind because it is a vital aspect of Buddhist ethics to remember that you are always included in the equation. In his primary teaching we find that the fourth assignment is presented as an eight-fold journey. It is, in essence, a guide to kind living. It forms the basis of what has come to be known within Buddhism as the five basic principals of ethical conduct. The acceptance and the adoption of these principals are a significant part of the formal ceremony that defines one as a Buddhist.

The five principals are a guide. They are not rules and regulations. They are not written in stone and you will never find areas that are entirely black and white. These principals are about you and your own development and bear no relation to the activities of any other being on the planet. Judgment of others forms no part of Buddhist ethical principals. Dharma practice is about the helpful development of the individual. It is about change and only you can effect change in you. You might influence others in a helpful way by your own helpful development, but you can't change any other being. So it's counter-productive and a complete waste of time and effort trying to do so.

Rules and regulations did creep into Buddhism as it developed institutionally. You will find the range very diverse and different throughout the many forms of classical Buddhism that exist today. For the most part, it is suggested here that these additions are more to do with the control and organisation of classical Buddhism than what the Buddha taught as being essential to the journey itself. And to be honest it is rare that anyone actually abides by them fully within the monastic system.

Actively engaging with Buddhist ethical principals in our daily life is not about trying to become a nice person. It's not about promoting the superficial aspects of Buddhism such as a smiley face and a soft and gentle voice. It isn't about the destruction of the ego by becoming pious, humble or self-righteous. These things are an expression of the self-biased mind. If you ever find yourself thinking that you are being humble, then what is actually present is pride. Authentic practice can be very confrontational. You need to accept from the outset that some people will not find you warm and cuddly. Some people will not like you. Neither of these things need give you any cause for concern. Have no doubt that once you begin to engage with Buddhist ethical principals in an authentic way, others will judge you. Many of those who will be doing the most severe judging will be people who consider themselves to be **'proper Buddhists.'** It is suggested here that if you ever find yourself in a position where you are worrying about what people will think of you and you change your behaviour on that basis alone, you will be at the start of a very long slippery slope.

To understand Buddhist ethical principals and why, as Dharma practitioners, we undertake to practice them, we have to view them within a wider context. It's a part of the whole journey that the Buddha proposed as a means to bring to an end our worries. This is the fundamental point of the Dharma journey that so many Buddhists lose sight of. If all you want to do is to be a good person and be liked, you might as well do that within the context of a theistic religion. The teachings of these and other religions or paths will provide you with what you're looking for. If you are practicing Buddhist ethics so you can be re-born next time as something nicer, or because you are racked with guilt about something you have done in the past the same applies. Of course none of these options are hip, cool, give you an air of mystery or make you seem special when you tell everyone you're a Buddhist. If that's what you are really looking for, even if you're not consciously aware of it, then you're probably in the wrong place as well. If you want to study Buddhism as a hobby, within a social context or just want to show off your knowledge at the local coffee shop go for it. It'll get you nowhere other than a continued life of worrying.

The point of the Dharma journey is the individual realization of clarity. So many Buddhists, even long-standing ones, either don't understand this or have lost sight of it. The Buddha taught the Dharma in many different ways to many different people, all with very different levels of understanding, ranging from the illiterate to the intelligent elite, from Kings to paupers. You are free to decide where you sit within those ranges. It is, in essence, a very simple and effective method that has been over complicated by those who created themselves as guardians of the teachings, whose status is assured all the while they continue to collude with their and your confusion.

To gain a clear understanding of Buddhist ethical principles we need a context. The context we are going to use here is the teaching of the **'Three-fold method.'** This clearly sets out why the Buddha proposed the ethical lifestyle he did. In turn we will discover, perhaps for the first time, why, as Dharma practitioners, we choose to adopt Buddhist ethical principals in an authentic way. This teaching, like so many others, is a complete package in itself. If you are serious about engaging authentically in Dharma practice you don't get to pick and choose the bits you like and disregard the bits you find difficult. It just won't work.

If you are intent on the realization of clarity and that, after all, is the whole point of the Dharma journey, you will be prepared to push through all of the many resistances that will occur on your way to that realisation. If we look to the historical story of the Buddha's own awakening experience, we can see that it wasn't a piece of cake. It was a massive struggle. It is accepted here that within our western culture, where our conditioning factors have been wholly based on the three poisons of want, not want and confusion, we perhaps might believe we start a little further down the hill than the Buddha. In fact we are told by classical Buddhists this is the reason why we can't find any awakened beings anymore. That form of self-interest propaganda is bent on supporting the status quo that maintains the institutions. It is the complete opposite of what the Buddha taught. In actuality our life of privilege today far surpasses the life of privilege that the Buddha had 2,600 years ago. The central message of the Buddha is one of simplicity and effort. Effort is the word to be emphasised. It doesn't matter where you start. It's about the journey and anyone can do it by their individual effort. The Threefold Path consists of:

1. **The practice of ethical conduct**
2. **The practice of meditation**
3. **The development of insight**

All share equal billing in this teaching and are self-supporting. In its most simplistic form, without one you don't get the other. Without the consistent effort to take your ethical conduct in the direction of being increasingly kind and helpful, you will never be able to take your meditation practice to the level of concentration where insight arises. If insight never arises then it follows that you will never realize clarity in accord with this developmental model of the Dharma journey.

In practice this is how it develops: We are drawn, for whatever reason, to Buddhism. We learn a little bit about it and it seems to suit us so we become a Buddhist or take up Dharma practice. We begin to effect small changes to our ethical lifestyle. We learn to meditate and try to do so regularly. Little flashes of insight bubble up, which show us that perhaps our actions are not being as kind and helpful as they could. We experience some discomfort with this. It effects our meditation so we practice our ethical life with a bit more effort. Our meditation practice settles down and another bubble of insight arises and we follow the same pattern as before and on it goes. Eventually, those insightful moments come to fruition and we find we've let a part of our former self go. It gets increasingly more uncomfortable when we behave in a certain way to the extent we just stop doing whatever it was. What we discover, from within our own direct experience, is that a little bit of worrying has been eradicated. This is what is meant by the individual development of conscience.

Meditation is at the centre of Dharma practice. If we look to the historical story of the Buddha we will find that it was in meditation that the awakening experience happened. When the term meditation is used within this context it is not referring to the kind of fluffy, feel-good relaxation sessions that pass themselves off as meditation. Without the developed skill of concentration, all you will be doing is daydreaming. As pleasant as this may be for you, if you think you are meditating it is suggested that you go back to square one and learn how to do it properly. Transformative insight will never arise without the development of the varying layers of concentrated states.

In general terms, Buddhist ethics is about what we think, say and do. It isn't just about the end result. This is so important to remember because, as human beings, Dharma practitioners or not, we will tend to judge and evaluate an experience by what we see and hear. A significant part of our interpretation of that experience will be fashioned by our on-going conditioning factors. We will experience so many difficulties and so much unpleasantness in life because we never clarify an unhelpful experience. The motivational factors of another human being are hidden from us and it is these motivational factors that will determine, within the context of Buddhist ethics, if an action is helpful or unhelpful towards the realization of clarity.

It's very much like a game of Chinese whispers. In that almost instantaneous moment when our mind begins the process of evaluating what we have seen or heard it gets altered and relayed back to us as something completely different. For example, what we are seeing is someone sitting with their legs crossed away from us. Our conditioning factors will tell us that when someone sits with their legs crossed away from us they are exhibiting negativity and we react accordingly and experience that negativity. In fact it may well be that this person has a damaged knee and finds it uncomfortable to sit in any other position. If we ask, we at least have the opportunity of finding out.

Genuine human communication is difficult at the best of times. How many times have we upset ourselves as a result of what someone apparently said to us when we haven't heard what they've said properly, or we've misinterpreted what they've said? How many times have others appeared hurt by something we have said and we stand there puzzled as to why they are upset? For some bizarre reason seeking clarification of an experience seems alien to our culture. In the practice of Buddhist ethics it is crucial that we learn to do this with integrity. We might not like what we hear, but at least we then have the option of choosing the most helpful response rather than reacting on the basis of being blind.

Our reactions to any experience are an important aspect of ethical training. By and large we are creatures of repeated behaviour patterns fashioned by our conditioned lives. Our self-biased mind will be formed in accord with this behaviour. This is how we will be recognised by others. When this happens, this is what we do. When that begins to change with practice it will inevitably be a cause of concern for others. Even if the change is a helpful one from our perspective, or maybe theirs, there will be discomfort because change has taken place. Humans are subconsciously uncomfortable with change. It's important to remember that choosing the Dharma journey will result in change. Living in accord with Buddhist ethics will mean changing how you live.

Having taken a brief look at meditation we need to have a brief look at the insight aspect of the threefold method because this is another area that's often misunderstood. Insight, in Buddhist terms has no relationship to knowledge or intelligence. You can read and memorise every Buddhist book ever written and remain confused. It could be argued that if this was your approach to being a Buddhist you'd probably increase your chances of confusion considerably. Dharma study does play an integral part of Buddhist development. But far too many westerners get themselves caught up in the cultural aspects of religious Buddhism where the Dharma becomes little more than holy scripture to be believed in and to have faith in, rather than contested and challenged from individual direct experience.

The vast majority of Buddhist books will tend to divert you away from engaging with authentic Dharma practice. You need to approach your reading selection with a highly critical eye, testing and challenging everything you read against your own life experience with honesty and integrity. Studying the Dharma in this way is supportive of development. Talking Dharma with other practitioners in a study context, rather than as conversational one-upmanship over coffee is supportive of development. Challenging and questioning your teacher is supportive of development and always to be encouraged. Insight in Buddhist terms means seeing through to the actuality aspect of any experience to the extent that the insight itself provides a transformation in the way you think what you think, say what you say and act as you do.

The overriding principal of Buddhist ethics is non-harm and kindness. You will notice straight away, that unlike most other formulations of ethical conduct found in mainstream religions, you get something to avoid and something to do. This is crucially important. Most ethical formulations focus on the unhelpful aspects of, don't do this or else. Buddhist ethics encourages you to actively engage with helpful actions. Take note that the principle is non-harm. Realistically, we have to accept that this is actually impossible. For a human being to survive, a certain level of harm is inevitable. This does not excuse us from the ideals of non-harm and in practice our aim is to search for ways to do less harm in all aspects of our daily lives.

So let's take a look at the wording of this first principle.

(Classical Buddhism) Ethical principal one: **I undertake to abstain from taking life.**

(Secular Western Buddhism): Ethical principal one: **I undertake the ethical training principle, to avoid wherever possible, doing harm and to practice loving kindness.**

Straight away you will notice that the classical Buddhist version is actually not possible. In effect you are undertaking to do some thing that you can't actually do. For you to live, something else has to die. That is the actuality aspect. The secular western version is not only possible but takes the principle a lot deeper and promotes the helpful aspect clearly.

Kindness, like many other words that have become slightly overused in Buddhist circles such as generosity and compassion, is a physical, emotional and psychological response to an experience. In practice, what we are developing is a kindly attitude to life in general and we are included in that. Sometimes we can be so busy trying to be kind to everyone else, we overlook the fact that we are doing ourselves some harm in the process. There is one other area that we need to be aware of in relation to kindness because it is very common in the Buddhist world. Whenever we collude, or go along with another person because we don't want to hurt their sensitivities, we are sorry for them, or we don't want them to think badly of us, we are not being kind or compassionate. Colluding with another's confusion is not being honest with them or us. Collusion is never compassion.

Although there are five basic ethical training principals, or precepts as they are known within classical Buddhism, it is always the overriding principal of non-harm and kindness that is paramount. It is helpful to bear this principal in mind when we are considering everything we think, say and do. In its traditional interpretation we find that the first of the five precepts is translated as abstention from killing living beings. As with all of the other precepts it is not as simple as the written word. There is always a sliding scale of responsibility that will determine the level of helpful or unhelpful action. At one end of the scale would be the willful murder of a human being. At the other end of the scale would be the un-mindful killing of a micro-organism that we inhale during the breathing process. Although both of these are extremes it does highlight the fact that to survive, we will inevitably be responsible for the death of other living beings. Whilst Buddhism does contend that all life is important and valued, it is clear that human life is understood to be the most important of all and within those terms our own individual life is the most important.

This first training principle is probably the most difficult to engage with as it can throw up some hugely controversial issues such as abortion, euthanasia, vegetarianism, animal welfare and others. Issues such as these can and will be supported, or defended in very aggressive ways, even by Buddhists. Before we take a look at such issues, you are reminded that we, as individual practitioners, are only responsible for our own decisions and actions. We will be unaware of the motivational factors of others and are not there to judge their actions as being helpful or unhelpful.

You will never find any rights and wrongs in Buddhist ethics. Many Buddhists do become vegetarians or vegans but, it would be accurate to say that, numerically speaking at least, non-vegetarian Buddhists are in the majority. Apparently, even the Dalai Lama has publicly acknowledged he has a fondness for the odd lamb chop. Does this really make him a lesser Buddhist?

As with everything else, we have to make decisions and accept the consequences of those decisions. The Buddha's teaching's on difficult subjects like these are a guide only. Ultimately, with time and practice, it is the development and observance of our individual conscience that will determine how we experience the degree of helpful or unhelpfulness of our actions. In doing so, we need to be so careful that we do not fall into the trap of simply avoiding the issue by indulging in trying to justify our actions to ourselves and others. It would be so easy to use the Buddha's teaching to do this.

The only recorded teaching the Buddha appears to have given in relation to what we choose to eat could so easily be used to negate our actions. In essence it says that, provided we do not kill an animal for food ourselves, or we do not see or hear it being killed for food by another, or it hasn't been specifically killed for us, it is permissible to eat meat. But, how can we square that teaching with the overriding principle of non-harm? Do we seriously not see that in order for us to eat meat another living being will suffer no matter how we dress it up as being done humanely. In actuality there is no such thing as a humane killing. Conversely do we really imagine that our veggies arrive on our plate with no aspect of harm being done to other beings? How many rodents, small birds and insects are destroyed when crops are harvested or when pesticides are sprayed all over them? We really do have to explore the actuality aspect here. Otherwise we have a situation where we have two groups. One wears the **'save the whale'** T shirt and the other a T shirt that reads **'what about the poor plankton?'**

No matter what view you take regarding Buddhist terms such as reincarnation or re-birth, according to all schools and forms of Buddhism, life begins at the moment of conception. The moment the sperm enters the egg, the birth clock begins ticking. Consciousness, according to Buddhism is understood to have started. Maybe the scientific and medical worlds and human rights groups take a different view, but that is the Buddhist position. There has always been and always will be a demand to terminate pregnancies. Conversely, in some countries birth control is a matter for the state and termination is the only option other than facing harsh penalties. Even with the most effective forms of birth control being freely available and used properly, pregnancies still occur. Clearly in many cases alternatives to termination could be explored, but without wishing to make judgments about the decisions made by others, and ones that will never apply to me as a male of the species, I can only point you back in the direction of the overriding principle of non-harm and kindness.

Perhaps at the other end of the life cycle we may have to make decisions about the continuance of the life of another. Maybe someone we love. This is yet another painful and emotive subject for Buddhists. The Dharma journey is often described as the journey to end suffering. If we looked at that statement in black and white in a Buddhist book, how easy would it be for us to justify a decision and say, I assisted in the death of another or did nothing to prevent the death of another because I could see they were suffering? The question we really need to examine first is who is suffering? Is it them, or us? Suicide is a different matter. It is not possible to commit suicide in a way that is helpful. No matter what the motivational factors are, the act itself is the deliberate and intentional ending of a life.

This first precept has enormous implications for us in our daily lives. If we accept the principle that all life is important and we are honestly aiming to do the least amount of harm as possible, we may have to examine closely things that we may enjoy doing recreationally. Fishing is considered to be both a sport and a recreation that is enjoyed by vast numbers of people. Some scientists will tell us that all fish are physically, emotionally and psychologically incapable of experiencing pain. As a result we could easily use that reasoning to give ourselves permission to continue. But does that honestly accord with our own direct experience of fishing? Have you ever seen a fish that appears to be OK with being caught on a hook, pulled through the water by its mouth, left to drown in a bucket or have its head bashed in? Do we really get a sense that given the option a horse would choose to have someone sit on its back, stick a lump of metal in its mouth and have that person kick them in the ribs every so often? Given the choice would the parrot prefer to be flying wild or sat in a cage? Every living being has its own nature and a general rule of thumb is, that if it appears to go against that nature it might be helpful to look a little closer at your own.

Bear in mind that none of these things in themselves are either right or wrong in the sense that the choices we make depend only on our fear of punishment or seeking some reward. Buddhism and Buddhist ethics in particular throws that option out of the window as being useless for the authentic development of the human conscience. The practice of ethics is about learning to live with our eyes open to actuality with total integrity. Realistically, the only person we have to justify our actions to is ourselves. Because it is us who is harmed the most by our unhelpful actions. If we always allow kindness to be present in our decision making process we will experience a greater sense of freedom from worrying. It's not that we stop doing the things we used to do with a begrudging sense of religious duty. It's more that we have come to experience worrying in those things and choose to let them go. The principal of non-harm and kindness can be developed even further when we look at things such as the environment. Buddhist teaching and practice points to the interconnectedness of all things so there is always plenty of scope for us to keep our eyes open with a growing awareness of that actuality. Always bear in mind that the quality of our next moment of mind state experience is directly linked to our previous thoughts, words and actions. Rest assured that if they are wholly based on kindness, oh how happy we would be.

(Classical Buddhism) Ethical principal two: **I undertake to abstain from taking the not-given.**

(Secular Western Buddhism) Ethical principal two: **I undertake the ethical training principle, to avoid wherever possible, taking anything that is not freely given and to practice generosity.**

There is just a slight variation between the two this time. We can see that the secular version again gives its helpful counterpart and is not written in the authoritarian language of abstention. This principle of not taking that which is not given goes much deeper than not stealing. The act of stealing involves a dishonest intention. It is suggested that if we looked hard enough at our daily lives we would find many instances where we have obtained something without ensuring that it has been freely given, because we habitually take many things for granted in our lives. It's likely that in each of these circumstances there was no element of dishonest intention, so the unlawful act of theft wouldn't be complete and we would legally be in the clear. But Buddhist ethical practice goes beyond simply trying to get away with something on a legal technicality. This is not only about physical property. We also can take someone's time and even some suggest their energy.

The workplace is a good place to start our examination of what we do in relation to this principle. Whatever our job is, we are employed and paid to do it. We are not paid to sit around chatting. When we do, we are clearly not doing what we are being paid for. Therefore it follows that we are receiving payment for something we haven't done. When we pick up the phone to make a private call, our intention isn't to dishonestly charge our employer for the call but someone has to pay the bill. We probably don't even give it a second thought. We take it for granted that it's OK. Everyone does it. How many pens, paper clips, envelopes, stamps and other little items have found there way home without any concern whatsoever? We might be entitled to ten days sick leave a year as part of our contract of employment, but if we use them up as part of our holiday leave or just when we fancy a day off can we really write it off as yet another accepted practice?

At the start of our Dharma life the subtleties surrounding the ethical principles are not clear. In time, as we engage with the three-fold method of meditation, ethics and insight, these subtleties begin to rise within our conscience. What can happen very early on is that we experience a sense of unfairness as we see everyone else around us continuing to do these things without the slightest concern. It's helpful to bear in mind that we are not responsible for their actions, only ours. There are helpful ways we can engage with this principle. We can ask permission. At first your boss might think you a bit odd when you ask if it's OK to use the phone, or use some stationary for private use. But at least your conscience will be clear. It's more than likely that they will say OK and that you don't have to keep asking, but you will have earned a little more respect from them along the way.

Generosity is said to be the first basic footprint of the Dharma life. We might not be the brightest star in the sky, we might not have built up a regular meditation practice, we might not have made any significant changes to our ethical conduct. But there is only one thing standing in the way of practicing generosity and that is our conditioning. If we can do nothing else at the moment we can learn to give. This is not as easy as it seems, especially within western culture where our conditioning factors have been based on living within a transactional economy. In the west we find it very hard to engage with generosity on an unconditional level and that is the level that Buddhism understands authentic generosity to be. Even in traditional Buddhist countries where Buddhism can only exist with the financial support of the populace, the level of giving is transactional, but there is a difference. Traditionally, apparent spiritual value in these countries is placed above material value. There is clear evidence that in these traditional Buddhist countries, as western culture continues to heavily influence their lives, traditional support continues to be in decline. This has led to an on-going corruption of the Dharma in favour of maintaining the status quo of the institutions which in turn has fed the gradual decline of authentic Buddhism in these countries.

Like every other ethical principle there is a sliding scale to be considered when we are exploring levels of helpful and unhelpful actions. At the top end of the scale is unconditional giving. That is giving for no other reason than giving. This in Buddhist terms is called 'dana,' the most helpful form of generosity. At the other end of the scale is giving when our intention is to gain some direct benefit from the act of giving. Both of these acts have a degree of helpfulness because the end result is that someone else will receive benefit from our giving, so we need not stop practicing giving because we are aware that it has a degree of unhelpfulness attached to it also. Like everything else within Buddhism we begin where we are at and aim towards the ideals at the top of the scale. That is what practice is all about.

(Classical Buddhism) Ethical principal three: **I undertake to abstain from sexual misconduct.**

(Secular Western Buddhism) Ethical principal three: **I under-take the ethical training principle, to avoid wherever possible, engaging in sexual exploitation, or manipulation and to practice stillness, simplicity and contentment.**

If we look at the root meaning of the term, translated from Pali as sexual, we find that it actually means to desire or to enjoy. This throws a very different light on what the Buddha was actually proposing and the approach to this principle is more consistent with the fundamental teaching of Buddhism, namely that the cause of worrying is wanting things to be other than they are. If when practicing ethics we are bearing in mind the overall principle of non-harm and kindness we would not be engaging in sexual acts that involve any kind of coercion or manipulation, be that in a regular or casual relationship. There's no work to be done if we just accept the traditional face value of this principal and that was never what the Buddha was about.

It seems clear that in essence, ethical principle three is about learning to deal with our wants for stimulation, intensity and excitement. What we take in and what we push out, under the sway of our wants make us what we are in each moment of existence. The way of practice here is to train ourselves to check our unhelpful reactive wants, in order to make space for helpful, creative needs to flourish. The root of all reactive want is the deep, but often barely conscious sense we have that somewhere, somehow, we are currently incomplete. We tell ourselves **"If only I had this or that, my life would be complete and I would be happy"** only to find that very soon after we get whatever it was that sense of dissatisfaction and emptiness surfaces and worrying returns.

We live in a consumer society. No other modern people have consumed as much as we do today. It seems that the level of worrying continues to rise even amongst those who appear to have everything in the sense of material worth. There are many probable factors that contribute to this rise, social fragmentation, the breakdown of the traditional family, the pace of change, the loss of religious belief or perhaps our constant subjection to brand advertising to name a few. But, the real issue is that deep down, at a part of our being we're barely conscious of, there is a sense of our own incompleteness. There is no fixed and unchang-ing essence that we can point to and say **"This is me. This is what I truly am."** We want above all else simply to be whole, to be complete, to be real. Advertisers tell us that we can achieve this by wearing their brand, or driving it, or drinking it. We carry on consuming, chasing after an elusive satisfaction that the world seems to promise: **"I shop - therefore I am".**

The point of the third precept is not that we have to give up chocolate, wine or the latest fashions. It is more about bringing awareness to the business of consumption. It's about getting the material aspect of our lives into proportion. It is about learning to maintain our humanity and creativity within the context of our consumerist society. Once a want has lodged itself in our minds it spreads like a virus, rapidly infecting other parts of our being with its intense clamour. So long as we constantly give way to reactive wants, such as the want to have and to own, then our more creative needs, our yearning for what is helpful for our development, will be weakened.

The helpful counterpart of this principle is contentment. Taking things as they come and not getting caught up in the dramas of life that are driven by our wants. It's about learning to let go of any expectations, because the expectations themselves are formed from our base wants also. Inevitably they will lead to disappointment and a heightened sense of worrying. Dealing with worrying such as a want has always been an issue for Buddhist practitioners. You can't live your life thinking thoughts and then expect them to vanish just because you sit down and close your eyes. This is why the threefold method is so important when we understand the clear link between ethical conduct and the degree of concentration to realize insight.

Although the Buddha suggests that living a simple life is more conducive to realizing clarity, what he does not say is that there is anything wrong with having stuff. There is nothing inherently wrong with stuff itself. It is our attachment to it and the idea that it will bring us happiness that forms part of our confusion. That is the problem. Happiness will never be found in anything that is impermanent and you can be assured of one thing, all stuff is impermanent - including you.

(Classical Buddhism) Ethical principal four: **I undertake to abstain from false speech.**

(Secular Western Buddhism) Ethical principal four: **I undertake the ethical training principle, to avoid wherever possible, unkind speech and to practice truthful and kindly communication.**

We may like to think that a little white lie never hurt anyone but it does. It hurts us, by keeping us confined in constricted states of self-concern and it hurts others, by perpetuating the smog of confusion. The deliberate pursuit of truthfulness, on the other hand, clears the air around us. It leaves us better off as we can see more clearly where we stand and where we're going. When we're honest, people know they can trust us and that makes our dealings with them much more straightforward. We know what we really need and others know us to be authentic. They know that what you see is what you get.

Developing kind speech is vital to our practice. It is the principal means of communication between human beings and it also occupies the central position between thought and action. It also happens to be one of the hardest things to work on and one that does an amazing amount of harm in our daily lives. Truthfulness is essential to the functioning of any society. Without truthfulness there can be no trust. Without trust human relationships fall apart and we are left with an atmosphere of suspicion and disharmony. Truthfulness, as an ethical principle has to be based on kindness and not used as a weapon to hurt others. Truthfulness, like all these ethical principles, begins with us. We need to be honest with ourselves, about what we think, what we experience, what we do and what we say. It's not easy to do this. It might mean facing up to unpleasant aspects of our character and it may seriously dent our pride and even put us in the position of needing to apologise to others. But if we can't be honest with ourselves we have absolutely no chance of being honest with others.

Truthfulness means, firstly, being factual in what we say or write. It also means steering clear of exaggeration, which is one of the great building blocks of egotism. Truthfulness means not understating things and it means not deliberately leaving relevant things out and of course truthfulness means not deliberately lying. When we tamper with the truth it is often because we want to be seen in a particular light, or we want to gain some advantage. We want to be liked, we want to be popular and bending the truth can seem an easy way to get attention and approval, or get whatever we want. Of course, if we do that as a matter of habit, we will ourselves become a kind of fiction and in our being we will be lonelier than ever.

Untruthfulness is rooted in want, ill-will or fear. If you tell a lie, it is either because you want something, or because you wish to harm or hurt someone, or because you're afraid to be truthful for one reason or another and is therefore a clear demonstration of unhelpful mental states. For speech to be unhelpful within the context of this principle there has to be an unhelpful intention behind the speech itself. There must be some intention to mislead in some way the person who you are communicating with. The range of untruthfulness is as vast as the ocean, from the mass deceptions of political organisations, now commonly known as spin doctoring, to those little white lies we tell to get us out of sticky situations. It doesn't even require the use of speech. We can equally take part in the lie by a simple gesture or nod of the head or a failure to correct something that's said which we know not to be accurate.

One of the biggest problems with telling lies is that you have to tell more and more lies to cover up the first and eventually you can no longer remember what you've said to individual people and it's only a matter of time before you are exposed and humiliated. The other danger with untruthfulness is that it can become a habit and people who go down this route begin to lose the plot as they can't make out what's real in their life and what's unreal. They are taken in by their own deceit. According to the Buddha the consequence of persistent lying is that you won't be believed even when you speak truthfully.

From a Buddhist perspective, the ethical dimension of how we communicate doesn't stop at being truthful. According to the Buddha, there is both helpful and unhelpful speech. Helpful speech is usually described as speech, which is truthful, kindly or gentle, helpful and productive of harmony and unity. Unhelpful speech is untruthful, harsh, harmful and promotes disharmony and disunity. So much worrying has to do with unhelpful speech and a good example of this is the all too familiar trend for gossip. The problem is that gossip is so seductive. It's really easy to start doing it without thinking.

How easy it is to find ourselves joining in with gossip when we are in a group situation. If we stay silent, that very silence singles us out and makes us uncomfortable, as we will be expected to have an opinion that conforms to the group. It takes an act of courage for someone to make a stand that goes against group think and behaviour and this is the working environment of the authentic Dharma practitioner. Even then, when making their stand clear they seek to develop ways of doing that in such a way that their response fits the criteria of the ethical principal.

When considering how we communicate this principal, it throws up some areas where we will have to make tough choices because of the overriding principal of kindness or non-harm. For instance if we take it as we must be truthful at all costs we could in fact cause more harm than if we lied. For instance, imagine that you're a Dutch householder during the Second World War. You are harbouring a family of Jews in your attic and have been for months. One day there is a knock on the door and there is a group of heavily armed SS officers and one says **"Do you have any Jews in your house?"** Are you going to be truthful because that is what the ethical principle says to do? Or do you fall back on the general principle of kindness and non-harm? Say yes and it is likely that they and you will be killed. Say no and there is, at least, the opportunity that you and they will live.

Obviously that is an extreme example and one that won't happen too often. But even on an everyday basis we can find examples where we may well struggle. What if you're going out for dinner with a very important client and your wife comes bouncing in the room in her brand new bright pink, hooped design dress and says **"Does my bum look big in this?"** Do you think you are going to get away with just saying "maybe the pink is a bit bright, or it might have been better with stripes?"

(Classical Buddhism) Ethical principal five: **I undertake to abstain from taking intoxicants.**

(Secular Western Buddhism) Ethical principal five: **I undertake to avoid, wherever possible, anything that will tend to decrease the clarity of the mind and to practice keeping the mind clear and radiant.**

The first question that usually arises within a discussion on Buddhists ethics around the fifth precept is **"Do I have to give up drinking alcohol?"** This arises because the traditional interpretation is described as abstention from intoxicants and we associate the word intoxicant with alcohol. So, let's use this as our starting point and understand that just as with all of the other precepts you don't **'have'** to do anything or give up anything. There is no authority figure commanding you not to do something and there is no external punishment if you do. What you are asked to do is be aware of the quality of your mind states and seek to keep them in as helpful a state as possible. You are urged to guard all of your senses against any possible unhelpful infiltration.

It naturally follows that the use of alcohol isn't conducive to developing the concentration of mind necessary to gain insight. But we can become intoxicated by many other things in our lives. It isn't all about alcohol. There are obvious ones like recreational drugs, but there are many subtle one's also. We can become intoxicated with relationships, with work, with hobbies, watching TV, social networking. All manner of things are there to distract us. In many cases, if we are honest with ourselves, we use these things to distract us from that sense of worrying, that is ever present when we want any experience to be other than it currently is.

The helpful aspect of this fifth precept is the practice of awareness. From a Buddhist perspective, awareness is just as fundamental as love. It is helpful to develop awareness that is saturated with love and compassion and our love and compassion then reflects back to us and helps us to grow. Love and compassion without awareness can degenerate into sentimentality and pity and awareness without love can be cold and alienated. So these two qualities, love and awareness, need to be developed in tandem, which is why, it is suggested, that it is helpful for those taking their first steps on the journey to insight to develop the awareness of the breath and the awareness of kindness as their core meditation practices.

Awareness begins with ourselves. We need to become more aware of our bodies and our actions. We need to become aware of our thoughts and our emotions as this forms the basis for the awareness of other people and awareness of the world around us to awareness of actuality itself. Awareness brings about change of a far-reaching and profound nature and is naturally expansive. As we become more and more aware we become more creative and full of life. Our energy becomes more focused and more available to us and we become more capable of taking responsibility for our lives.

Awareness gives us the possibility of a genuine individuality and more authentic relationships with other people. It throws the light of actuality onto our lives and wakes us up to what is really going on. It transforms us. The greater the awareness the more far reaching the transformation. There is no limit to how aware we can become. The awakening experience itself can be described as a state of refined awareness. Awareness of other people and awareness of the world around us shows us that we are interconnected with humanity and nature. It shows us that beauty is everywhere.

Awareness of actuality is a constant immersion in the fact that all life is simply process. All life is flow and change. All life is interconnected and interdependent. To be constantly immersed in this actuality, to experience this all the time is to be free from all ill-will and possessiveness. This awareness gives life a quality of lightness and a vast prospective that turns all personal fears and anxieties into absurdities and makes much of what seems important in the world around us look ridiculous. Perhaps that's why society usually equates the Buddha with a serene smiling face. However, because of the presence of compassion there is no arrogance or impatience in this awareness. There is rather a tender regard for the worrying and the pain and suffering of the world.

When you start exploring ethics it can seem at first that if you take them up, life is going to be so boring from now on. But one thing you need to bear in mind is the basic Buddhist teaching of the middle way. No extremes - one way or another. These precepts are simply a set of guidelines for us to work with to try and practice ever more deeply to an idealised refined state eventually and that is the key phrase - eventually. One step at a time.

So far we have been exploring the subject of ethics from the perspective of the first period of Buddhist development that is known today as the Therevada which is most prominent in countries like Thailand, Sri Lanka and Myanmar. Within that school the ideal of awakening is often understood and practiced as being the path of the individual and for the individuals own benefit. It has very rigid rules and regulations and is wholly supported by a lay populace who are not really expected to make any significant progress towards the awakening experience themselves. Often their role is to settle into a routine of simply going along with the rights, rituals, dogma and beliefs of religious Buddhism. Lay practitioners are encouraged to abide by the five basic ethical principles but, as is often the case, when these rules are understood to be cast in stone, what happens in practice is that a way round them is sought so they can just get on with their life and leave it to the elite few. After all it's them who pay their bills in exchange for their blessings and a promise of an apparent better future life next time

At some point in its history, somebody somewhere, cottoned on to the fact that a lot of what the Buddha taught went in the opposite direction of being self-centred in respect to the awakening experience. It was recognized that the Buddha not only taught the Dharma by what he said, he also taught the Dharma by what he did and how he existed in the world. When you consider that the primary motivation for his search was for the cause of worrying and a way to end it and it was for the benefit of all beings, it will become clear that change was inevitable.

That recognition resulted in the arising of the second reformation period of Buddhism known as the 'Mahayana.' Within the Mahayana period arose the concept of the 'Bodhisattva.' A Bodhisattva is a being, either human or symbolic who is intent on awakening but with the primary motivation that they are doing so for the benefit of all beings. This is a clear demonstration of the altruistic aspect of the Buddha's teaching. The basic premise of the concept is that a practitioner dedicates his own practice to the benefit of others and politely declines the option of realizing the full awakening experience out of compassion for others. As noble as this seems at first, it does appear to ignore the fact that awakening would be of greater benefit to all beings more than only going to the brink. So, no matter how noble, it is suggested here that it is the motivational factor that takes precedence and one need not hold back from realizing clarity at all. Dedicated Theravada practitioners would say that they too practice for the benefit of all beings because they recognise that their awakening would be of greater benefit to humanity. So often in this day and age this is all little more than historical one-upmanship which causes unnecessary division and disharmony but that, for so long has been a significant difficulty within classical Buddhism.

Within the Mahayana period of Buddhism the practitioner still engages with the five basic ethical principles, but they move from being ethical guidelines to become vows. This is because with each new expression of the Dharma, as it moves further and further away from its origins, it begins to become more and more religious in its approach. Often, what we find is that many of the things that are being taught now do not originate from the historical-Buddha and are not a part of his Dharma. Other things are introduced and re-introduced from other systems and gradually, as a result ethics move further away from personal responsibility to a system that is rule-bound. There is nothing more binding than a vow and some of the punishments that are added in by the third period are definitely of the fire and brimstone variety.

What follows is an example of the four great vows of the wan-nabee bodhisattva.

Conscious beings are innumerable. I vow to meet them with loving kindness and compassionate interest.

Anxiety is inexhaustible. I vow to challenge it with integrity, patience and love

The Dharma life is unexcelled. I vow to surrender to it freely

The Dharma is infinite. I vow to explore it fully, realize it and actualize it

We now come to the third reformation period of Buddhist development known as the Vajrayana. It was a variant of the Mahayana in that it still promoted the Bodhisattva ideal but its focus was, it is suggested here, a bit of a throwback to the days of the Tibetan Bon religion prior to the arrival of Buddhism with a few other eclectic gatherings along the way. Vajrayana is translated as the diamond vehicle but is more widely known as the tantra. Again we find within Buddhism the apparent need to promote one form of Buddhism over another as the Therevada and Mahayana are collectively known as promoting the sutrayana or the vehicle of the sutras or texts whereas the Vajrayana promotes the tantrayana which it claims is the speedier path to awakening. It has as its basis the concept that our base passions and desires, which are the root of our anxiety, can be transformed by powerful rites and rituals and actively encourages the pursuit of pleasure.

This approach is probably the most fraught with dangers. In the first place it attracts the type of personality that is attracted to the rites and rituals like a moth to a flame. They become attached to the apparent specialness of it all because it is all so alien to their own culture and serves often just to bolster the self-biased mind rather than concentrating on practices to deflate it. The second danger and probably far more dangerous is that it tends to adopt an anything goes attitude as regards to ethical conduct and almost any type of behaviour can be justified or rationalised within the freedoms it offers.

It wasn't that long ago when I received a death threat from an apparent high Tibetan Lama who runs a Vajrayana Buddhist Centre in Istanbul because he claimed I was trying to destroy the Dharma and therefore he had a sworn duty to destroy me. He was a very angry Buddhist indeed. He said that he would summon a wrathful demon and that I would be dead within 24 hours if I did not stop communicating my heresy. Needless to say, just as when I was threatened to be struck down by God years ago by a Christian Vicar, I encouraged him to give it his best shot. Being a Dharma communicator within a secular western Buddhist context, I accept, is going to push a few buttons, but threats of murder? From Buddhists?

The most well-known aspect of the tantra is the way it actively promotes sexual activities between advanced practitioners, including its teachers. This is never a helpful idea. It claims to do this to help the individual break free from their gender bias with a union of the male and female sexual energies and also serves to lessen our attachments to others. Tantric sex retreats are now big business and are basically a free-for-all run by people who are not even tantric practitioners themselves and is very much part of the New Age movement. Surprisingly, with everything it offers and claims the Vajrayana has yet to take off in any big way in the west.

We have now looked at the approach to ethics from within the three 'currently recognised' periods of Buddhist reformation. Many western Buddhists have come to recognise that due to the misrepresentation of the Dharma as a belief based religion and the gross corruptions within the classical Buddhist institutions it is time for a fourth reformation period. When Buddhism came to the west, from whatever direction in the east, it brought with it an amazing amount of cultural baggage. For the first fifty years of Buddhist development in the west the only option to engage with the Dharma was through the filter of an alien culture. Many early western practitioners took themselves off into the jungles of Thailand, the temples of Tibet and into the hills of India to meet and study with great teachers. When they came back to the west, to a great extent, they simply brought with them the on-going belief systems of classical religious Buddhism and created identical institutions in the west that still exist today.

In more recent times, some of these now respected teachers have realized the elementary mistake of trying to teach the Dharma on the back of someone else's conditioned belief system and have broken free of the institutions of Buddhism to teach the Dharma in the same way it has been taught throughout its history as it travelled the globe. Originally, the Buddha taught the Dharma on the back of Brahmanism in India. As it travelled it was taught on the back of Bon or Siddhism in Tibet, or on the back of Taoism in China. It's incredible to think that it has taken so long for us in the west to follow suit and teach it on the back of our own ingrained conditioned belief systems.

What we have now, it is suggested here, is an opportunity for a fourth reformation period, or turning of the Dharma wheel. It is the development of Buddhism for the modern age that is aligned with scientific discovery and will move along with it and can never become stuck again. This has become to be known as secular western Buddhism. Its aims are to de-institutionalise Buddhism from its religious imposition to get back to the essence of the original communication. It recognises the inherent need to let go of almost all of this alien baggage and cultural interference so that practitioners can engage with the Dharma from within their own conditioned existence in a totally authentic way. It places a greater emphasis on the journey of individual development through the practice of ethics and meditation as the primary method to non-reversible insight and the realization of clarity.

At its centre, the approach to Buddhist non-rule-bound ethics is about the development of empathy, compassion, kindness and equanimity. It is set out in such a way that each individual practitioner is encouraged to take 100% responsibility for everything they think, say and do by observing the quality of their own mind states that will arise in dependence of that awareness and then learn from that experience. The connection with karma and ethics is not meant to be some kind of mystical belief system, but a practical method of awareness. When we are paying attention we will notice that thoughts, speech and actions that take into account the sensitivities and needs of others will result in contentment for us, although that is not our primary motivation. Thoughts, speech and actions that do not take others into account will result in us worrying.

Whenever we are motivated by the three poisons of want, not want and confusion we are being self-centred. It is all about us and that will never actually be helpful for us. Whereas when we bear in mind others we open ourselves up to actuality and provide the opportunity for compassion, generosity, empathy, kindness and love to be present which will, in turn, give rise to peace of mind. What the Buddha was trying to show people when he used the pre-existent idea of karma as a learning tool, was that it was all about ethical conduct and the consequences in each moment and not as part of some linkage with beliefs about other things.

His approach could be said to be very much akin to the approach of cognitive behavioural therapy which challenges our habitual patterns of thinking and behaving so we can see through to a level of actuality that will alleviate our worries.

The Buddha's connection between karma and ethics provides us with a real opportunity to identify for ourselves patterns within causality which we have been exploring. By engaging in awareness practices and meditation we can learn to pay attention with some integrity and see how things which arise from our own observation of our own mind states happen and their causes and conditions and that is what the Buddha's approach to ethics was all about.

Some try to suggest that there are such things as moral absolutes, but in actuality there is no such thing. There could be a circumstance where the most compassionate response to a situation would be to kill another human being. Sometimes the most compassionate thing you could ever do is to take something that is not freely given. Sometimes the most compassionate thing you could ever do is to lie.

Many other aspects of what we consider to be ethics are little more than the transitional norms of an ever changing society. It is the model of which is bound tight by group think and behaviour and beliefs that are not founded in actuality. We are all bound by the laws of any country that we live in or visit, but it is our responsibility not to just stick to them blindly, but to question their validity within our own direct experience like any other principle. In doing so, we still have to experience the consequences of any decisions that we make.

Chapter Seventeen: The Three-Fold Method – 2. Meditation Practice

What is meditation? Within this context it is the development of a way to pay full attention to the flow of ever changing physical, emotional and psychological experience without, as best as we can, judging them as good or bad, or seeking to change them into different experiences. In other words, it is the moment-to-moment non-judgmental awareness of one's thoughts, emotions, body sensations and motivations. To assist this development a combination of formal sitting practices are suggested and the on-going development of the skills learned in those practices into an everyday living awareness practice.

What is not meditation? Within this context it is anything that adds something external into your experience. This could include background music or other sounds like gongs and bells. It could include somebody leading you into a story or a visualization of something. It could also include creating vast images in your mind. This is not suggesting that any of these things do not have any value. Some of them can bring short-term relief from worry because the mind is being distracted away from it. The nature of the music that is promoted within this field is to relax. The mind clings to the movement and finds it pleasant. This is relaxation not meditation. When someone leads you into a story or a visualization session they are using auto-suggestive relaxation techniques. They are doing the work. You are doing nothing. There is no long-term benefit for you. It is in this area where there is an inherent danger though. There are a number of groups and organisations that operate under the disguise of meditation that use this technique to gain control over the vulnerable. Many people have found themselves hooked within the first couple of sessions which has resulted in severe financial and psychological difficulties.

The system of meditation that is promoted within this context of secular western Buddhism can be traced back, via textual material, to the Buddha himself. The human species is a thinking and emotional being. The two formal sitting practices that are promoted here, when practiced in balance, provide a helpful integration process of the entire mind/body complex we call us. To practice one too much either way would lead to imbalance. It is suggested that if you grow to favour the awareness of the breath practice, you are, in effect, avoiding facing your emotional side. If you favour the awareness of kindness, you are, in effect, avoiding bringing some discipline into your thinking mind. For this reason it is suggested that they are practiced in equal measure.

Within this system, the two practices are suggested as disciplined training practices that involve sitting. As regards to posture there is no need to try and get yourself into a position that resembles a pretzel. You get no brownie points for making yourself uncomfortable. There is no special or magical position. Just make sure that you can find a position where you are comfortable, but also able to keep the spine upright but not rigid as this helps to keep you alert and not fall back into relaxation mode. Make sure that the hand are well supported in the lap or a belt so that the shoulders do not pull you forward or take you off balance. Once you are in that position if you imagine you are looking straight forward, you just then tilt the head towards the chest very slightly so as to give a slight stretch at the top of the spine and so the crown of the head is level with the ceiling. Now you are good to go.

In both practices it is recommended, as best as you can, to use the nose for breathing in and breathing out and to make no effort in the breathing process. Any effort to manipulate the breath will be unhelpful. It is also recommended, as best as you can, to leave all expectations outside of the sit and not cling to any particular experience that may be pleasant or unpleasant. Within these practices it is unhelpful to try and solve problems or issues during the sit. You can always pick them up again afterwards if you choose, but if you engage with them during the sit you will not actually be helping yourself as each practice has a point of focus that you will be drawing yourself away from. There will be enough distractions and stories going on without adding any deliberate ones in. At the start of each session it is helpful to begin by taking three full inhalations through the nose, to the extent that the entire body is inflated. Hold momentarily and then exhale through the mouth with some force. The more energy you release on the out breath the more of a letting go process takes place. You breathe in the next moment of life with gratitude and exhale or let go of any stress, anxiety or worry on the out breath. If you do that three or four times it will enable you to settle into your position and then just spend about a minute in silence before you begin the practice allowing the breath to return to its normal pattern. Allow the eyes to close gently but if that causes any worry that you find too difficult, then have them slightly open and focus on an area about one metre in front of you on the ground.

Some people, prior to beginning the formal practice, find it helpful to prepare the mind by engaging in a period of chanting. Others spend some time working on their physical body, observing any tensions and working to release them or observing sensations within the body. If this is something you choose to do then it is suggested that you start at the point of contact between your feet and the surface they are in contact with and then slowly work your way up the body. If at any time during a session you experience light-headedness or a sense of floating, which is a very regular experience for some, then bring your awareness back down through the body and re-connect with the ground. Contrary to popular mythology nobody levitates in meditation. It is a mind game and there are plenty of those.

The mind does not want to be quiet and there is no point trying to force it to be quiet as that will make it worse. Contrary to popular belief, meditation is not about trying to empty the mind or have no thoughts. There will be thoughts going on most of the time. The practice is to be aware of thoughts but not engaging with them by bringing your attention back, time and time again, to the point of focus of the meditation. I would suggest that if you attend any meditation class or session and you are told it is about emptying your mind, or deleting your memories or anything like those things that you run out the door with your hand on your wallet or purse as quick as you can. Because what happens in these situations is that someone is intent on replacing what was there with something of their own and it always ends in tears.

So, you've settled in and you may be sitting there fully engaged with the structure of the practice and a sense or thought will arise that you are hungry. In an instant the mind will begin exploring the subject of hunger. It will search its memory to see what it is it fancies. It finds its target, a Pizza. A thought will pop up. It's cheap Tuesday. Shall I have Dominoes or Eagle Boys? What toppings shall I have? What crust? The next thing you know, there you are sitting in meditation and in your imagination you are munching your way through a stuffed crust Peperoni pizza with extra chilli. The work in meditation is to catch that story as soon as possible, acknowledge its presence, not give yourself a hard time over it, let it go and return your attention to the focus of the meditation.

'Awareness of the Breath' in four stages. This is the recommended core concentration practice and is the foundation practice for the development of the level of concentration required to engage in the process of insight. In the first stage we use a system of counting one to ten. We breathe in through the nose, breathe out through the nose. At the very end of the out breath we quietly say to ourselves one. We breathe in through the nose, breathe out through the nose. At the very end of the out breath we quietly say to ourselves two. We follow this sequence until we arrive at ten and then begin again at one and keep that sequence going until the end of that particular stage. Ten is not a goal or a target. It is simply a reminder to start again at one. It doesn't matter how many times you get distracted, (and you will) it is the letting go, not giving yourself a hard time, and returning to the focus of the practice that is the discipline aspect. If you lose the count along the way or become distracted on a story like the pizza, it is helpful always to start again at one.

The term distractions relate to the wandering mind. Often you will be told that it is helpful just to sit through distractions but it is vital to understand that they only relate to the wandering mind. If you begin to experience that your heart begins to beat fast, your chest becomes tight, you are flushed or feint that is not a distraction. That is your body telling you need to do something. What is most helpful to do in these circumstances is to stop what you are doing, open your eyes, take a few deep breaths, allow the panic or anxiety to quiet down and then start again if it seems OK. If you really need to cough then do so. Don't sit there and go blue in the face because you are scared to make any noise. Every person in the session is there to take responsibility for their own welfare and how they respond to any disturbances in the studio.

In the second stage it is almost the same process. Except this time we count to ourselves first. We count one, breathe in through the nose, breathe out through the nose and count two, breathe in through the nose, breathe out through the nose, again in sequences of one to ten. You may find eventually that there is a subtle difference in the emotional or psychological experience to these first stages. One thing to be aware of in both of these stages is not to develop the habit of counting and breathing at the same time. As best as you can, place the count in the gap between the breaths and breathe into silence.

In the third stage, we drop the counting and begin taking an interest in the entire breathing process in connection with our physical experience of it. We observe each in breath and out breath and see what happens. Not in an analytical way, but more simply becoming aware of differences. This breath might be long. This one might be short. This time the breath went as far as the abdomen. This one seemed to stay high in the chest. If we become distracted bring the awareness to a part of the body that is inflating and subsiding like the belly or chest for a few breaths and then relax back into the observation of sensations in connection with the breathing process.

In the fourth stage we turn our attention to one particular spot of the body. It is the point where we actually experience the breath arriving and leaving the body. When we breathe in there will be a slightly colder sensation somewhere around the nose area. When we breathe out that will become a slightly warmer sensation. We place our attention on the sensations and remain at their location and allow the breath to do its own thing and only meet it in each cycle on its way in and out of the body. If the mind wanders away, we gently bring it back and start again. As we move further into this session we aim to refine those experiences further to see if we can find the very centre of the experience.

The recommended period of time for each stage, is to begin with five minutes for each stage and gradually increase to ten minutes for each stage. Of course as your practice becomes more established and you begin to experience the helpful benefits there is no upper limit to the amount of time spent in each stage and eventually even the stages fall away.

'Awareness of kindness' in five stages. This practice is still a concentration practice, but it is an active concentration practice that is very much dependent on the imagination and the emotions. It uses a series of four people that are known to you as the focus point for awareness and they are as follows: It is recommended that you use people who are still alive.

1. Yourself

2. A good friend

3. A neutral person

4. A person you are experiencing low level difficulty with

Within western culture it's not that unusual for people to struggle with the first stage. Possibly, because we live in a culture that is based on success and performance in the pursuits of perfection. It seems to have developed over time into problems such as low self esteem or self-worth. Added to this is the conditioning of putting others before ourselves first and not being selfish. Within this context putting yourself first is about the most selfless thing you could possibly do. Developing yourself to think, speak and act in helpful ways is always going to be of more benefit to you, others and the world around you than doing those things on the basis of worry. What we are exploring within this practice is the development of kindness towards ourselves. There are many ways this can be done and all are equally valid. It is one of those practices in which you are encouraged to experi-ment to see what works for you. Some people use imagery, others use memories, others use phrases. For instance some people give a warm pink colour to the breath to represent kindness and breathe that in and out of the body. Others imagine that parts of the body are glowing in warm golden light, pulsating kindness through-out the body. Some people use their memories to recall times when they have done acts of kindness for others and recall the emotion of that experience. Whatever way you find works for you, it is always helpful every now and then to drop in a phrase into the experience like, **"may I be well,"** **"may I be content,"** **"may I realize peace of mind,"** **"may I be free from worry,"** or something along those lines. When you introduce a saying, just allow it in and then observe how the mind and emotions react without judgment.

In the second stage we turn our attention to a good friend. It is recommended that you find someone where there is no romantic or sexual connection. It is all just about friendship. Just a good mate as we say in Australia. Again, how you choose to work in this stage is for you and you are encouraged to explore and experiment. Bear in mind that this practice is about your transformation. Nothing you do in this practice is travelling across the airwaves and having any effect on any other person. The effect is noticed when you are in contact with them. The practice develops the way you interact with others. It is not uncommon for newcomers to this practice to report, after they have been doing it for a while, how people around them seem nicer, kinder somehow and some can often to cling to an idea that this practice has some mystical or magical element to it. It doesn't. It is you who is changing and as a result you meet people differently. When you start living with kindness, others reciprocate. The phrases we would use in this stage would be **"may you be well,"** **"may you be content,"** **"may you realize peace of mind,"** **"may you be free from worry,"** or something similar. As before when you drop a saying in, just sit back and observe the mind and emotions react without judgment.

In the third stage we turn our attention to a neutral person. A virtual stranger, but someone we can identify with. Maybe someone we see on a regular basis behind the counter at the shops, maybe the post person, or maybe even a work colleague who is there in the background but we've never made any contact with. What we're working to do here is to recognise a shared humanity. They too will want to be well, will want to be content. So, as we can do that with ourselves and our friend we can make the effort to do that with a neutral person. We can reflect on all of the things that we might have in common. We can even make up our own story about them in our head as long is it is of a helpful nature. The phrases we would use in this stage would be **"may you be well," "may you be content," "may you realize peace of mind," "may you be free from worry,"** or something we find helpful. As before when you drop a saying in just sit back and observe the mind and emotions react without judgment.

In the fourth stage we turn our attention to someone we are currently experiencing some difficulties with. It is important when we start this practice that we choose someone where the difficulty is of a low level. Something niggly or slightly frustrat-ing. No ex-partners, no employers and no politicians. Someone who basically is getting on your nerves. And the key to this practice is understanding that this practice is all about you. It is not about even touching on the difficulty. It is about seeing through the difficulty to the human on the other side. They are not bad or nasty people. They just do what they do. You experience the effect of your reaction to what they do. They can't make you angry. Only you can do that. The phrases we would use in this stage would be **"may you be well," "may you be content," "may you realize peace of mind," "may you be free from worry,"** or something of a similar nature. Here our observation of the emotional and psychological response gives us an opportunity to see how honest we are prepared to be with ourselves. It may take time and even if we have to say those things through gritted teeth to begin with it is more helpful than kidding ourselves.

The fifth stage is divided into two segments. First we bring all four characters together in a shared scenario. Us, our friend, our neutral person and the person we have difficulty with. Here we are working to equalise the sense of kindness for all. Sharing those warm pink breaths, the pulsating golden bodies or whatever method we have found useful. The phrases we would use in this stage would be **"may we all be well," "may we all be content," "may we all realize peace of mind," "may we be free from worry,"** or whatever we have found helpful. We observe now if we tend to favour one and not the other and work to equalise that. We then begin to expand our field of awareness outwards to include more and more people in all directions. It's a bit like having a still lake of kindness and throwing a love pebble into it and the ripples move outwards in waves allowing thoughts of kindness to be there eventually for all beings. The phrases we would use in this stage would be **"may all beings be well," "may all beings be content," "may all beings realize peace of mind," "may all beings be free from worry,"** This is a very expansive process and one where you are encouraged to put your imagination to good use.

The recommended period of time for each stage, is to begin with five minutes for each stage and gradually increase to ten minutes for each stage. Of course as your practice becomes more established and you begin to experience the helpful benefits there is no upper limit to the amount of time spent in each stage. These two practices are the preliminary training practices. Gradually, over time, other practices may well be added in, but the best advice is to keep to these two for a very substantial length of time, if not for the rest of your life. You really do not need anything more, but will certainly want more and that is very different. It is recommended that you work closely with a meditation teacher who is experienced in these practices and to discuss any changes before acting on them.

Over time the discipline aspect of these practices decreases and they move more towards the open awareness approach where the stages are reduced or removed and there is just unattached awareness of the breath or unattached awareness of kindness with each experience as it arises and subsides without judgment or a want to change anything.

Throughout the meditative process a whole range of experiences happen. That is all they are, experiences. The moment you start giving a story to them you then start clinging to them and wanting them again or not wanting them again and this kind of thing is unhelpful. What is happening is just a story in your head or a sensation in the body. The meditative process itself is set out well in a teaching that is aligned with the twelve link of causality teaching that we explored earlier. So, this will give us an opportunity to explore that within the context of meditation.

Chapter Eighteen: The Three-Fold Method – The Meditative Process of Concentration

In his attempt to communicate an experience that is beyond words and intellectual understanding, the Buddha communicated a number of different progressive methods that are all connected in some way with each other. Possibly the most well know of these is the eight-fold journey, where each theme needs to be worked on all at the same time, but is still also progressive by nature at the same time.

Another example would be the three-fold way of ethics, meditation and insight, which operates on a circular basis with each aspect supporting the other. By working on our ethical lives, we create the conditions for the mind to be clear of unhelpful obstructions, which in turn gives rise to insights that may include the fact that perhaps we need to go a little further with our ethical life, which clears a deeper level of unhelpful obstructions that gives rise to insight that may include the fact that perhaps we need to go a little further with our ethical life and so on.

Having explored the twelve links of causality earlier in detail, you could be excused if you began to form an idea that the Dharma journey appears, in many respects to be an unhelpful one. It seems, at first, to be all about trying to get rid of things within the process of worrying. In practice, it is about undermining the process of the conditioned reactive way we think, speak and act in accord with our pre-conscious and subconscious habitual patterns of thought and resultant actions. When we do this effectively it sets free the creative responsive mind which brings forth a worry free world of endless positive opportunity.

This approach is set out in this teaching that I will call the **'spiral journey'** and it begins at that point in the twelve link chain where we find the gap in the link that connects the pre-conscious reaction of pleasant or unpleasant to the want for the experience to be different than it is if it is unpleasant or a want to cling to it or have more of it, if it is pleasant. This journey could be described as the meditational guide to awakening and sets out, in detail, an upwardly mobile, ever increasing, subtle, graduated journey of meditational experience that lead us all the way to the realization of clarity within the direct experience of causality.

The spiral journey could be said to be the helpful counterpart of the seemingly unhelpful aspect of the twelve link chain of causality. In a discourse found in the early Buddhist texts, the Buddha sets out the twelve links in their positive formulation in words to the effect:

Birth gives rise to worrying. Worrying gives rise to confidence. Confidence gives rise to calmness. Calmness gives rise to alertness. Alertness gives rise to tranquility. Tranquility gives rise to thought-less-ness. Thought-less-ness gives rise to directed thought. Directed thought gives rise to clear thinking. Clear thinking leads to non-attachment. Non-attachment gives rise to clarity. Clarity gives rise to knowledge about destruction.

Obviously, we couldn't even begin the Dharma journey unless we were born in the first place, so perhaps we can take that as read. Let's also be honest here, we wouldn't even be considering starting the journey unless we have discovered, within our own experience at least, some degree of worrying. So, these two factors could be said to be the motivational drive to begin to explore, even tentatively at first, what the Buddha has to say. We read and we listen. We spend time with like-minded individuals. We begin to meditate and take a look at our ethical lifestyles and all the while we do these things with a mind set of test and challenge and checking results against our own experience.

As a result of our own experience we then begin to develop a degree of confidence or trust that we are in the most helpful place and doing the most helpful thing and within the most helpful context. We discover for ourselves things are beginning to move us away from worrying into a more content state of well-being and calmness begins to surface as we have found something at last that seems to work on a very practical level.

From that moment on it is all about working towards the integration of our pre-conscious and subconscious drives and our newly discovered authenticity releases the unhelpful energy and transforms it into the creative energy of calmness, alertness, tranquility and thought-less-ness which is the gateway point of the working ground for the arising of insight into the totality of the human condition. This eventually leads to the later stages of directed thought, clear seeing, non-attachment and clarity with the resultant destruction of the idea of being a fixed or separate and enduring ego-identity, personality, self, soul, spirit, essence, mind-stream, conscience, energy or any other thing that can be identified and referred to as you, me, or I.

So, as always, it starts with openly acknowledging the actuality of our worrying about the apparent insecurity of the human condition. We humans put a great deal of effort bemoaning facts of life of which we have no control. **"If only the sun was shining, I won the lottery, my wife had loved me more, I lived on a Caribbean island, I was five inches taller, I was able to sing and dance, I had been kinder to my kids…. Then everything**

would be alright." Generally speaking we think we are OK when we're getting what we want and like. It's the other end of the see-saw where we find we notice our worrying the most, in the moments when we're trying our hardest to avoid or escape from anything we experience as unpleasant. In many ways it is when we are in this state of mind that we have the greatest opportunity to bring some awareness to our situation so we can respond in more creative ways. We might even begin to notice that it is us who are the major contributory factor in creating our own worries and often it is nothing to do with any external factor including other people. So, it is our awareness of worrying that creates the opportunity for the development of confidence.

What is that we begin to develop confidence in? This can be broken down into two self-supporting aspects. First we begin to have confidence in ourselves. We begin to experience the helpful changes that our practice brings into our daily lives. As a result of that we gain a greater confidence in the actual Dharma journey. We begin to recognise that the Buddha is the very symbol of our own potential for the alleviation or eradication of our own worries. We begin to recognise that he provided, within his body of work, a very down to earth, practical, step by step developmental method to realization that is based on direct personal experience and not belief. We begin to recognise that, although the journey is individual to us, a crucial aspect of that development is being supported by like-minded individuals, especially those that may have a greater experience of the journey.

It is suggested here that confidence in the Dharma journey is developed in three different ways. There is the intellectual aspect where we listen, read, reflect on, contemplate or discuss with others, the Buddha's teachings. Then there is an emotional response where we may be inspired by one of our Dharma friends when we observe the helpful qualities of their practice. Some people find that they develop some kind of devotional aspect to their emotional response to the journey, maybe by creating inspirational shrine areas, or engaging in devotional practices such as prostrations, chanting or puja (ceremony). Maybe that emotional aspect will arise as some kind of emotional response to the journey itself. The area where I suggest our confidence grows more than anything is in the doing aspect of the journey. We have confidence in our capacity to live the Dharma life as best as we can, within our own individual life circumstances and lifestyle option. Perhaps we begin to take a closer look at our ethical lifestyle and are prepared to stand up and be counted when it comes down to those core values. Perhaps we even drag ourselves out of bed every morning in the depth of winter to meditate.

Confidence needs to be developed on the basis of intelligence, reason and direct experience. Why would we even get started unless we had some kind of idea that it might be helpful? We see something, hear something or read something of the Dharma and it quite naturally sparks our curiosity. And that initial thought might throw us in head first and we can't get enough if it. Don't worry. It soon wears off and starts to settle down. The Dharma journey could easily be described as a long distance hurdle race and it's this first of many hurdles along the way that is the hardest to jump over. This is because the initial worrying that brought you through the door in the first place may have been lessened to the extent that it is now manageable or comfortable. If we manage to look past the hurdle to the non-existent finishing line that is way off in the distance and continue to question, test and challenge our practice, then our confidence grows because it is grounded in a reason to continue. That final element of confidence brings everything together in a realized experience of the benefits of making the journey our own.

It's possibly that moment when we have actually landed on the other side of that first hurdle. Or maybe even the first few hurdles as they do tend to come thick and fast sometimes, especially if we're running too fast. It's a moment when that first glorious experience of calmness pops up and gives us a big hug and a sloppy wet kiss. It's that moment when that first wave of doubt, (and I can assure you that there will be many more) is overcome. In different Buddhist texts you find that the experience of calmness can not only arise as a result of confidence in the journey, but it can equally arise from simply the sense of the freedom from guilt, regret or remorse as our ethical lifestyle begins to clear away a lot of the worrying that arises when we are not being aware of what we think, say and do and the way that impacts on us, others and the world around us.

We also find in the early Buddhist texts another route to the experience of calmness that arises from insightful attention. This approach focuses on reflective thinking or contemplation of thoughts and ideas that go beyond conventional thinking, to discover what is actually going on. It's a bit like peeling an onion, starting with a thought and then peeling back layer after layer of conditioned thinking until you get to the actuality of the thought. Big subjects like impermanence and interconnectedness help us to loosen our grip on our self-biased mind. Reflecting on the certainty of death and its unpredictability can help us to lessen our fear of it and can actually help us to engage with life more fully. We can also use this type of thinking to help us work on our relationships with others, perhaps recognising that even people we have difficulties with have good qualities and are not inherently bad people who are intent on making our lives a misery. Each time we eat even gives us an opportunity for reflection as to how interdependent and interconnected we are on each other for life.

So, there you have it. According to the early Buddhist texts there are three different ways to move us to the experience of calmness on the spiral path. There is the development of confidence in ourselves and trust in the Dharma as we notice the helpful changes we experience in ourselves. There is the freedom from guilt etc as we develop our ethical lifestyle and there is insightful attention. Just think for a moment how fast we would progress if we did all three at the same time.

This first stage post of 'calmness' arises at a point when we have discovered at last that we have some direction, some sense of purpose. We may have only had a tentative glimpse through the curtain of conditioning, but it is enough to move us forward. At this stage calmness and trust are intermingling and self-supportive. Just be aware that it is not always as cut and dried as this. We all begin the journey from where we are at and it needs to be acknowledged that each individual will have their own conditioned baggage to work through at their own pace. For those that struggle at first to identify with calmness we need to be actively looking for any element of it within our experience. We need to nurture it and enjoy it when it is present even momentarily as it will set the scene for the arising of the next stage of the spiral journey.

It is worth exploring this first stage of concentrative absorption in detail. It is the stage where many meditators, especially if they only engage with meditation on an irregular basis and have not built up a regular daily practice, or do not spend time regularly on retreats, remain for long periods, if not years and maybe forever. This stage of calmness arises when the five hindrances have been let go of to some extent. The first of these hindrances is 'a want for material things to make us happy.' In an ancient text the Buddha sets it out in a variety of ways to the effect of:

Just as this body lives on nourishment, lives dependent on nourishment, does not live without nourishment. In the same way, the five hindrances live on nourishment, depend on nourishment, do not live without nourishment. There are beautiful things; frequently giving unwise attention to them. This is the nourishment for the arising of a want for material things to make us happy that has not arisen, and the nourishment for the increase and strengthening of a want for material things to make us happy that has already arisen. There are unhelpful things, (used for meditation) frequently giving wise attention to them. This is the de-nourishing of the arising of a want for material things to make us happy that has not yet arisen, and the de-nourishing of the increase and strengthening of a want for material things to make us happy that has already arisen. These six things are conducive to the abandonment of a want for material things to make us happy.

1. **Learning how to meditate on unhelpful things**
2. **Devoting oneself to the meditation on the unhelpful things**
3. **Guarding the sense gateways**
4. **Moderation in eating**
5. **Dharma friendship**
6. **Helpful conversation**

The Buddha then provides us with a descriptive simile to help us understand what a want for material things to make us happy is all about with words to effect:

If there is water in a pot mixed with red, yellow, blue or orange colour, a man with a normal faculty of sight, looking into

it, could not properly recognise and see the image of his own face. In the same way, when one's mind is possessed by a want for material things to make us happy, overpowered by a want for material things to make us happy, one cannot properly see the escape from a want for material things to make us happy, which has arisen; then one does not properly understand and see one's own welfare, nor that of another, nor that of both; and also texts memorised a long time ago do not come into one's mind, not to speak of those not memorised.

In another ancient text we find a very different helpful description of a want for material things to make us happy with words to the effect:

There is a man who has incurred a debt but has become ruined. Now, if his creditors, when telling him to pay back the debt, speak roughly to him or harass and beat him, he is unable to retaliate but has to bear it all. It is his debt that causes this forbearance. In the same way, if a man is filled with a want for material things to make him happy, for a certain person, he will, full of a want for material things to make him happy, be attached to it. Even if spoken to roughly by that person, or harassed or beaten, he will bear it all. It is his want for material things to make him happy, that causes this forbearance. In that way, a want for material things to make us happy is like being in debt.

The second of the hindrances is 'not want.'' In an ancient text the Buddha sets it out in a variety of ways with words to the effect of:

There are things causing not want; frequently giving unwise attention to them. This is the nourishment for the arising of not want that has not yet arisen, and for the increase and strengthening of not want that has already arisen. There is the liberation of the practice of kindness; frequently giving wise attention to it. This is the de-nourishing of the arising of not want that has not yet arisen, and the decrease and weakening of not want that has already arisen.

The Buddha advises that there are six things that will help us eradicate not want with words to the effect of:

1. Learning how to meditate on the awareness of kindness
2. Devoting oneself to the meditation on the awareness of kindness
3. Understanding that you are the owner and responsible for the consequences of what you think, say and do
4. Frequent reflection on it (in the following way) Thus one should consider: "Being angry with another person, what can you do to him? Can you destroy his integrity and his other helpful qualities? Have you not come to your present state by your own actions, and will also go hence according to your own actions? Anger towards another is just as if someone wishing to hit another person takes hold of glowing coals, or a heated iron-rod, or of excrement. And, in the same way, if the other person is angry with you, what can he do to you? Can he destroy your integrity and your other helpful qualities? He too has come to his present state by his own actions and will go hence according to his own actions. Like an unaccepted gift or like a handful of dirt thrown against the wind, his anger will fall back on his own head.
5. Dharma friendship
6. Helpful conversation

The Buddha then provides us with a descriptive simile to help us understand what not want is all about with words to the effect of:

If there is a pot of water heated on the fire, the water seething and boiling, a man with a normal faculty of sight, looking into it, could not properly recognise and see the image of his own face. In the same way, when one's mind is possessed by not want, overpowered by not want, one cannot properly see the escape from the not want which has arisen; then one does not properly understand and see one's own welfare, nor that of another, nor that of both; and also texts memorised a long time ago do not come into one's mind, not to speak of those not memorised.

In another ancient text we find a very different helpful description of not want with words to the effect of:

If a man suffers from a bilious disease, and receives even honey and sugar, he will not enjoy its flavour, owing to his bile sickness; he will just vomit it, complaining, "It is bitter, bitter!" In the same way, if one of angry temperament is admonished even slightly by his teacher or preceptor who wishes his best, he does not accept their advice. Saying "You harass me too much!" he will leave the Order, or go away and roam about. Just as the bilious person does not enjoy the flavour of honey and sugar, so one who has the disease of anger will not enjoy the taste of the Buddha's dispensation consisting in the contentment of the meditative absorptions, etc. In that way, not want resembles illness.

The third of the hindrances is 'restlessness and worry." In an ancient text the Buddha sets it out in a variety of ways with words to the effect of:

There arises listlessness, lassitude, lazy stretching of the body, drowsiness after meals, mental sluggishness; frequently giving unwise attention to it. This is the nourishment for the arising of restlessness and worry that have not yet arisen and for the increase and strengthening of restlessness and worry that have already arisen. There is the element of rousing one's energy, the element of exertion, the element of continuous exertion; frequently giving wise attention to it — this is the de-nourishing of the arising of restlessness and worry that have not yet arisen and of the increase and strengthening of restlessness and worry that have already arisen.

The Buddha advises that there are six basic things that will help us eradicate restlessness and worry with words to the effect of:

1. Knowing that overeating is a cause of it
2. Changing the bodily posture
3. Thinking of the perception of light
4. Staying in the open air
5. Dharma friendship
6. Helpful conversation

The Buddha then provides us with a descriptive simile to help us understand what restlessness and worry is all about with words to the effect of:

If there is a pot of water, covered with moss and water plants, then a man with a normal faculty of sight looking into it could not properly recognise and see the image of his own face. In the same way, when one's mind is possessed by restlessness and worry, overpowered by restlessness and worry one cannot properly see the escape from restlessness and worry that have arisen; then one does not properly understand one's own welfare, nor that of another, nor that of both; and also texts memorised a long time ago do not come into one's mind, not to speak of those not memorised.

In another ancient text we find a very different helpful description of restlessness and worry with words to the effect of:

A person has been kept in jail during a festival day, and so could see neither the beginning nor the middle nor the end of the festivities. If he is released on the following day, and hears people saying: "Oh, how delightful was yesterday's festival! Oh, those dances and songs!" he will not give any reply. And why not? Because he did not enjoy the festival himself. Similarly, even if a very eloquent discourse on the Dharma is going on, a practitioner overcome by restlessness and worry will not know the beginning, middle or end. If after the discourse, he hears it praised: "How pleasant was it to listen to the Dharma! How interesting was the topic and how good the similes!" he will not be able to say a word. And why not? Because, owing to his restlessness and worry, he did not enjoy the discourse. In that way, restlessness and worry are comparable to imprisonment.

The fourth of the hindrances is 'boredom and remorse." In an ancient text the Buddha sets it out in a variety of ways with words to the effect of:

There is unrest of mind; frequently giving unwise attention to it. That is the nourishment for the arising of boredom and remorse that have not yet arisen, and for the increase and strengthening of boredom and remorse that have already arisen. There is quietude of mind; frequently giving wise attention to it. That is the de-nourishing of the arising of boredom and remorse that have not yet arisen, and of the increase and strengthening of boredom and remorse that have already arisen.

The Buddha advises that there are six basic things that will help us eradicate boredom and remorse with words to the effect of:

1. Knowledge of the Dharma
2. Testing and challenging it by asking questions
3. Engaging in the five ethical training principals
4. Association with like-minded individuals who may have made progress on the journey
5. Dharma friendship
6. Helpful conversation

The Buddha then provides us with a descriptive simile to help us understand what boredom and remorse is all about with words to the effect of:

If there is water in a pot, stirred by the wind, agitated, swaying and producing waves, a man with a normal faculty of sight could not properly recognise and see the image of his own face. In the same way, when one's mind is possessed by boredom and remorse, overpowered by boredom and remorse, one cannot properly see the escape from boredom and remorse that have arisen; then one does not properly understand one's own welfare, nor that of another, nor that of both; and also texts memorised a long time ago do not come into one's mind, not to speak of those not memorised.

In another ancient text we find a very different helpful description of boredom and remorse with words to the effect of:

There is a slave who, with the help of a friend, pays money to his master, becomes a free man, and is henceforth able to do what he likes. Similarly a practitioner, perceiving the great obstruction caused by boredom and remorse, cultivates the six things opposed to them, and thus gives up boredom and remorse. And having given them up, he is like a truly free man, able to do as he wishes. Just as no one can forcibly stop a free man from doing what he likes, so can boredom and remorse no longer stop that practitioner from walking the contented path of renunciation. Therefore the Buddha declared the abandonment of boredom and remorse as being similar to winning freedom from slavery.

The fifth of the hindrances is 'doubt & indecision." In an ancient text the Buddha sets it out in a variety of ways with words to the effect of:

There are things causing doubt and indecision; frequently giving unwise attention to them. That is the nourishment for the arising of doubt and indecision that has not yet arisen, and for the increase and strengthening of doubt and indecision that has already arisen. There are things which are helpful or unhelpful, blameless or blameworthy, noble or low, and (other) contrasts of dark and bright; frequently giving wise attention to them. That is the de-nourishing of the arising of doubt and indecision that has not yet arisen, and of the increase and strengthening of doubt and indecision that has already arisen.

The Buddha advises that there are six basic things that will help us eradicate doubt & indecision with words to the effect of:

1. Knowledge of the Dharma
2. Testing and challenging it by asking questions
3. Engaging in the five ethical training principals
4. Firm conviction concerning the Buddha, Dharma and Sangha
5. Reflection, on the levels of concentrative absorption within the meditative process
6. Investigation of the actuality of causality.

The Buddha then provides us with a descriptive simile to help us understand what doubt and indecision with words to the effect of:

If there is a pot of water which is turbid, stirred up and muddy, and this pot is put into a dark place, then a man with a normal faculty of sight could not properly recognise and see the image of his own face. In the same way, when one's mind is possessed by doubt and indecision, overpowered by doubt and indecision, then one cannot properly see the escape from doubt and indecision which has arisen; then one does not properly understand one's own welfare, nor that of another, nor that of both; and also texts memorised a long time ago do not come into one's mind, not to speak of those not memorised.

In another ancient text we find a very different helpful description of doubt and indecision with words to the effect of:

There is a strong man who, with his luggage in hand and well armed, travels through a wilderness in company. If robbers see him even from afar, they will take flight. Crossing safely the wilderness and reaching a place of safety, he will rejoice in his safe arrival. Similarly a practitioner, seeing that doubt and indecision is a cause of great harm, cultivates the six things that are its antidote, and gives up doubt and indecision. Just as that strong man, armed and in company, taking as little account of the robbers as of the grass on the ground, will safely come out of the wilderness to a safe place; similarly a practitioner, having crossed the wilderness of unethical conduct, will finally reach the state of highest security, the deathless realm of clarity. Therefore the Buddha compared the abandonment of doubt and indecision to reaching a place of safety.

Having explored what is required to be done before this first stage concentrated absorption of calmness is present during a meditation sit, you will understand why this is the most difficult stage to engage in. You could sit there for years thinking to yourself that you have transcended this stage and are sitting there in another of the other layers of concentration but you will be just kidding yourself. This is why it is helpful to work with an accredited meditation teacher who can unpack your practice and assist you to go further. There are a couple of descriptions given in the texts that give an indication of what being in the state of calmness is like experientially, but bare in mind this is just the way it was or is for others. It may not be the same for you.

Suppose that a wild deer is living in a wilderness glen. Carefree it walks, carefree it stands, carefree it sits, carefree it lies down. Why is that? Because it has gone beyond the hunter's range. In the same way, a practitioner, quite and withdrawn from a want for things to be other than they are, withdrawn from unhelpful qualities, enters and remains in the first concentrative absorption of calmness born from withdrawal, accompanied by directed thought & evaluation. This practitioner is said to have blinded Mara. Trackless, he has destroyed Mara's vision and has become invisible to the self-biased mind.

The meditator, secluded from a want for things to be other than they are, enters and dwells in calmness. He steeps, drenches, fills and suffuses his body with the calmness of things as they are, so that there is no part of his entire body that is not suffused with this calmness. Just as a skilled bath-attendant or his apprentice might strew bathing powder in a copper basin, sprinkle it again and again with water, and knead it together so that the mass of bathing soap would be pervaded, suffused, and saturated with moisture inside and out yet would not ooze moisture, so a practitioner steeps, drenches, fills and suffuses his body with the calmness born of things as they are, so that, there is no part of his entire body that is not suffused with this calmness with things as they are.

My own description would be the experience of coming to the end of an exhilarating and challenging black run mogul field on freshly laid powder snow in your budgie smugglers (swimming trunks) on a skiing holiday and falling into a hot mountain spa. A period of intense concentrative focus combined with that ah moment as the cold body melts into the warmth of the hot spring.

The next stage of the spiral path and the second level of concentrative absorption within the meditative process is that of 'alertness.' It arises in dependence on calmness. More often than not alertness is usually associated with meditation, but it is definitely not confined to that. It is a very difficult word to try and explain because it is experienced very differently by different people. Some classical descriptions could range from a blissful experience in the body that has a vibrant sense of enthusiasm, happiness, gladness, pleasantness, serenity, an escalating energy or an intense thrill running through the body from top to bottom. Others include a sense of weight-less-ness or a kind of firework light show behind the eyelids or even the hairs standing up on the back of the neck. Outside of meditation, alertness could occur perhaps just being in the peace and quite or beauty of nature, or chilling out to some great music. I've even known it to happen when engaged in open communication with a good Dharma friend or listening to a Dharma talk.

The experience of alertness seems to rise up in different layers of intensity for most people. Eventually though you are left with this sensation that can only be described as fullness or completeness. It could be described as something like the release of blocked energy that falls away when something from the pre-conscious or sub-conscious has become integrated into conscious awareness or resolved in some other way.

From a meditation perspective, alertness can sometimes be an experience that people tend to try and cling on to or recreate because it is such a highly charged emotional experience that is extremely pleasant. The level of pleasantness can take you by surprise and therein lies an inherent danger. Because it is so pleasant, we want to keep it or want more of it and that, as we know, sets up the conditions for worrying to arise. I can't emphasis enough that it is really helpful for your own meditation development that you just accept all experiences in meditation as just that. They are just experiences which are not good or bad and it isn't helpful to add in any kind of value system to the experience. If you don't work in meditation that way, it is more than likely you will get stuck in that stage and not move on to the next stage.

It is suggested here that it is when the experience of alertness begins to arise, either in or outside of meditation, it is a sure sign that the Dharma journey is opening up in a very healthy way for us. As we begin to work on integrating the hidden or obscured elements of the sub-conscious, we automatically begin to let go, little by little, of our habitual patterns of conditioned thoughts and resultant behaviour. Some of our minor worries get resolved because we are learning to see and know them for what they are. Combined with our newly adopted ethical guidelines we are beginning to experience for ourselves the direct consequences of what we think, say and do within our physical body as sensations, and in our thought process where we can begin to notice the differences emotionally in our reactive or responsive actions to situations that present themselves to us. Once again our level of enthusiasm for practice can be recharged and our trust in the Dharma deepens a little further which in turn helps us to go further along in the journey.

In a text we find this description of alertness to the effect:

With the stilling of discursive thoughts and evaluations, the practitioner enters and remains in the stage of concentrated absorption of alertness born of calmness, unification of awareness free from discursive thought and evaluation and internal assurance. This is said to have blinded Mara. Trackless, he has destroyed Mara's vision and has become invisible to the self-biased mind.

The next stage of the spiral journey and the third level of concentrative absorption within the meditative process is that of 'tranquillity', which arises in dependence on alertness. If we have allowed the alertness to run its course and not gotten attached to it because we are enjoying the intensity of the pleasurable experience, it will subside and be replaced with a real deep sense of calmness within the physical body. Combined with this will be a state of mind that is at ease with itself. It is a sense of contentment that recognises a deep sense of well-being as the tensions that arise when we are resisting something melt away.

When the mind is in this state of tranquillity it provides the opportunity to utilise the very strong level of concentration that is now present, to prepare to open up areas of insight as we are no longer being distracted by the busyness of the mind. In classical Buddhism this is known as **'Samadhi'** which means something like the bringing together of thought and it is this state that, according to the Buddha, can help sustain a genuine and on-going contented state of mind. The Buddha points out in several places in the ancient texts how important it is to develop and maintain this state, as sometimes it can be very easy to think that the Dharma journey is all about suffering. In one such text we find him talking to the leader of the Jain religion that promoted the idea that suffering was the way to cleanse the mind and body of the karma of our past.

In the conversation the Buddha asks if he thought that the King, with all his wealth and power could live, experiencing tranquility without moving his body and without speaking a word for seven days and the reply came back as no. The Buddha then went on to say that he can live experiencing tranquility without moving his body and without speaking a word for seven days and nights. Now, it would be very easy to jump straight in and say that the Buddha was bragging or being egotistical but, as usual, he was simply illustrating the point that one would think that if one was all powerful and rich and can do basically anything you want you'd be happy. What he is pointing out is that happiness is not dependent on any external factors and that this level of tranquility is an internalised experience that is refreshed and maintained by this level of concentration.

As our trust in Dharma practice develops, as we develop our ethical lifestyle and we develop a regular pattern of daily formal meditation practice, the natural development of those things help us to begin leading a contented or at least happier life. Lots of the angst we used to carry around in regard to our thinking, speaking and behaving is being resolved in more helpful ways. This new outlook on life can be the inspiration behind us taking greater interest in what we appreciate in others and ourselves and in itself can be the motivational factor behind trying to maintain this state on a more regular basis.

Realistically, if our life is not transforming in this way as a result of engaging with the Dharma journey, then we need to ask ourselves if we have misunderstood something, or are we not taking it seriously enough, or even are we on the right journey for us at all. I'm not suggesting that the journey is always moving in a helpful direction and that is a very normal thing to be happening during this process. But, generally speaking it is only when you notice the helpful aspects that inspiration arises

It doesn't just end with tranquility. Tranquility is just the springboard to the development of insight. Until insight begins to arise and becomes established, there is always the danger of letting go of the concentrated state as a reaction to our habitual patterns of thinking, speaking and behaving. These powerful pre-conscious and subconscious drives need to be pruned right back within the process of integration to become an authentic individual that is not subject to group think and behaviour. Then and only then can the real work begin to establish the irreversible insight of clarity that arises within the realization of causality when even that authentic individual we have spent so much time developing has to be let go of in a moment of surrender. Until that moment, we work from where we are at, developing different layers of insight into different aspects of actuality, so we can begin to look at them deeper in bite size chunks and gradually integrate them into our daily lives by allowing them to influence the way we think, speak and act.

In a text we find the description of the state of tranquility to the effect:

Then again, with the fading of alertness, the practitioner remains in equanimity, aware and alert. He enters and remains in the third concentrated absorption of tranquility of which the Buddha declares: With equanimity and awareness established, he is experiencing tranquility. This practitioner is said to have blinded Mara. Trackless, he has destroyed Mara's vision and has become invisible to the self-biased mind.

Arising from tranquility the next stage of the spiral journey and the fourth level of concentrative absorption within the meditative process is that of 'thought-less-ness.' The term bliss often gets used within classical Buddhism for this stage but it is not a helpful term as it gives a totally inaccurate idea of what is actually going on. If anything the term bliss would possibly be best served to describe the previous stage of tranquility or even to some extent alertness or even calmness. The experience of thought-less-ness is not about a sense of happiness or joyfulness or sitting there thinking you are a fluffy pink bunny. It really is a state that goes beyond our emotional reactions or responses. I would describe it as a state of sustained non judgment happening. There are no worries present. There is just this untroubled awareness that is silence. Now, let's face it, the average human being is not too keen on silence at the best of times. There seems to be this need to have some kind of background noise going on within our life in order to fill in some kind of mysterious gap in our experience that we don't understand, or to bring us some kind of comfort. Yet silence is really the foundation of the world of the contemplative or meditator who embraces silence as their best friend and there is a sound reasoning behind that. Silence, as a regular practice and a prelude to meditation is so beneficial in arriving at the stage of thought-less-ness that moves us onto the next stage.

In the texts we find a description of thought-less-ness to the effect:

Then again, with the abandoning of want and not want, the practitioner enters & remains in the fourth stage of concentrative absorption of thought-less-ness: purity of equanimity and awareness, neither-pleasure-nor-pain. This practitioner is said to have blinded Mara. Trackless, he has destroyed Mara's vision and has become invisible to the self-biased mind.

At last we have arrived at the point of the spiral path where it all kicks off. Arising from the silence of thought-less-ness we move into the 1st stage concentration stage of **'directed thought'**. Up until this point it could be said that our thought process is out of our control and runs amok, hence the traditional terminology of the monkey mind and the image of the monkey swinging from branch to branch trying to grab on to any fruit that is available. Now it is a very different experience. From this moment on, specific thoughts are re-introduced that are designed to give rise to insight and as concentration deepens to the 2nd stage of concentration **'clear thinking'** arises and the insight becomes stronger and clearer and then the concentration deepens to 3rd stage concentration of **'non-attachment'**. This, in classical meditation is called the **'Vipassana'** period of development.

The term Vipassana, like many other words within Buddhism has been over commercialised and become a bit of a buzz word that people use in the same way they use the term meditation to mean relaxation or Yoga to mean a workout. Vipassana is a stage of concentration and nothing else. It is not a defined meditation practice in itself and can arise in any period of any meditation practice when the preparatory work that in classical Buddhism is called samadhi has taken place. There is a whole industry out there called Vipassana meditation and most follow a particular pattern of a nine or ten day silent retreat.

Personally, I don't recommend this type of retreat until I know something about the mental state and progress in meditation of someone I have been working with. Historically speaking, there have been many people psychologically damaged as a result of involving themselves at this level of intensity too soon. There have also been a number of reported suicides so I will always err on the side of caution.

This type of retreat is very helpful when you are ready for such a challenge, but the fact is that quite a lot of people sign up, pay their money or make their donation and never get past the first few days. The thing that they do not seem to realize is that the first few days are just the preparatory stage. Another strange phenomena of these types of retreats is that many people do not stick to the instructions that were given at the start and don't stay with the program and do their own thing and sit there thinking they're doing Vipassana and then tell everyone it's the best thing since sliced bread and want to buy and wear the **'I survived a Vipassana retreat 'T' shirt'** etc.

The stage of Vipassana is the point when meditation moves from being something you do to relax, or loosen your worries, or deal with any issues. It now becomes a work in progress to develop and maintain a level of clear and undisrupted conscious awareness. It is only at this point when this level of concentration is present can we let go of the intellectual thinking mind and direct thoughts to specific topics that will help us move in the direction of that final stage of clarity. This is what I suggest the term Vipassana actually means. It is a break-through moment when a big light bulb goes off in your head, or a very large penny drops and you finally actually get something for the first time. It's that big aha moment and as a result something transformative takes place.

The next stage of the spiral journey is **insight into the way things are in actuality.'** Actuality has, according to the Buddha, three defining characteristics and these now become the focus of our insight practice which moves them from an intellectual understanding into a lived experience of them. These three characteristics are:

1. **All conditioned things are impermanent**
2. **All conditioned things have the potential for worry**
3. **All conditioned things have no self-essence**

These are three huge areas for exploration that we will take a look at in depth in the next chapter as they do form the basis of the realization of awakening which is the realization of causality. But for now, so we can move forward exploring the spiral path all we need to be aware of is the very basics.

Because every thing is conditioned, all things can only ever be constantly changing in accord with surrounding circumstances, causes and conditions. Our physical body, our emotional reactions and responses and our thoughts are constantly changing. Everything that is experienced is engaged in the process of change. Because of that change there is nothing that can give us this thing we call happiness that most people seem to think is the purpose of life. As a result we can't find any external thing that can provide us with lasting satisfaction. Leading on from those understandings we will find that because of change and non-satisfaction we will eventually see that no thing in itself has any independent self dependence, including us.

It is this stage of the spiral journey where these insights become established and irreversible. In classical Buddhism this is known as the point of stream entry or the point of no return. Once established the journey changes from the journey towards realization to the journey of actualization, which becomes the work in progress and is on-going, up to and including your very last breath, heart beat or flicker of brain activity. This initial awakening moment of clarity changes everything and nothing all at the same time. What it does not create is this infallible, faultless human being. There is just no longer any hiding place from the actuality of the way things are, including your thoughts or emotional responses because those pre-conscious and sub-conscious aspects have become integrated into that actuality.

When it becomes known that things can never be depended upon, we no longer go off chasing them. The need for gratifying external stimulus falls away and we are more content to simply go with the flow of things as they are. In many ways we can actually enjoy life more, because we know for certain that pleasure is not sustainable. Therefore we do not experience disappointment when it ends. It is the same with expectations. They just seem to drop away. We all probably have an idea of something that is akin to non-attachment. Think back to when you were young. Maybe you used to have loads of toys and games but eventually you just grew out of them. Maybe you kept hold of them for a long time, but you no longer played with them. You may still have one or two items that you keep for nostalgic reasons but that is about it.

So, whilst non-attachment could be said to be the actual process that moves us away from the things that used to create our worries, non-self awareness could be said to be the mind state that develops as a result. Non-self awareness has the flavour of letting go, which is expressed as a lack of being upset, not easily excited, a kind of calm and composed demeanour. To the outside observer it could be seen as coldness, or seemingly standoffish, or remoteness but it is nothing like that. The full range and entirety of human emotional experiences are present and available. It's just that the drama's that are usually associated with those emotions are not there. The presence of non-attachment and non-self awareness are a good indication of the initial awakening experience, but it can easily fool some, as similar things begin to happen as part of the gradual method of development within the Dharma Journey.

In a text we find the description of the state of directed thought, clear thinking and non-attachment to the effect:

Directed thought: Then again, with the complete transcending of perceptions of physical form, with the disappearance of perceptions of resistance, and not heeding perceptions of diversity, perceiving, "Infinite space," the practitioner enters and remains in the dimension of the infinitude of space. This practi-

tioner is said to have blinded Mara. Trackless, he has destroyed Mara's vision and has become invisible to the self-biased mind.

Clear thinking: Then again, with the complete transcending of the dimension of the infinitude of space, perceiving, 'Infinite consciousness,' enters and remains in the dimension of the infinitude of consciousness. This practitioner is said to have blinded Mara. Trackless, he has destroyed Mara's vision and has become invisible to the self-biased mind.

Non-attachment: Then again, with the complete transcending of the dimension of the infinitude of consciousness, perceiving, 'There is no thing,' enters and remains in the dimension of no-thing-ness. This practitioner is said to have blinded Mara. Trackless, he has destroyed Mara's vision and has become invisible to the self-biased mind.

The next stage of the spiral journey is 'breakthrough.' This is that moment of surrender. The complete letting go of this idea that there is a fixed or separate and enduring ego-identity, personality, individual, self, soul, spirit, essence, mind-stream, conscience, energy or any other thing than can be identified or established as being you, me or I. This is the moment the self-biased mind is awakened from its confusion. It no longer clings to, needs to, or wants the idea of a separate self. It no longer operates in reactive mode of living. It is free to respond creatively and in a way that is helpful to each circumstance as it arrives and its default mode is compassion.

In a text we find the description of breakthrough to the effect:

Then again, with the complete transcending of the dimension of no-thing-ness, enters and remains in the dimension of neither perception nor non-perception. This practitioner is said to have blinded Mara. Trackless, he has destroyed Mara's vision and has become invisible to the self-biased mind.

The final stage of the spiral journey is the 'awareness that breakthrough has taken place.' The three poisons of want, not want and confusion have been destroyed. This is the end of the realization journey. Yet, and here is the paradox, there is also an awareness that there is no-one who has broken through and that nobody has reached the end of the journey. In one of the early Buddhist texts there is a description of what awakening is all about that says in effect:

'One understands as it actually is. This is worrying. This is the origin of worrying. This is the ending of worrying. This is the journey to the ending of worrying. These are the pollutants. This is the origin of the pollutants. This is the ending of the pollutants. This is the journey to the ending of the pollutants. As one is knowing and seeing this, one's mind is liberated from the pollutant of wanting things to be other than they are and the confusion of the self-biased mind. When breakthrough happens, the knowledge arises, breakthrough has happened. It is known that birth is destroyed, the Dharma life has been lived, what was to be done has been done and there is no further existence like this.'

In another text we find words to the effect:

Then again, with the complete transcending of the dimension of neither perception nor non-perception, enters and remains in the cessation of perception and experience. And, having seen that with discernment, his mental formations are completely ended. This practitioner is said to have blinded Mara. Trackless, he has destroyed Mara's vision and has become invisible to the self-biased mind. Having crossed over, he is unattached in the world. Carefree he walks, carefree he stands, carefree he sits, carefree he lies down. Why is that? Because he has gone beyond the self-biased mind.

Here, we can see that the culmination of the Dharma journey to realization is set out in terms of causality. The worrying aspect of all experience that arises from the self-biased conditioned mind ceases with the realization that there is no fixed or separate and enduring ego-identity, personality, individual, self, soul, spirit, essence, mind-stream, conscience, energy or any other thing than can be identified or established as being you, me or I that has ever been born, is incapable of worrying and will never die. This is the knowledge of breakthrough and there is no belief aspect within that experience. It is just as it is.

The difficulty, as always, is trying to communicate the direct experience of infinite creativity and freedom to anyone who has yet to realize the experience. It sounds so far fetched, unbelievable and tantalizing and can often inflame a want to achieve it, gain it, get there, or have it. This is why it is more helpful to voice it in terms of what is lost along the way and not what is gained as there is no thing to gain. It is just a different way of seeing the way things are, that results in a different experience. It is just a different perspective or viewpoint. It is not higher, superior or special. It is just different.

The Buddha attempted to communicate this experience and its resultant effects in so many different ways. The cyclic wheel of existence and the spiral journey are just two. Two helpful descriptions of the Dharma journey are found in the ancient Buddhist texts. The first is the image of a tall mountain with a natural spring at its uppermost point. The water flows down the mountain side, finding its way eventually to the sea. This imagery represents the same twelve link system of the cyclic wheel. On its way down it fills up streams, lakes, ponds, wells and gives life.

The second is an image of a tree, which in early Buddhism symbolised the awakening experience long before the first images of the Buddha began to emerge. The image of the tree, as it reaches maturity and comes into bloom, represents the aspect of the journey that develops from ethical conduct, to freedom from guilt, remorse or shame. The inner core of the tree is where the growth takes place and the outer surface is the result. Eventually that inner core will be replaced with new growth and the previous core will now be in bloom.

However the Buddha chose to communicate his experience of causality, it always arises on the basis of the Dharma journey being a progressive model that moves the individual along the journey in stages of development with each unfolding supporting the next unfolding. When exploring how to engage with and approach walking the Dharma journey, it is helpful to bare in mind advice found in many ancient Buddhist texts. It is not so much the case of making willed effort or simply hoping that it will all be OK if you stick to the formula in a half-hearted way. What the teaching of causality is pointing to is to experience directly for ourselves how one mind state simply flows into the next and how the journey itself unfolds very naturally as a result of our engagement with its foundational practices of ethics, meditation and the development of insight.

According to the Buddha, we need to let go of any idea of trying to get somewhere, or trying to achieve any kind of state. Be that in meditation, or in our everyday life of living the Dharma life. He suggests that if we simply pay attention to our ethical lifestyle in a non rule bound way with openness and integrity, our meditation practice will unfold naturally and reveal insights that will move us along the journey towards the realization of clarity. Nobody can force you to take this journey and you cannot force yourself to make it.

There is a good illustration of the breakthrough moment found in one of the ancient texts when a wanderer came to see the Buddha for a teaching but was told he was out on his daily food collection trip. The wanderer chases after the Buddha and catches up with him and asks for a teaching. Apparently he was unaware that it was the custom of the Buddha to collect his food in silence, so he appeared to ignore the request and carried on his walk. The wanderer was not prepared for this so he asked a second time and got the same nil response. He persisted again and made a third request. Now, apparently, not only was it the custom of the Buddha to collect his food in silence, it was also his custom to reply on the third occasion to any request. (Have you noticed when it's the Buddha doing something it's a custom and when anyone else is doing it it's a habit?) The Buddha turns to the wanderer and says words the effect of:

"In the seen only the seen. In the heard only the heard. In the touched only the touched. In the tasted only the tasted. In the smelled only the smelled. In the thought only the thought"

and then carried on walking.

The wanderer, it is said, broke through on that very spot by just hearing those words. What the Buddha in effect was saying, is do not react. Let it be what it is. If sound impinges on your eardrums, it is just sound. It is not good sound, or bad sound. It is just a sound experience that you do not need to label as anything. You do not have to like it, or dislike it. You do not have to want it to continue, or to stop. As with all the other sense experiences you do not need to react, or analyze. You can just allow the bare experience to be there, as it is, without judgment, simply paying full attention to it. What he is saying is, if you can do that you can step off the wheel in an instant.

This immediate stepping off the wheel is quite a rare thing to happen. But it does happen. It can be so easily misunderstood though and for most it will be a transformative experience but they will very quickly be back on the wheel. The gradual unfolding of continuous progress on the other hand is marked by increasing awareness, by increased ethical sensitivity and by increased emotional positivity. This is the preferred model that was set out by the Buddha as being the most helpful for most people. This is why he sets it out in so many different ways and formulations. To try and get a handle on why he did that lets explore what he is pointing to within a modern context that could easily represent life for most in western society in the 21st century.

Chris is in an acute state of worrying. His long-term girlfriend has just left him for a work colleague. Since then, Chris has found his life to be more and more unsatisfying. It's not just that he's got no girlfriend. He also has to face his work colleague's smug sympathy in the office every day. It'd be easy to get another girlfriend, or job, but there is more to it than that. The experience has raised questions in his mind about the direction he is taking in his life. Yes, he has a few pleasures. He likes fine wines, surfing, music and yes, he is good at his job and earns much more than his father did, but where is it all going? What is life all about? Surely there must be more to it than this? These are the first two links of the spiral journey which lead upwards through the gap on the wheel between pre-conscious reaction and want. It is also the flickering of the initial vision, the sense that there must be more to life than this worrying.

Walking around town one day, Chris passes a rack outside one of those catch-all apparent spiritual shops. Those that sell everything from incense and dream catchers, to instant psychic readings, colour therapy and angel cards. What really catches his eye is a leaflet saying **"No Worries."** It has a big smiley sun face as a logo. It is advertising meditation classes at the local Buddhist meditation centre. Mmmmmm I wonder? That could be interesting. After all, that Dalia Lama bloke always comes across as a very happy and a wise kind of guy. He's doesn't seem stuffy and puffed up and never seems to get stressed out about anything. (What a great advert that man is for the Dharma)

So, Chris attends his first meditation class. He likes the people he meets there. He enjoys the meditation. After a few sessions he finds it is really making a difference to his life as he notices people around seem to be very different and less reactive towards him. (He hasn't quite worked it out yet that it is him that has changed and not them.) He decides to see what else is on offer at the centre as he has noticed that there are some discussion groups and courses on Buddhism also available. So, he starts attending on a regular basis. He starts to put into practice what he has learned at the classes into his daily life. In time, he increasingly experiences the direct benefits of his practice of ethics and meditation. He is somehow lighter and clearer in his thinking. He seems to be happier more often than not. In fact these days he just finds joy wells up inside him, almost for no reason. He is OK when it's sunny. He is OK when it rains. It's good to be here on this planet. It is good just to be alive. This is the first link on the spiral path, the experience of calmness and joy.

Chris is now convinced that Buddhism and meditation is for him. He decides to formalise his commitment to the Dharma journey and asks to be accepted into the community that has provided the context of what he has learned so far. In time he commits himself to go on a meditation retreat and he finds his meditation practice being expanded, going deeper and deeper. At times all those knots of worry just seem to unclick and fall away. This is the second link of alertness kicking in. Still meditating, still concentrating, this alertness seems to spill out into a still lake of meditative silence, where it is absorbed and pacified and all physical, emotional and psychological experience are expressions of tranquility. This is the third step of the spiral. At some point Chris or no thought of Chris is any longer within the experience and there is just thought-less-ness. This is the fourth part of the spiral.

At some point, that seems outside of time and space the idea of Chris re-appears but now there is an opportunity to bring in thoughts "All conditioned things are impermanent." "What is this?" "All things are insubstantial." "Who am I?" Points are made, questions are asked and then he sits back and simply sees what happens in that silent space. Yes, yes, how could I have not seen that before? That's it! And at that point there is a reaction from the self-biased mind and the session comes to an end.

Of course the Dharma journey is not as smooth for the vast majority of us, as it was for Chris. Nor do we usually move along it so quickly. Sometimes we go up the ladder and sometimes we slide down and land on a snake. Sometimes we may even spend what seems like forever kind of stuck in the Dharma doldrums where we have bursts of intensity and then a slacking off. There really is no normal on the Dharma journey.

What Chris has done has found something that works for him. He has found something for him to do and something to commit himself to. He has created supportive conditions by joining others who are also on the same journey who are there to act as a support network of Dharma friendships for each other.

Chapter Nineteen: The Three-Fold Method. 3. Insight

Having explored the middle way philosophy and the methods of practice set out by the Buddha, we now turn our attention to the overriding Dharma principle of conditioned causal continuity that is no-thing-ness. This is what everything he ever communicated leads to. It is this insight that he points to. It underpins every-thing the Buddha ever communicated as a means to move us away from our worries towards peace of mind. According to the Buddha the realization of causality is the direct experience of the way things are in actuality. Although it is often stated as being an ultimate truth, it is suggested that it is as actually more helpful to see this as an on-going current theory of actuality so it can become a learning experience rather than a belief.

He states that every thing arises in dependence on preceding causes and conditions, which means that all things are condi-tioned. Every thing that we experience, physical, emotional, psychological or a combination of those things arises as a result of certain conditions and will end when those conditions are no longer present. He supports this realization by setting out three things that characterize all things that come into existence.

1. **All conditioned things are impermanent as they are de-pendent on the conditions which created them, all of which are also impermanent.**
2. **All conditioned things have worrying contained within them, because no permanent satisfaction, contentment or fulfillment can be gained by any thing that is impermanent.**
3. **All conditioned things have no enduring essence or inde-pendent is-ness.**

To begin with, let's deal with the first two as they are not too difficult to grasp with the intellectual thinking mind. All conditioned things are unsatisfactory because they are all impermanent. Every thing that comes into our field of awareness exists only in dependence on preceding causes and conditions. The flowers in your garden have grown from seeds and exist in dependence on sunlight and water. According to current theory, the planet earth came into existence around 4.5 billion years ago at the same time as the known solar system in something that is called 'Big Bang.' But even that, according to causality, had preceding causes and conditions otherwise it could not have happened. It could be said that each and every atom of which all things are made might not even last forever, as every thing that is conditioned is just a condition for another condition and another ad infinitum. In an ancient text we find the Buddha sets this out when he says words to the effect:

"**All conditioned things are impermanent. Seeing this with insight, one tires of worrying. This is the journey to peace of mind.**"

By understanding the nature of impermanence intellectually, we begin to see directly that all things are subject to change. Actuality itself is no thing but change. It is the continuity aspect of no-thing-ness. In another ancient text we find the Buddha explaining this to his followers something like this:

"**There are three conditioned characteristics of what is conditioned. What are the three? Arising is to be recognised; passing away is to be recognised and change in what continues to exist is to be recognised. These are the three conditioned characteristics of what is conditioned.**"

On a surface level it isn't too hard to get to grips with this idea of impermanence. But the difficulty is that we are not only thinking animals, we are significantly emotional animals as well and it is within our emotions that we usually find ourselves stumbling. When we are in love with someone, somehow we suddenly become oblivious to the actuality that it is as transitory and dependent on causes and conditions as everything else. It is very difficult when we are caught in a depressed mode of thinking to remember that it is not a permanent state and it too will pass if we just stop hating it or resisting it.

There is a really helpful aspect to this actuality of impermanence from a practical application point of view. When we look around at our ever changing world, it can bring it home to us that we could bring so much more of ourselves fully into our aspiration to realize peace of mind within the awakening experience of clarity before it is too late. This amazing opportunity is missed, as the inevitability of death and the uncertainty of its timing could be in the very next moment. This powerful insight is reflected in a verse that is purported to have been written by an aged follower of the Buddha.

"Black as the black colour of bees were my curls; age makes them like hemp-bark fibres. Scented like a basket full of flowers was my head. Age makes it smell like dog's hair. Like wonderful jewels my eyes were dark and large. Age has long ruined their beauty. My singing was as sweet as the wood-wandering nightingale. Age finds me faltering at each note. These are the words of one who speaks from actuality."

This powerful and valuable insight reminds us how growing old cannot be avoided and how death lingers in the shadows over our conditioned arisen existence. But this is a liberating insight not a depressing insight. If we approach it in a way that recognises what it is that we set out to do in the first place, which was to move away from our worries towards peace of mind within the awakening experience of clarity, it helps us to do that. The other helpful aspect of impermanence is that if all things were not impermanent then we would not have the opportunity to effect change and make progress along the journey. What the Buddha is pointing to is that all the while we continue to seek lasting satisfaction in any conditioned thing, we will be setting up the conditions for the arising of our worries.

When we talk of worrying, we are of course using modern terminology for what in classical Buddhism is called dukkha, which is often poorly translated as suffering. This has caused problems for many as they do not recognise that they suffer in any serious way, so the term worrying is a more helpful description as it describes a kind of a discontented mood with our on-going wish for experiences that we don't like to be other than they are.

Worrying is broken down into three different aspects, each distinguishable from the other:

1. The actual physical sensation aspect of what we call pain. Things like a black eye, a broken toe, a boil on the bum or sunburn

2. The dissatisfaction that is there in the thought process that creates an emotional mood that arises when we observe or experience things arising and passing away

3. The discontent that arises as a result of change, that disappointment we experience when those things we have accumu-

lated, be they material or emotional do not last forever and we have to start again

At face value this whole subject of impermanence and worrying can, for some, be quite disconcerting and difficult in itself. But it is just another obstacle to jump over that is in our way on the journey. The closer we move in the direction of realizing these two facts, our tendency to cling to our habitual patterns of beliefs and conditioned fixed views about some mythical infallibility begin to collapse under the weight of actuality. The development of conscious awareness of actuality provides us with the impetus for making significant progress along the journey, away from our worries towards peace of mind within the awakening experience of clarity.

We now move on to the third aspect that the Buddha says characterises all things that come into existence. This is the aspect that causes the most difficulty for the majority of people. I will do here the best I can to set out some practical observations to try and help you to understand it, even if it is only as an intellectual understanding at first. I am talking here about **'no-thing-ness.'** The first thing to be aware of is that the hyphens are crucial to this understanding as it often gets confused with nothingness which is completely different and takes people off in the wrong direction.

Let's begin by taking a look at what the Buddha is purported to have said in one of the ancient texts:

"All things are not-self. Seeing this with wisdom, one wearies of worrying. This is the path to the realization of clarity."

Back in the day of the Buddha and throughout modern history people have gone off and engaged in a variety of apparent spiritual quests in search of finding their **'true self.'** But the realization experience of the Buddha totally rejects that idea as his communication of no-thing-ness revealed that there is no fixed or separate and enduring ego-identity, personality, individual, self, soul, spirit, essence, mind-stream, conscience, energy, vibration or any other thing than can be identified, labeled or established as being you, me or I.

He replaces that confusion with the actuality that reveals that all there ever has been, since the arising of what we call human consciousness and all there ever is and all there ever will be in dependence on that human consciousness, is existence as a flow of ever-changing physical, emotional and psychological experiences in a process of what is best described as the becoming process.

This is so hard to get our heads around. It seems obvious to us that this same 'I' that existed yesterday, exists now and will exist tomorrow and we are this same ego-personality from cradle to the grave. This is no different really from the prevailing belief system that was within Indian culture at the time of the Buddha. He too would have been conditioned to some extent to believe this. Even back then he often struggled to communicate what, for most, seems crazy. This is shown in one of the early texts when a wanderer is purported to have engaged the Buddha in conversation about this subject. He begins by asking **"Is there a self?"** The Buddha does not reply. He then asks **"Does the self not exist?"** Again the Buddha does not reply. Not satisfied with the silence the wander gets up and leaves. Ananda, the Buddha's faithful and constant companion has been observing this and asks the Buddha why he did not give a reply. The Buddha replies words to the effect:

"Had I answered that a self exists, that would have meant agreeing with those ascetics and Brahmins who teach eternalism. Had I answered that a self does not exist, that would mean agreeing with those ascetics and Brahmins who teach nihilism. If I had simply answered those direct questions in a way that he seemed to want, he would have become even more confused."

This is a classic example of the Buddha showing that he is not willing to collude with people just so they will think well of him or his teachings. Collusion for the Buddha, or us, is never compassionate. What the Buddha sets out is another example of his middle way approach. He sets out a sense, concept or idea of self that is based on perception and the thought process of human consciousness that sits between the extremes of eternalism and nihilism. So, we can see already, that our everyday assumption that we exist is not entirely wrong and not entirely right. It really is just a case of seeing the actuality of things from the perspective of two different filters. The first is the conditioned self-biased mind and the second is the awakened mind and before you ask, neither is higher or lower, better or worse, apparently spiritual or special in any way. It is just a different way of knowing how things are that gives rise to different experiences

OK, let's get into some practical examples and see if we can crack this open a bit. Let's take an everyday thing such as a motorcycle. It can be pointed to and be recognised by everyone as a motorcycle. That is the label that it has been given for communication purposes. It appears to us to be a separate thing in its own right. But, if you were to take it apart and lay out on the garage floor all of its component parts, you would no longer have a motorcycle. What you would have is a collection of other things that have the potential to become a motorcycle if you put them back together.

When you contemplate this for a while you will eventually come to realize that the motorcycle can only come into existence in dependence on this collection of other things and only when they are arranged into very specific relationships with each other. If you destroy or disrupt those relationships, the motorcycle disappears. The motorcycle could be said to be the thing, whilst the parts of the motorcycle could be said to be the basis of the becoming or the potential of the thing.

Years ago, when I first starting writing for the theatre, I bought an ancient second-hand typewriter for next to nothing as it did not work properly. I took it to pieces and cleaned it all up and then put it back together again and it worked perfectly. But, I was left with this little pile of bits and pieces that I couldn't remember where I took them from. So, I started with something that was called a typewriter but did not actually perform the function of what a typewriter was meant to be. I then ended up with some, but not all of the component parts of that previous thing that now functioned as a typewriter but did not have the component parts of what a typewriter is supposed to be.

I recently underwent major surgery and had a part of my inner workings removed. What was removed, either went off to a laboratory to be dissected, found itself in a jar of preserving fluid or disposed of by incineration. So, where was 'I' in this? Was 'I' lying there in the recovery room or was 'I' in the jar?

Here's another example to contemplate and one that might be more practical, especially if you don't own a motorcycle or a typewriter to take apart. If you roll up your fingers into the palm of your hand and make a fist, you can point to it and recognise it as a fist. Then when you unroll your fingers, you see that the fist immediately disappears. So what then is a fist? It is no more than a concept or idea to which we give a label. If it were a thing in its own right, existing inherently from its own side, in and of itself, how would it be possible to make it appear and disappear so easily?

If you are beginning to follow this it will become apparent eventually that our entire world would have to be identical to its parts and yet somehow be separate from them, and it would also have to exist in that form for all eternity. This would be accurate of absolutely every thing and on every scale. Objects are made of parts, which are made of chemicals, which are made of molecules, which are made of atoms, which are made of subatomic particles, which are made of more fundamental particles, which are made of something else as yet unknown, but still something else. This is what no-thing-ness is saying.

It is suggested here that the relationships between the parts which comprise the thing are entirely imagined. They are created by this thing we call the mind. Imagine for a moment that you could put the entire universe through a blender so that you end up with just a brown liquid. Where are the motorcycles, the type-writers, the fists and all the other things now? It still weighs the same as the universe, and all the atoms and other blibs and blobs are still present, but the relationships between the parts at every level have been disrupted. Relationships which, it is suggested, is only held in this thing we call mind.

Bring to mind an image of a pile of bricks. Imagine yourself taking some of the bricks and piling them up to look like a house. In actuality, all you still have is bricks. It is this thing we call mind which creates the idea of a house based on the artificial relationships between the bricks.

Take a cup and then smash it. Now the cup is gone. All you have is some pieces of china. Some of you may say that no, what you have is a broken cup, but that would be a mistake because that view is reliant on you knowing that the pieces of china were once in relationship to each other in a form that could be given the label **'cup'**. That is not how it is in the present moment. If you had never seen the cup before it was smashed, there would be no way for you to know that they had once formed a cup. From this you can see that a cup has no self-essence. It has no **'cupness'** about it. It is merely an imagined object.

OK, the next example is nothing to do with me as I'm not that clever, so I borrowed something from a very clever person to see if any rampant intellectuals out there might be able to get to grips with this in your own way. Think about a photon (a particle of light). If you were a photon, what would the world look like to you? We apparently know from Einstein's special theory of relativity, that when you reach the speed of light some strange things happen. Your mass apparently becomes infinite (not a problem for light, as it has no mass). Time, for you, apparently stands still. Your size in the direction you're travelling becomes zero. This means that not only do you have no dimensions (there is no space), but your entire life takes zero time. You are born and destroyed in the very same instant and because there are no spacial dimensions for you, you exist everywhere all at once. OK, I have no idea what all that means but if this kind of thing is your thing maybe it might be helpful.

Obviously, one of the most important questions about no-thing-ness is **"What is the point of knowing this, let alone actually realizing it?"** Well, the answer lies within your own direct experience. If you explore that experience fully and if possible by doing so within the meditative process and are prepared to be totally honest with yourself, you will already know that you cannot find full satisfaction with any thing. It is suggested that you will come to see for yourself that all of the satisfaction you experience is transitory and you live in the centre of a world that is a see saw, going up and down all the time and never coming to rest for any significant amount of time. It is like being caught in a cycle of seeking pleasurable experiences and avoiding unpleasant ones.

For many, this manifests as a sense of incompleteness, or a sense that there should be more to life than this. This is where no-thing-ness, even at an intellectual level and that is possibly where most have to start, becomes a tool for development. This is its point. If things, including you, don't ultimately exist in the way you think they do, what then is there to have a want or not want towards? No-thing-ness is such a challenging thing isn't it? Perhaps now you can begin to understand why there is so much resistance to even taking a cursory glance at it. It cuts away at the very fabric of everything we have ever believed to be true. It totally destroys any idea that somebody or something out there is in charge or that the universe actually gives a damn. Yet at essence it is so blindingly simple and obvious. No luck, no chance, no fate, no destiny just conditioned causal continuity that is no-thing-ness. No first cause or end effect of any thing, including you.

The essence of non-dual perception, or the awakened view, or the view from the perspective of the awakened mind, or whatever current terminology is in vogue, is that no-thing looks out and sees that it is every thing. Rather than being a discrete, substantial entity, the apparent perceiver realizes that they are no-thing ie not an object that can be defined or confined. One knows oneself as infinite open awareness, empty of any form, yet full of potential. As this open, empty, formless conscious awareness contemplates form it sees that form is an expression of itself. The appearance of duality begins to collapse and life begins to be experienced as it is, undivided, seamless and whole.

By exploring no-thing-ness, at first by intellectualizing it and then when you meditate, or even better are experienced enough in meditation to enter the points of directed thought and clear thinking which follows the state of thought-less-ness, its actuality gradually allows you to let go of the idea that you are a fixed or separate self-biased mind.

As we test and challenge our on-going experiences against the initial intellectual understanding of no-thing-ness it begins to move the intellectual understanding to a realized experience and it is here that the transformation from the self-biased mind of the pre-conscious and subconscious gradually becomes integrated into the conscious awareness of the awakened mind. It may take some time and be a slow gradual process, which at times will be painful and confusing. That is why it is helpful to be in contact with someone who knows something of the experience to act as a mentor and others who are making the same journey of discovery.

The more unusual way is that it will be an instant awakening. This can range from being very dramatic to the point of insanity, or very ordinary. There really is no set pattern. Whichever way it happens it doesn't end there like the way it is promoted within classical religious Buddhism. What follows is a lifetime's actualization process. This is the nature of actuality that is no-thingness. The existence of space, time and objects is no thing other than mere confusion as is this fixed or separate self-biased mind.

So, what are the practical implications of this fundamental communication of the Buddha? At a very basic level it means that we don't have to take everything so personal anymore. As we move further and further into this way of thinking about ourselves, we will find out, for ourselves, that this belief that we have had that we are the same one moment to the next, or one year to the next was always a confusion of this thing we call mind. We will find that all aspects of this thing we call us is constantly in a process of change.

A useful way to explore this is to get out your old photo albums, or old home movies, or even look at things you wrote years ago. You will find, if you do this, that your interests, views, beliefs and relationships have all changed in some way. Eventually, we will work out that we can't find one thing that corresponds to the idea that there is such a thing as an unchanging self that we call 'I.' It doesn't mean that there is no 'I,' it just means that this I' is constantly evolving in a process of becoming. In this exploration of the confusion of 'us,' we will come to see that our thoughts are just that. They don't define us. External events are just that. They aren't happening to us personally. Our thoughts are therefore real, but not true. This is the liberating factor of the Buddha's communication. It is only when we come to see that we do not need to identify with thoughts or a fixed idea of who we are, or supposed to be, that we open ourselves up to the actuality of change and the potential for awakening and the realization of peace of mind within the experience of clarity.

In the early stages of our Dharma life our practice revolves around developing a greater sense of integration. We use meditation and ethical living as a way of developing a more helpful outlook on life so that we can prepare ourselves emotionally and psychologically for the arising of insights that will slowly chip away at and eventually change everything we have ever believed to be true about us and the world around us.

That is why, it is suggested, that the Buddha took a great deal of time setting out different methods of approaching this. One of the most popular methods he sets out is by way of observation and intellectual analysis of the five aspects of what it is to be a human being. He suggests that we pay attention to our physical body and the external stimuli via the senses in detail. For instance when there is the presence of this book within our experience, we see it with the eye sense as a physical thing that can then be held in the hand and when we read the words it is then processed in this thing we call mind. There is so much going on within that simple experience for us to pay attention to and learn something from.

He then suggest that we pay attention to the next part of the experience which will be the pre-conscious reaction of, I like it or I don't like it, that arises in dependence on what it is we have read, seen, heard etc. This gives us a great opportunity to challenge any habitual patterns of reactions. Then we can observe and explore the labeling system that we create for any particular part of an experience. We can see if what we perceive, is as it is, or are we adding in a kind of story that isn't actually there. This leads on to exploring the ways in which we think about our experiences and of course all of this is done within a field of awareness that we call consciousness which is the ability to be aware of being aware of being a human being with a thinking process.

In classical Buddhism these five aspects of becoming are listed as:

1. Form
2. Pre-conscious response
3. Perception
4. Formations
5. Awareness

and this is what the Buddha sets out as being the basic starting point of what it means to be human.

In one of the ancient texts, which many claim was the second discourse he gave to his initial band of five followers he begins to set out his core realization of conditioned causal continuity that is no-thing-ness something like this:.

"Form is without self. If form were self, then it would not be disposed to illness and with regard to form it would be possible to say, may my form be like this, may my form not be like this. Because form is without self, then form is disposed to illness and it is not possible to say with regard to form, may my form be like this, may my form be like that."

He then goes on to say the same thing about the pre-conscious responses, perceptions, formations and consciousness and then continues:

"If the five aspects of becoming are not in our control, if our bodies get ill, or we are unhappy or experiencing stress, does it make any sense to say that they are my self? If I am not able to dispose of my body, experiences, perceptions, formations or awareness as I want, are they really what I am?"

He then directly challenges the group with some questions. He asks if the five aspects of becoming are permanent or impermanent and of course they say impermanent. He then asks as they are impermanent is that satisfactory or unsatisfactory and of course they say unsatisfactory. Then he hits them with the big one. If, as you say, that the five aspects of becoming are impermanent and unsatisfactory because they are subject to change is it helpful for you to regard these things as being yourself?" They all agree that it is not.

The Buddha's communication of no-thing-ness really gets to the centre of the actuality of there not being a fixed or separate and enduring ego-identity, personality, individual, self, soul, spirit, essence, mind-stream, conscience, energy, vibration or any other thing than can be identified, labeled or established as being you, me or I. It is there as a constant reminder to undermine our conditioned and habitual patterns of thinking, speaking and acting on the basis of our self-biased mind. Let's be honest it's always those repetitive habits that cause us the most problems.

Let's take an everyday occurrence of just being around someone that we don't particularly get on with. Just the sound (form) of their voice (perception) can be the trigger for the arising of a (pre-conscious) response which creates a reaction like trying to avoid seeing or speaking to that person (formation) and all the time throughout this process even if we are not paying attention to it there is no escape from it (awareness) as it will just slip down into the subconscious and reinforce the habit time and time again.

By identifying ourselves with the five aspects of becoming the sense of self creates itself. By observing any experience on the basis of analysing those five aspects whilst it is happening, we will notice that they are impermanent and dependent on preceding causes and conditions and it isn't actually us against them. It is just not want happening on the basis of conditioned habit. We really have to ask ourselves if we want to live a life that is forever being bounced around by simply believing all of these thoughts and resultant damaging emotions are us, or do we want to commit ourselves to a life that is an on-going work in progress to lessen those fixed beliefs and habits that cause us to worry. If we move away from a goal orientated mentality to one of taking just one step at a time with integrity then it can be said that we are really engaged with the Dharma life.

It is not enough just to have faith or believe that the Buddha got it right. This approach is not going to help us in any way to alleviate or eradicate our worries. We have to accept that no matter how long we may have been living the Dharma life, until such time as we have begun developing insight into the actuality of no-thing-ness there are going to be worries arising and subsiding. But even the intellectual knowledge that we do not have to cling to them as being ours, will begin to make life easier for us. This communication of no-thing-ness is a potential for awakening. It provides us with creative opportunities to take responsibility for what we think, say and do and learn from that process. As we make progress, which is inevitable if we put into practice what we learn along the way, we will find that we will become less and less attached to this self-biased mind that we created and as a result we will realize a greater sense of clear thinking and purpose.

On the subjective and relative, everyday level of realty, it isn't that difficult for the average human being to accept that all things are impermanent and therefore have an element of worrying built within them. This is because it is not that difficult to look at things that are external to us and see those things. But somehow, even that knowledge is not enough for them to change the way they think speak and act in light of that knowledge so that it is in accord with actuality and not cause any further worries. So, it is understandable and very natural that the aspect of no-thing-ness that explores the actuality of the non-separate-self is going to be even more challenging and confusing for most, if not all, simply because it is outside of our ordinary human experience. There is always this 'us' telling us we are existing. The difficulty is that no matter how challenging and confusing it is, unless we go there and work through it, we will never make the breakthrough to peace of mind within the experience of clarity and that is the point or purpose of the Dharma path.

A reasonable starting point is to contemplate that if this non-self-ness that the Buddha talks about is an aspect of actuality then how did this confusion become such a permanent feature within the minds of well educated and intellectual human beings? Why, does it not make sense? Why can't they get it? A reasonable question to ask would be what is it like to see through it? What's in it for me? One of the ways the Buddha tried to answer those kinds of very tough questions is to present a variety of different ways that the human process could be observed by the individual. In his teaching of the twelve links of causality he shows us the moment by moment process of the sense of self arising and all the potential difficulties within that for us, others and the world around us. What we are talking about here is the constantly becoming process of the self-biased mind that we think of as 'I' and of course this 'I' can be so easily hurt and offended.

There is a great example of this in one of the ancient texts when one of the ruling class came to see the Buddha in an angry state of mind because one of his people had recently gone forth and taken refuge with the Buddha. He lets rip with a barrage of abuse and insults and of course all the Buddha did was sit there and let him get everything off his chest and then engaged him in a discussion which was a teaching. He asked the man: **"Do your friends and companions, family members and relatives come to visit you?"** "Yes," says the man. **"Do you serve them food or refreshments?"** asked the Buddha. **"Of course I do"** says the man. The Buddha then asks, **"If they do not accept the food or refreshment to whom does it belong?"** **"Me"** says the man. I imagine a bit of a pause here for dramatic effect and then there is the teaching.

"You insult someone who does not insult you back. You taunt someone who does not get annoyed. You quarrel with some-one who does not quarrel and I do not accept these things. These things belong to you. If I traded insults, paid back taunts or argued back it would be like me joining you for the meal and all I would get is indigestion or heartburn."

In other words, thanks but no thanks.

At some point in our lives we all know what it is like to be on the end of some kind of verbal abuse. It doesn't matter even if it could be rationalized or justified we know what it was like to experience that. I suggest that we would have taken it very personally and there would have been a strong reaction from us in some way or another. This is the personality aspect of the self-biased mind that is eradicated within the experience of clarity. The Buddha did not react to the insults of the other person because he was restrained from doing so because of some special, spiritual, or magical woo woo. It was because the reactive mode had been eradicated within the experience and all that remained is the response mode of compassion. Did the other person recognise it as compassion? Probably not. He might well have thought the Buddha was being arrogant, smug, egotistical, proud or self-righteous but as will always be the case, it was him adding in his own story in reaction to the need to protect and defend his own self-biased mind.

By way of example, years ago I was standing in a very long queue at a South London Post Office during the lunchtime peak period. I had just finished leading a meditation class at the local Buddhist centre so was in a very passive and aware frame of mind. I was just standing there minding my own business waiting my turn so I could post a parcel to a friend overseas. Standing directly in front of me was the archetypal, stereotypical, fourth generation West Indian young man, aged about 18, complete with head to toe bling bling. His hat was on backwards and his trousers were hanging down around his butt cheeks. I never said anything to him or made any kind of visual indication that I was judging him in any way, although I clearly was.

So, for no apparent reason he turned directly to face me and got right up close and personal and started ranting in my face in a very loud kind of psuedo American gangster rap voice, complete with accentuated hand movements and body swaying. Although it didn't go on for long, I could sense the tension in the room as this part of London was known for its violence. I just stood there in a deadpan non-reactive way. There was no fear or anxiety present and when he finally stopped, there was a moment of silence and then came my response. I wasn't being sarcastic or trying to be clever but I said to him in a very soft and friendly tone **"Sorry, you clearly are very angry with me for some reason and if I have said or done anything to contribute to that I apologise. But I do need to let you know, I have no idea what it is you have said to me. I didn't understand a word of it."** What followed was a beautiful silence in the entire room that was only broken when he shrugged, swore, kicked over the display stand and stormed out of the post office. There was an outbreak of applause and verbal positive affirmations and I was invited to the front of the queue by everyone who was in front of me. All that had happened was an experience was met in a way that was helpful to the experience.

Imagine for one moment that you've arranged to meet a friend for lunch at noon. It's now 12.15pm and it's a no show. No text. No phone call. No instant messenger. You've been sitting there for fifteen minutes being bored and restless and frustration begins to surface within your thought process. Next to arrive are the stories in your head that will now seek justification as to why you are beginning to get angry with your friend who has stood you up. When you see your friend in the distance running towards you out of breath, you've already decided that whatever they tell you is just them lying to make themselves look good. Even while they're apologising profusely and telling you how they stopped to give the kiss of life to some old lady who had collapsed on the bus, your mind is going **"oh yeah really"** and then maybe, just maybe, you catch yourself doing it and you get to see how your mind habitu-ally works against you.

The power of human imagination is immense but it does get us into trouble at times, especially when it is in expansive story telling mode. We think we can tell the future and recall the past as it actually was. We can fly ourselves anywhere in the world with a single thought and we can amuse ourselves no end, but when this thing we call mind is in expansive story telling mode it can increase the level of our selfish greed. It can increase our level of ill-will and also serves to feed and enhance the illusion of us. In an instant it can go from us having thoughts to thoughts having us because the self-biased mind is in the driving seat. When you take a look at human history you can see for yourself the effects of this expansive story telling mode that has resulted in genocide, torture, persecution and more.

The world of the awakened mind is very different. With conscious awareness established, this expansive and reactive story telling mind is lost and is replaced with the responsive mode that arises on the basis of compassion. It could be described as the middle path position, or the gap between want and not want as in the like, don't like response to sense experience and the want for it to be other than it is. In an ancient text the Buddha gives a description of such a person, who he calls the wise sage as something like this:

"The sage at peace is not born; not being born, such a one does not die, is not disturbed and is without the want for things to be other than they are. For there is no thing by which he might be born; not being born, what will age? Not ageing, what will die? Not dying, what will be disturbed? Not being disturbed why would a person want things to be other than they are?"

Although we know, according to the traditional life story of the Buddha, that he did in fact physically die, what this text is pointing to is an explanation of the subjective experience of the awakened mind of Buddha. What it is saying is that although there is the experience of the deathless, physical death is still inevitable.

There is one aspect of no-thing-ness that causes even more difficulties for people to come to grips with. Here, the Buddha is saying that all things, be they physical, emotional, psychological or a combination of those things are conditioned by preceding causes and conditions, yet he also tells us that the awakened mind is the unconditioned, so it sounds very paradoxical or contradictory which can then give rise to confusion or worse it can lead to doubt. There are a few examples to be found in the ancient texts where the Buddha tries to explain why it isn't contradictory. In one he says words to the effect:

"I will teach you the unconditioned and the path to the un-conditioned. What is the unconditioned? The eradication of want, the eradication of not want and the eradication of the confusion of the fixed or separate and enduring ego-identity, personality, individual, self, soul, spirit, essence, mind-stream, conscience, energy, vibration or any other thing than can be identified, labeled or established as being you, me or I."

So, from this we can establish that the unconditioned is a state of mind that is totally free of want and not want and has seen through the confusion of the self-biased conditioned mind. This thing we call mind is free from all habitual reactions that arise from the pre-conscious and subconscious as they have become integrated into conscious awareness and the mind is at peace. Well, I guess we could all say that on a good day we experience something a bit like that as well, but it never lasts does it? Well, within the unconditioned it does. There are no worries.

This state of calm and clarity was once described as follows:

"Just as in the midst of mountains there was a lake whose water was clear, transparent and undisturbed, so standing on the bank someone with eyes might see oysters and shells, gravel and stones and shoals of fish on the move or stationary."

It is a description, as to how the awakened mind just plunges into the actuality of the lake and forms just one expression of the many ways the Buddha used ideas and images to communicate, as best as he could, an experience that is beyond words and description and can only be realized by the individual.

In one of his most famous communications he says words to the effect:

"There is an unborn, an un-become, an unmade, an uncon-ditioned. If there were not an unborn, an un-become, an unmade, an unconditioned, there could be no escape from what is born, become, made and conditioned. But, since there is an unborn, an un-become, an unmade, an unconditioned, an escape can be made."

The very nuts and bolts of what the Buddha teaches us is simply to pay attention to our sensory experiences and see them for what they are and not what we believe them to be or want them to be. He encourages us to observe and look out for patterns in how we react differently between things we like and don't like. He suggests we observe when we are and we are not in the expansive story telling mode through the process of associated thoughts. Can we catch ourselves having thoughts at all or are thoughts just happening? This is why meditation is promoted so heavily as being crucial to the Dharma journey. It is practically impossible to do any of these things with the distracted everyday mind. We do need to learn the skills we are taught within the meditative process so we can bring them, at least to some degree, to clear thinking in our everyday life if we are to make progress towards the unconditioned awakened mind.

Ever since the Buddha first communicated his realization of causality over 2,600 years ago it has led to significant misunderstandings. This is because it is not an intellectual understanding, but a realization experience. Without that experience we can only get a taste of it, but it can never result in the same effect as the realization itself. Throughout history the essence of the experience has been communicated by a number of other awakened minds, both within Buddhism and outside of it, which has also added to the confusion. Even within Buddhism it is communicated in very different ways and a very different language. So before we move on lets take a look at how the development of this fundamental and source teaching has been expanded upon and why would it not? All things are subject to change, including Buddhism, although at times it can be difficult to acknowledge that within classical Buddhism.

After the Buddha died, his followers more or less dispersed and went their own way in small groups and began to develop his teachings in a variety of ways that suited each particular group. This came about because the Buddha refused to name a successor and basically said that they had to make their own way in the world with just his Dharma as their guide. During his lifetime nothing of what he communicated was ever written down. Initially we are told that his followers memorised his teachings and kept them alive by constant recitation. Although we are told that this was an effective process that was kept alive until such time as they could be written down years later, when you explore the origins of what is known about the development of what we have today as Buddhism, then it is helpful to be cautious about the origins of texts and see them as pointers for exploration, study, testing and challenging rather than accepting them as some kind of holy word of the Buddha. For instance one of the major selling points as to their authenticity and reliability was the fact that his faithful companion Ananda had an amazing memory and was responsible for the transmission of most of the teachings at the first council. But it seems, from what we think we know now, that Ananda didn't even enter the scene until about twenty years after the Buddha's awakening and wasn't even present during his most prolific teaching period. It also seems apparent that he wasn't even taken seriously by his fellow wanderers as he was only invited to the first council as a servant.

One of the major diversions that occurred soon after his death was the arising of the Abhidharma school. This began a new phase of Buddhism which was academic based. It involved analytic interpretation, a kind of early form of mind mapping that explored patterns and relationships in all experiences that eventually arrived at a conclusion. It is suggested here some of those conclusions were not consistent with what the Buddha had originally set out. They came to a view that things, be they physical, emotional or psychological were things in themselves rather than dependently arisen.

Other groups began to focus on different aspects of the Buddha's teachings and what was once a very practical down-to-earth method of personal development seems to have got itself stuck in an early form of an institutional mind set that created more and more rules and regulations and became more and more remote from its original intention. To some extent the only surviving school from that era, the Theravada has been stuck ever since. By the time of the first Buddhist council who took on board the job of collecting and compiling a set of written teachings that took into account the various views and changes that occurred during this period, it is clear that much would have been lost and much would have been added in so that Buddhism could again be unified, but this time with a clear agenda to create a new hierarchical religious belief system.

The reaction to this many years later was the emergence of an entirely different philosophical approach to what the Buddha communicated in the form of the **'perfection of wisdom'** literature that formed the basis of the Mahayana school of Buddhism which was developed in the second century by Nagarjuna. This is where the terminology of sunyata and emptiness was first used as an effective counter argument to the Abhidharma in an attempt to return to the middle way approach as taught by the Buddha. In a part of that literature, that as far as we know has no direct linkage back to the Buddha we find the following words to the effect:

'We claim that dependent arising (conditioned casual continuity) is emptiness (no-thing-ness). Which notion, once acquired, is truly the middle way. Since there does not exist any thing which is not dependently arisen. So there does not exist any thing that is not empty.'

What he tried to point out was that although the Abhidharma approach is a very helpful tool for the exploration of this thing we call mind and our thought process, it is limited by its intellectualism. Even during his lifetime there were many that couldn't grasp what Nagarjuna was saying and dismissed this new approach in favour of the more regimented and ever growing religious elements of the very conservative Theravada school which found favour amongst the lay followers as all they were expected to do is fall back on ritualism and support for the monks for their own salvation.

They seemed to think, or maybe were even were encouraged to think Nagarjuna was advocating a form of nihilism, which of course was not what the Buddha taught. They viewed him as saying that as nothing exists, nothing matters despite constant rebuttals by Nargarjuna such as **"When viewed wrongly by those of weak intelligence, emptiness is disastrous."** This problem eventually gave rise to what's called the doctrine of the two truths, but again the use of the word truth itself always leads to further difficulties.

It is more helpful to see causality that is no-thing-ness as a current theory of actuality. It is there to be tested and challenged and every effort needs to be made to refute it. It is in those attempts to refute it that its actuality becomes realized on a deeper level. If it were ever thought of as an absolute truth then it would surely be counter-productive as it would defeat what it sets out to establish straight away as it becomes a fixed thing.

It is suggested that a more helpful way to engage with this subject is to see it as a single theory of actuality that is viewed through two different filters. The first filter is that of the conditioned self-biased and subjective mind of the separate ego-identity. This is our everyday world where we can observe things arising and subsiding in dependence on preceding causes and conditions. We can talk about them as if they exist because it is helpful to do so in order that we can communicate on a practical everyday level. Even the Buddha used terms such as you, me, us, I, trees, flowers, water etc. The second filter is through the unconditioned awakened mind that realizes and sees that all things have no intrinsic self-essence, they have no existence that goes beyond just the on-going process of the arising and subsiding experience of causality that is no-thing-ness.

It seems that Nagarjuna, having recognized that the Dharma had become misrepresented by the religious institutions that had grown out of its original communication was attempting to get it back on a more philosophical basis. This idea can be supported in one of the ancient texts during an apparent conversation between the Buddha and his loyal companion Ananada. He says to the Buddha

"You have said that the world is empty. What does this mean?" The Buddha replies **"It is because it is empty of the self or anything to do with the self that I say it is empty."**

When we explore that on the basis of those two filters we can see that on a conventional level of everyday subjective reality the world is not empty but actually full up with people who believe they exist as separate selves. But through the filter of actuality there is no self-existent world. Nor are there any self-existent beings inhabiting it.

The Buddha continues with his teaching to Ananda as follows:

"And what is empty of a self or anything to do with the self? The eye, is empty of a self or anything to do with a self. Form is empty of a self or anything to do with a self. Eye consciousness and eye contact are empty of a self or anything to do with a

self. Whatever arises with eye contact as its condition, to be experienced as pleasant or unpleasant, that is empty of a self or anything to do with a self."

He then repeats the sequence in relation to the ear, the nose, the tongue, the body and this thing we call the mind. He concludes by saying:

"It is because these things are empty of the self or anything to do with the self that I say that the world is empty."

In this text it is clear that the Buddha, when he uses the word 'world,' he is talking about actuality as it is, not in the conventional and relative sense. He is using the language of relative reality to try as best as he can to communicate an experience of actuality. This will always be an uphill struggle for any Buddha, including the original one.

To explore this further it may be helpful to take a quick look at one of the most famous teaching on this subject. It is called the Heart Sutra. What follows is a version formulated using the language of secular western Buddhism.

The Buddha, whilst seated in meditation, realized that all five aspects of becoming are no-thing-ness. Realizing this gave rise to peace of mind.

From this realization, he communicates, that this body is no-thing-ness and no-thing-ness is this body. This body is no thing other than no-thing-ness and no-thing-ness is not other than this body. It is the same with the other five aspects of becoming namely; physicality, emotional experiences, perceptions, thought process and consciousness.

All things embrace the actuality of no-thing-ness; their nature is of no birth, no death, no being, no non-being, no defilement, no purity, no increasing, no decreasing.

This is why, in no-thing-ness, physicality, emotional experiences, perceptions, thought process and consciousness are not separate self-created things. The six sense organs, the six sense objects and the six consciousnesses are also not separate self-created things.

The twelve links of conditioned causal continuity that is no-thing-ness, arising and subsiding are also not self-created entities. The causes of worrying and the arising of peace of mind, the Dharma journey, insight and realization are also not separate self-created things.

One who realizes this has no thing to attain. One who lives in accord with this realization that brings us to the other shore has no obstacles within this thing called mind. Because there are no obstacles, there is no fear, all perceptions are destroyed and they reside in peace of mind.

All beings, past and present, who practice this realization with integrity are capable of realizing peace of mind. Let it be known therefore that the insight that leads us to the other shore is a great mantra, a mantra that illuminates the mind, the highest mantra that is beyond compare. It is the realization of actuality that puts an end to worrying and re-becoming.

Let us all give voice to the mantra that proclaims the insight that will bring us to the other shore.

Gone. Gone. Gone beyond. Gone beyond the beyond.

Gate, Gate, Paragate, Parasamgate, Bodhi Svaha!
Gate, Gate, Paragate, Parasamgate, Bodhi Svaha!
Gate, Gate, Paragate, Parasamgate, Bodhi Svaha!

What we have to come to terms with is that we live in a conventional world of relative reality. We may have jobs to work at, families that keep us occupied, we have bills to pay, housework to be done, food to cook and eat, Facebook to attend to and a million and one other things to keep us busy. That's life. But, the more we bring the actuality of no-thing-ness into our everyday activities, by keeping it at the forefront of our mind so it can be explored within whatever it is we are doing or experiencing, the greater the opportunity there is for us to see for ourselves directly how our worries have preceding causes and conditions that we can search for.

We can come to experience for ourselves that they too have no intrinsic self existence and can be changed by simply changing our thought process. Although when we first begin to explore this subject matter it can seem almost farcical at times and scary at others, which is why many practitioners possibly do not engage with it with integrity. It is the pure genius of its practical application in our moment by moment everyday experience that will reveal to us directly the mistaken view that lies at the heart of the confusion that gives rise to worrying. The term no-thing-ness is not that attractive and can be confused at times with nothingness which is why I suggest much of the confusion has arisen around this source experience of the Buddha. Now that we have managed to unpack it a bit further perhaps we can now see why those two hyphens become so important.

In a later development of the Mahayana approach which began in the sixth century, originally in China and then later in Korea and Japan, we find a reintroduction of magical and mystical elements. Possibly because of the nature of those things that were pre-existent in these new cultural additions that formed a wider spread of Dharma communication. To facilitate this, an entire mythical context was created to provide a credible link back to the historical Buddha that at times stretches the imagination beyond irrational belief. But on another level it provides some very helpful practice methods and teachings that explore a very different aspect of causality that can help us to understand this fundamental source communication that is so difficult to get our heads around.

One of the great images and stories of this period is that of 'Indra's net.' When you first explore it you could be excused in thinking that it is some kind of left over remnant from the Hinduistic belief system of the Buddha's times as it makes reference to heavenly abodes occupied by the god Indra who is portrayed as the creator of the net. In some respects, when accepted in that way it has served to create the irrational belief aspect that now exists in a number of classical Buddhist schools. Once you can see your way through the fantasy element to what it is actually trying to communicate, you will find that it is showing yet another aspect of no-thing-ness. It invokes the imagination to see the universe as one giant net stretching out in all directions into infinity. At each intersection of the net there is a jewel that is a reflection of and at the same time reflecting all of the other jewels which in total represents the interconnectedness of all things in the field of actuality.

There is a possible danger here though, because this appears to have developed in line with Taoist thought which would point to things coming into existence simultaneously and being dependent on each other at the same time. This can then create the idea of what is often called oneness, the divine etc or a kind of unification of all things having a single identity, soul, spirit or God that underpins the connected parts of nature and is responsible for it in some way. That approach will work against the principle of causality that recognizes that things, on the relative level of reality, are things in themselves, but in actuality have no self-essence and are interconnected without any external controlling influence. So it is a very subtle difference to bear in mind.

Although it seems clear from the ancient texts that the Buddha did not deny or accept the existence of any kind of creator entity, if we understand the implications of his communication, then it becomes clear that it does not allow for such a thing to be remotely possible, just as it dismisses things such as randomness, luck, fate, chance and destiny.

It is suggested here that the view of interconnectedness that is more in-line with what the Buddha communicated is really a very practical method of thinking about and coming closer to the realization of causality. In its most simplistic format we could say that as all things emotional, physical, psychological or a combination of those things arise in dependence on an infinite number of interconnected preceding causes and conditions they depend on other things but are not the same thing at the same time.

There is so much reflection opportunity provided in relation to the interconnectedness aspect of causality. For example, if you just think of any household item in your cupboard like a packet of biscuits, just start to consider the implications of its existence. How many human beings has it taken throughout the history of mankind just for that one packet of biscuits to now exist in your cupboard? Look at how many component parts there are in that single packet of biscuits and the cupboard they are in. All of those components have their own infinite stream of preceding causes and conditions. All it takes is for one single cause or condition at any point in history not to have taken place and that packet of biscuits could not exist. This is the essence of under-standing this source realization of no separate self-essence. All things exist as separate things but are also connected with everything else and everybody else by virtue of conditioned causal continuity that is no-thing-ness.

What it does not mean, on the everyday level of relative real-ity, is that all things are interdependent as in circumstances like when you wake up in the morning in a depressed state or mood and it is somehow connected with the state of mind of the bloke down the chip shop. Nor does it mean that there is a direct connection between the tea you are drinking and the milk you put in it prior to drinking it. All of those things have their own set of specific causes and conditions that bring them into being but at the level of causality that is no-thing-ness there is interconnectedness because all things are simply inexpressible no-thing-ness.

Chapter Twenty: The Dharma Practitioner

Having established that there is only one thing in common to all Buddhists, as in the central act of going for refuge to the three jewels, we can now explore the major difference in approach between being a classical religious Buddhist and a secular western Dharma practitioner. Unlike previous reformations secular western Buddhism does not claim to be higher, better, deeper or superior to anything that has come before it. It salutes and respects the glorious past and its many dedicated participants, but will not collude with it.

The Buddha communicated actuality and that, as far as secular western Buddhism is concerned, needs to be applied to all aspects of Buddhism and its religious institutions. Within the context of this book a Buddhist therefore would be defined as someone who goes for refuge to the three jewels but is content to remain in the Buddhist world of hierarchical belief systems. A Dharma practitioner is someone who abandons the institutions and its obligations to explore the experiential aspects of the Dharma, as a living embodiment of it, within the fields of ethics, meditation and the development of insight.

Within this context what would not be consistent with being a Dharma practitioner falls into four categories:

1. If you cannot accept, even provisionally, that all things are impermanent, or if you believe that there is some essential essence to any thing

2. If you cannot accept, even provisionally, that all sensory and emotional experience contains an aspect of worry or if you believe that some of them can be sustained as pleasure

3. If you cannot accept, even provisionally, that all things are an expression of no-thing-ness, or if you believe things do exist in and of themselves

4. If you think that awakening exists within the spheres of time, space or power and is a permanent thing

In classical Buddhism these are known as the four seals. It is one of those teachings that doesn't get aired that often. Possibly because it is very confrontational and pulls no punches, so doesn't seem to fit with the usual warm and cuddly stuff. Their importance cannot be underestimated because they point directly to the source realization of the Buddha and that, after all, is why we have undertaken the journey to our own realization of it.

Within the awakening experience of clarity, the Buddha realized that all physicality, including our flesh and bones, all our emotions and perceptions are assembled. They are the product of two or more things coming together. When any two components or things come together a new thing emerges. Nails and wood becomes a table, water and leaves becomes tea. Fear, devotion and a saviour becomes a creator entity. This end product doesn't have an existence independent of its parts. Believing it truly exists independently is the greatest deception of all time. Just by meeting each other, the character of the parts has changed altogether. They have become some thing else. They are compounded. The Buddha realized that this applies not only to human existence but to all physical, emotional and psychological things in the known universe. This is because every thing is interconnected and subject to change. He could find not one single thing that had an autonomous, permanent state of being. Not this book you are reading, not atoms not even apparent gods. He found, that so long as some thing exists within reach of our mind, even in our imagination or our dreams, then it depends on the existence of some other thing. What he found was that impermanence did not mean death. It meant change.

With realization the Buddha found a way around the worries about death, or more importantly about non-existence. Having realized that change is inevitable and that death is just part of this cycle, he also realized that there was no almighty power that could reverse the path to death. Therefore there was no opportunity for him to be stuck in the world of fear driven belief. If there is no blind hope there can be no disappointment. If one realizes the actuality of impermanence, there can be no grasping. If one does not try and cling to stuff, there is no thought of having or lacking and therefore one lives a full and active life without the worries. By realizing that all things are assembled and have no state of permanence he was free.

By nature, the act of assembly is bound by time. It has a beginning, middle and an end. This book did not exist before it existed now and eventually it will be gone. Similarly the self that existed yesterday, that is 'you' is different from the self that exists today. Your bad mood has become a good mood. You may have learned something new. The cut on your hand has healed a little. Our apparent continuous existence is just a series of beginnings, middles and ends. Even an apparent creation moment like the Big Bang requires a time before existing, a time of coming into existence.

Those who choose to believe in a creator entity do not seem to understand this aspect of actuality. To give credit to an all-powerful, omnipotent creator defies actuality. If this world has always existed there would be no need for creation. Therefore it must have existed for a period of time before creation and thus a sequence of time is required. Since the apparent creator entity must, by virtue of actuality also be subject to the same rules of actuality, they too must be subject to change and must have only come into existence as a creator by some thing that preceded it which then negates it as being the creator.

If there is no paper, there is no book. If there is no water, there is no ice. If there is no beginning, there is no end. The existence of one is dependent on the other. If you explore this you can see that there can be no independence of any thing. Because of interdependence, if just one component part of a thing makes even the smallest shift, then the integrity of the thing is compromised and it changes into some thing else. If just one condition in a process spanning thousands of years, that includes thousand of people and thousands of other things that led to this book did not happen, then this book would not exist now.

Every change contains within it an element of death. Today is the death of yesterday and tomorrow will be the death of today. Most people accept that everything born must eventually die. But our definitions of everything and death may differ substantially from that of the Buddha. When he refers to death he means all created things, not just flowers, brussel sprouts and human beings, but every thing that comes into existence. This realization was not perhaps as spectacular as discovering a new star and having it named after you. It was not designed to propound moral judgments, or to establish a social movement or religion. Nor was it a prophesy. Impermanence is a simple mundane fact. Will, at some point in a possible yet to come future, this actuality be overturned? We can't say no, because that would be to deny impermanence. What we can say is that for at least 2,600 years the brightest minds of every age have done their damndest and continue to do their damndest to refute it, which may give us a reasonable clue. Yet the vast majority of the human species appears to choose to settle for a bind faith belief system that has no basis in verifiable actuality. How crazy is that?

2,600 years after his death at a time of year millions of people were celebrating, making merry and anticipating a new start some thing happened. It was a time to remember the birth of Jesus Christ for some. For others it meant preparing to take advantage of the New Years sales. For others a catastrophic tsunami shook the world to its foundations and it went into shock. The only possible response from a Buddha could be compassion, but com-passion that recognized the actuality aspect of it. This planet is made of volatile magma. Every land mass, including Australia, is like dew about to drop from the grass. Our insatiable deforesta-tion for the sake of disposable chopsticks and junk mail only invites impermanence to act more quickly. It should not surprise us to see this, but we are very hard to convince because of our drives of want, not want and confusion.

Yet, even after a devastating reminder like the tsunami, the death and destruction will soon be camouflaged and more or less hidden from us. Luxurious resorts will be erected on the very spot where families came to identify their loved ones. Many of those countries that were affected were traditional Buddhist countries and to add to their pain they were told by some within classical Buddhism that it was as a result of their karma, just as the people of Nepal were blamed for their earthquake by many Tibetan Buddhists.

No matter how many times an airplane flies into a building, no matter how many times famine strikes, no matter how many unnecessary conflicts kills off a significant number of a population and causes a refugee crisis, no matter how many bombs go off, human beings will continue to be caught up in compounding and fabricating actuality with hopes of achieving happiness. Wishing for 'happy ever after' is nothing more than a want for permanence in disguise. Fabricating concepts as 'eternal love,' 'everlasting happiness' and 'salvation' generates more evidence of impermanence. Our intention and the results are at odds with each other. We intend to establish ourselves and our world, but we forget that the corrosion begins as soon as creation begins. What we aim for is not decay, but what we do leads directly to it.

At the very least, the Buddha advises us that it is helpful to keep impermanence in mind and not to try and conceal it, or kid ourselves about it. By maintaining an awareness of assembled things we become aware of interdependence. Recognizing interdependence we recognize impermanence. When we remember that things are impermanent, we are less likely to be gripped by assumption, rigid beliefs, value systems or blind faith. Such awareness helps us not to get caught up in all kinds of personal, political and relationship dramas. We begin to understand that things are not under our control and never will be, so there is no expectation for things to go according to our hopes and fears. We can never find someone to blame, because what has happened has happened simply as a result of an infinite number of preceding causes and conditions.

When the Buddha spoke of all assembled things he was referring to more than just obviously perceivable things such as DNA, your cat, Ayres Rock or eggs and sperm. Mind, time and even the idea of a creator entity are also assembled. Each assembled component in turn depends on several layers of assembly. Similarly, when he taught impermanence, he went beyond conventional thinking about **'the end,'** such as the idea that death happens once and then its over. Death, in this context is continuous from the moment of birth, from the moment of creation. Each change is a form of death and therefore each birth contains the death of some thing else. When all the innumerable causes and conditions come together and there is no obstacle or interruption, the result is inevitable. Many mistake this to be fate, luck or destiny. But that is not what it is.

Life is little more than a vast array of assembled things. It is a constantly shifting set of transitory experiences that are impermanent. It neither has meaning nor is it meaningless. Although millions of life forms exist apart from us, we all have one thing in common. None of us wish to suffer. We all want to be content. But the definitions of suffering and contentment differ a great deal even within the small human realm. For some being content means managing to survive. For others, it means owning hundreds of pairs of shoes. Sometimes the price of that contentment can depend on the life of another being, like a want for shark fin soup or another bucket of fried chicken. Some consider the gentle tickle of a feather to be erotic, while others prefer cheese graters, whips and chains. Even within one individual those wants change over time.

Perhaps at your first school you noticed that all the other kids had the latest craze, designed pencil case. You developed a want to own one so you can fit in. You tell your mum about it and your happiness depends on whether she buys it for you or not. This continues throughout life. The next door neighbour has a plasma TV and you want the same, only bigger and newer. Some of these cultural definitions of happiness do work to some extent. In general, a sense of having a bit of money in the bank, comfortable shelter, enough food to eat, decent shoes and other basic comforts does make us happy. But then again, the sadhus of India and wandering hermits of Tibet experience happiness because they have no need for a key ring. They have no fear that their possessions will be stolen because they have nothing to be locked up.

We human beings occupy ourselves with the pursuit of happiness and the avoidance of our worries more than we do any other hobby or profession, employing innumerable methods and materials. This is why we have elevators, laptop computers, rechargeable batteries, battery operated nose hair clippers, toilets with heated seats, Viagra. But inevitably these conveniences provide an equal measure of headache and Viagra certainly does, or so I'm told.

Nations pursue happiness and the end of worries on a grand scale, fighting for territory, oil, space, financial markets and power. They wage pre-emptive wars to prevent anticipated worry. Individually we do the same by getting preventative medical care, taking vitamins, vaccines, blood tests, entire body CAT scans. We search for signs of impending worry and once we find the worry, we immediately try to find the cure. Each year new techniques, remedies and self-help books attempt to provide long-lasting solutions for worries and promise an end. But they never do.

The Buddha was also trying to end worries. But he was not dreaming up solutions such as starting a political revolution, migrating to another planet, or creating a new world economy. He wasn't even thinking about creating a religion or developing codes of conduct. He explored worries with an open mind and through meditation he realized that the root of our worry is found within our emotions. One way or another, directly or indirectly, all emotions are born from selfishness, in the sense that they involve clinging to the self-biased mind. He realized that, as real as they may seem, emotions are not an inherent part of one's being. They are not inborn, nor are they some sort of curse or implant that someone or some entity has thrust upon us. Emotions arise when particular causes and conditions come together, such as when you rush to think that someone is criticising you, ignoring you, or depriving you of some gain, then the corresponding emotions arise. The moment we accept those emotions, the moment we buy into them, we have lost awareness and sanity. We are worked up. If you examine emotions as the Buddha did, if you try to identify their origin, you will find that they are rooted in confusion and therefore fundamentally flawed. All emotions are basically a form of prejudice. Within each emotion there is always an element of judgment.

When we look at the body as a whole, we don't think in terms of its separate pieces, molecules, genes, veins and blood. We think of the body as a whole and we also prejudge that this is a truly existing organism called the body. Being convinced of this, we wish for a flat tummy, artistic hands, imposing height, dark & handsome features or a curvy figure. Then we become obsessed, investing time, money and energy into gym memberships, moisturisers, slimming tea, the Atkins diet, yoga, crunches and scented oils. As his meditation deepened the Buddha began to see the illusory quality of all things. He could now see that his own physical body was no-thing-ness. He discovered that as long as one believes that such things exist, either momentarily, or for all eternity one's belief is rooted in confusion and a lack of awareness. And when awareness is lost, that is what the Buddha refers to as confusion. It is from this confusion that our emotions emerge.

We are familiar with emotions such as love and hate, guilt and innocence, devotion, pessimism, jealousy and pride, fear, shame, sadness, joy. But there are so many emotions that we are unaware of. Apparently, in some parts of Asia there is no word that would describe romantic love but in Spain they have several words that describe different kinds of love. Some emotions are seemingly rational but most are irrational. Some seemingly peaceful emotions are rooted in aggression. We might even think someone is completely impassive or detached but that is itself an emotion. Emotions can be childish, like when you get angry because another person isn't angry and you think they should. Or you might be upset because your partner is too possessive and the next day be upset because they are not possessive enough. Some emotions manifest as arrogance such as the political power houses imposing their ideas of liberty on the world. Forcing our personal views on others through strength, blackmail, trickery or subtle manipulation is also a part of our emotional activity.

All of these various emotions and their consequences come from the root of confusion, the clinging to the self-biased mind. We assume that each of us is a self, that there is an entity called me. But the notion of a self is simply a misunderstanding. We are conditioned to view this notion as consistent and real. When we raise our hand we think 'I' am this hand. We think this is 'my' body. We think this body is 'me,' 'I' am tall. We think 'I' dwells in this body, pointing to the chest. We do the same with emotions, perceptions and actions. 'I' have emotions, 'I' am my perceptions. But the Buddha realized that there is no independent entity that qualifies as the self to be found anywhere, either inside or outside the body. The self is illusory. It is a fallacy, fundamentally flawed and ultimately non-existent. When we look at our own bodies, emotions, perceptions, actions and consequences, we see that these are different elements of what we think of as 'me.' But, if we examine them, we would find that 'me' doesn't dwell in any of them. Clinging to this fallacy of the self is a ridiculous act of confusion. It perpetuates our 'selves.' So if this perception is based in confusion then that confusion permeates everything we do, see and experience.

However, as unsound as the label 'self' may be, destroying it is no small task. This label called 'self' is the most stubborn of all concepts to break. From time immemorial we have been conditioned to be addicted to the self. It is how we identify ourselves. It's what we love most dearly. It's also what we hate most fiercely at times. Its existence is also the thing that we work hardest to try to validate. Almost everything we do or think or have, including our journey, is a means to confirm its existence. It is the self that fears failure and longs for success, fears hell and longs for heaven. The self loathes worry and loves the causes of worry. It stupidly wages war in the name of peace. It wishes for awakening but detests the journey to awakening. It wishes to work as a socialist but lives as a capitalist. When the self experiences loneliness, it wants friendship. Its possessiveness of those it loves manifests in passion that can lead to aggression. Its supposed enemies, such as paths designed to conquer the ego are often corrupted and recruited as the self's ally. Its skill in playing the game of deception is nearly perfect.

One might have a view that not all emotions are worry. What about love, joy, peace, fulfillment? Whilst emotions such as aggression, jealousy and headaches have an obvious unhelpful quality, others that we would normally see as helpful have much more subtle layers of worry. For the Buddha, anything that has a quality of uncertainty and unpredictability is worry. For instance, love may be pleasant and fulfilling, but it doesn't spring independently out of the blue. It depends on someone or something and therefore it is unpredictable. At the very least, one is dependent on the object of love and in a sense, always on a leash and the additional hidden conditions are uncountable. For this reason it is also futile to blame our parents for our unhappy childhood or to blame ourselves for our parents disharmony, because we are not aware of the many hidden dependent conditions involved in these situations.

There are of course things we can do to bend conditions to our advantage, such as taking vitamins to become strong or drinking a cup of coffee to wake up. But we can't hold the world still so that it won't stir up another tsunami. We can't prevent a bird from hitting the windshield of our car. We can't control the other drivers on the road. We might think that we aren't really worrying and even if we are, it isn't so terrible. After all, we aren't living in the gutter or being massacred in the latest conflict. Many people think, I'm OK, I'm breathing, I'm having breakfast, everything is going as well as can be expected, I am not worrying. But what do they mean? Do they mean 100%? Have they stopped preparing for things to get better? Have they dropped all their insecurities? If such an attitude comes from genuine contentment and appreciation for what they already have, this kind of appreciation is what the Buddha recommended. But rarely do we ever witness such content. There is always this constant nagging sense that there is more to life, and this discontent leads to worry.

The Buddha's solution was to develop awareness of the emotions. If you can be aware of emotions as they arise, even a little, you restrict their activity. They become like teenagers with a chaperone. Someone is watching and the power of the self-biased mind is weakened. So how do we develop awareness? The answer comes within the story of the Buddha's awakening experience. What was it that led to this experience? It had little to do with living an ethical lifestyle. It had little to do with living as a renunciate. These were thing he suggested that would be helpful. It had little to do with doing 100,000 prostrations or the endless lighting of candles and incense or chanting for hours some meaningless mantra or the wearing of particular garments. It was whilst seated in meditation, almost as a silent observer to the war going on in his head as the self-biased mind battled for supremacy that he discovered the solution to the cessation of worries.

By defeating the self-biased mind in meditation, the Buddha realized the no-thing-ness of inherent existence. He understood that everything we see, hear, emote, imagine and know to exist is simply no-thing-ness onto which we have labeled with certain trueness. The activity of labeling or perceiving the world as true is born out of a strong individual and collective habit. We all do it. The forces of habit are so strong and our concept of no-thing-ness is so unappealing that few have the will to pursue a realization such as the Buddha's. Instead, we wander like a disoriented desert traveler who sees a lush oasis in the distance. The oasis is actually just the reflection of heat on sand, yet out of desperation, thirst and hope, the wanderer identifies it as water. Using his last ounce of strength to get there, he discovers it is only a mirage and becomes filled with disappointment. Even though we don't consider ourselves to be so desperate, and believe that we are well educated, sane and sober, when we see and experience that everything truly exists, we are behaving like the man in the desert. We rush to find authentic companionship, security, recognition and success, or simply peace and quiet. We may even succeed in grasping some resemblance of our wants. But just like the wanderer, when we depend on external substantiation, eventually we are disappointed. Things are not as they seem. They are impermanent and they are not entirely within our control.

If we were to analyse, as the Buddha did, we will find that labels such as physicality, time, space, direction and size are easily dismantled. The Buddha realized that even the self exists only on a relative level, just like the mirage. His realization brought an end to his cycle of expectation, disappointment and worry. At the precise moment of his liberation a thought arose that was something like this: **"I have found a journey that is profound, peaceful, non-extreme, clear, wish-fulfilling and nectar-like"** No sooner had this thought subsided another arose, **"If I attempt to express it, if I try to teach it, there is no one capable of hearing, listening or understanding"**. As this thought fell away another arose, **"I shall remain in this peaceful state in the forest"**. Within the legend of the Buddha, at this juncture it is said that he was so overwhelmed by compassion for the suffering of all beings that he made the decision that he should at least attempt to teach what he had discovered and this marks the very beginning of what we now call Buddhism.

The Buddha was right to think that teaching would be no easy task. In a world that is driven by greed, pride, materialism, even teaching basic principles such as love, compassion and generosity is very difficult, let alone the actuality of no-thing-ness. We humans are stuck with our short-term thinking and bound by practicality. For us, something must be tangible and immediately useful in order to be worth our investment of time and energy, let alone actually paying for something. By those criteria, no-thing-ness as defined by the Buddha seems completely useless. With our limited rationale, we have a set definition of what makes sense and what is meaningful and no-thing-ness goes beyond that limit. It's as if the idea of no-thing-ness can't fit inside our heads. We operate as if thousands of years of history have preceded this moment and if someone were to tell us that the entirety of human evolution took place in the duration of a sip of coffee we would not be able to comprehend. But, imagine a week's holiday with your nearest and dearest. It goes like the snap of the fingers. On the other hand, one night in a cell with a rowdy rapist or serial killer would seem to last forever. Perceived in this way our concept of time might start to seem not so stable.

Some of us may permit a little bit of the unknown into our system of thinking, allowing some space for the possibilities of clairvoyance, intuition, ghosts, spirit guides, soul mates and so on. But for the most part we rely on black and white, scientifically based logic. A few people might have the courage to go beyond convention and as long as their view isn't too outrageous they might build up a bit of a following and there are some who deliberately go a little further beyond convention and are venerated as some kind of divine madmen. But, generally speaking, if you try and teach no-thing-ness you will be written off as abnormal, crazy and irrational and possibly either be assassinated as a threat to the status quo or find yourself in a straight jacket and padded cell. Is it no wonder then that those who have realized its actuality have at least an initial drive to keep it to themselves?

But let's be clear, the Buddha wasn't irrational, nor abnormal or crazy. He was merely asserting that conventional, rational thinking is limited. We cannot, or will not, comprehend that which is beyond our own comfort zone. It's much more functional to work with the concept of yesterday, today and tomorrow than to say time is relative. We continuously confine ourselves with safe and narrow perspectives that have been handed down for generations. When these perspectives are examined, however, they don't hold up. For example, take the concept of time upon which this world relies so heavily. How can time have a beginning and an end? For beginning to exist something must have existed prior to it to bring it into being and that we would have to call beginning and so on and so on. Using this rationale, we measure or label things as truly existing. Function, continuity and consensus play a major part in our process of validation. We think that if something has a function, for example your hand holding this book, then it must exist in a permanent ultimate sense. A picture of a hand doesn't function in the same way, so we know it isn't really a hand. Similarly, if something seems to have a continuous quality, for example if we saw the local coffee shop yesterday and it was there again today we are confident it is real and will be there tomorrow and the next day. And when other people confirm that they see the same things we see, we are even more certain that these things truly exist.

Of course, we don't walk around consciously rationalising, confirming and labeling the true existence of things, but subconsciously we operate in the confidence that the world solidly exists and this affects how we think and emote every moment of the day. On rare occasions, perhaps when we look in the mirror, or at a mirage we do appreciate that some things are mere appearances. After all, there is no flesh and blood in the mirror. There is no water in the mirage. We know that these mirror images are not real, that they have no inherent actuality of their own. This kind of understanding can take us much further, but we only go as far as our rational mind allows. Of course, we say that some things change. A bud blooms into a flower and we still think of it as a truly existing flower as it changes. That growth and change is part of our fixed idea about the nature of the flower. We would be much more surprised if it became permanent. A river flows with fresh water, always changing and we still call it a river. If we visit that place a year later we think it is the same river. But how is it the same? If we isolate one aspect or characteristic, this sameness falls apart. The water is different, the Earth is in a different place in its rotation through the galaxy, the leaves have fallen and been replaced, all that remains is an appearance of a river similar to the one that we saw last time. Appearance is quite an unstable basis for actuality.

The Buddha found that the only way to confirm something as existing is to prove that it exists independently and free of interpretation, fabrication or change. For the Buddha, all of the seemingly functional mechanisms of our everyday survival, physical, emotional and conceptual fall outside of that definition. They are all put together from unstable, impermanent parts and therefore always changing. We can understand this within the confines of the conventional world. For example, you could say that your reflection in the mirror does not truly exist because it depends on you standing in front of it. If it were independent, then even without your face, there should be a reflection. Similarly, no thing can truly exist without depending on so many unaccountable conditions. Because we don't see things as parts we settle for looking at them as a whole. If all the feathers are plucked from a peacock, we are no longer impressed by it. But we are not eager to surrender to seeing the entire world in this way. It's like being curled up in bed having a good dream, slightly conscious that you are dreaming and not wanting to wake up. Or seeing a beautiful rainbow and not wanting to get too close because it will disappear. Having the courage to wake up and examine is what Dharma practitioners do.

You may still be pondering what is the benefit of understanding no-thing-ness? Well, by understanding no-thing-ness, you maintain an appreciation for all that appears to exist, but without clinging to the confusion as if they were real and without the incessant disappointment of a child chasing a rainbow. You see through the confusion and are reminded that the self-biased mind created them in the first place. You may still get stirred up or emotional, sad, angry or passionate, but you have the confidence of someone at the cinema who can leave the drama behind because there is a clear understanding that it is just a movie. When we have not realized no-thing-ness, when we don't fully understand that all things are viewed by the self-biased mind, the world seems real, tangible and solid. Our hopes and fears also become solid and uncontrollable as a result. For example, if you have a solid belief in your family, you have a deep-seated expectation that your parents will take care of you. You don't think that way about a stranger on the street. They have no such obligation. Understanding assembled things and understanding no-thing-ness allows for some room in the relationship. As you begin to see the various experiences, pressures and circumstances that moulded your parents, your expectations of them change, your disappointment lessens. When some of us become parents ourselves, even a little understanding of interdependence effectively softens our expectations of our children, which they may interpret as love. Without that understanding, we might have good intentions to love and care for our children, but our expectations and demands can become unbearable.

Similarly, by understanding no-thing-ness you lose interest in all the trappings and beliefs that society builds up and tears down – political systems, science and technology, global economy, free society, the United Nations. You become like an adult who is not so interested in children's games. For so many years you have trusted these institutions and believed that they could succeed where past systems have failed. But the world has not yet become safer, more pleasant, or secure. This is not to say that you should drop out of society. Having an understanding doesn't mean that you become blasé. What arises is a sense of responsibility and compassion. More often than not, many of us choose to stay in the dark. We aren't able to see the confusion that creates everyday life because we don't have the courage to break out of the network that we're plugged into. We think that we are, or will soon be, comfortable enough if we continue on as we are going.

It's as if we are entering a maze through which we already have a habitual route and we don't want to explore other directions. We are not adventurous because we think we have so much to lose. We fear that if we see the world from the view of no-thing-ness, we may be cast out from society, lose our respectability and along with it our friends, family, job etc. The seductive allure of the confused world of the self-biased mind doesn't help because it is packaged so well. We are bombarded with messages about soap that makes us smell like heaven, how miraculous the seaweed diet is, how democracy is the only viable system of government, how vitamins will increase our stamina. We rarely hear more than one side of the story and when we do it's usually in the fine print at the bottom of the page. Like a child at the cinema, we get caught up in the confusion. With this arises all of our vanity, ambition and insecurity. We fall in love with the illusions we have created and develop excessive pride in our appearance, our possessions and our accomplishments. It's like wearing a mask and proudly thinking that the mask is really you.

Nirvana, enlightenment, awakening, liberation, freedom, heaven. These are words that many people like to utter and few have time to examine how it would be to enter into them. Within classical Buddhism many Buddhists have come to believe that nirvana is a place. Even though they may think that nirvana is far different from theistic heaven or paradise, their versions of heaven and nirvana have roughly the same characteristics. Heaven/nirvana is where we go when we die after many years of paying our dues, doing practice and being good citizens. We will meet many of our old comrades because it is a place where all the 'good' people gather, while the not so-good people suffer down below. We finally have a chance to solve life's mysteries, finish unfinished business, make amends and maybe see into our past lives. Small babies without sex organs fly around doing our ironing. Our dwelling meets our every want and is well situated in a community of other nirvana/heaven dwellers who obey the rules. We never have to lock the windows and doors and there is probably no need for police. If there are politicians, they are all reliable and honest. Everything is exactly to our liking. It's like a very pleasant retirement home. Or perhaps some of us imagine the purest of white light, spaciousness, rainbows and clouds upon which we rest in a blissful state practicing our powers of clairvoyance and omniscience. There is no death to fear because you are already dead and there is nothing to lose. The only concern we might have is worrying about some of our dear friends and family members whom we've left behind.

The Buddha found these versions of the afterlife to be fantasies. Under close scrutiny, the typical version of heaven is not that attractive and neither is that vision of nirvana. Retirement, honeymoons and picnics are pleasing, but not if they're infinite. If our dream vacation lasts too long, we become nostalgic for home. It wouldn't take very long for an ardent Jimmy Barnes fan to be fed up with all that harp music. Immortality is another attribute commonly assigned to nirvana or heaven. Once we arrive at our new home in the clouds, we will never die again, so we have no choice but to live on forever. We are stuck. There is no escape. We have everything we ever dreamed of except a way out. Surprises, challenges, satisfaction and free will are no longer part of our experience because we don't need them anymore. From this perspective this image of heaven is beginning to look now like the ultimate state of boredom. But most of us don't critically examine our version of an afterlife; we prefer to keep it vague, with a general sense that it is a good final resting place. Or some may think that they can come back for a visit as a sort of deity or higher being that possesses special powers we mortals don't have. But then the question arises, if some of these new immigrants have their own set way of thinking that might distract other heavenly beings won't heaven have a problem? And if all the 'good' people are given membership to heaven or nirvana, whose version of happiness prevails?

No matter how we define it, the ultimate goal of every being appears to be happiness. It's no wonder that happiness is an indispensable part of the definition of heaven or nirvana. A good after life should include finally getting what we have always strived for. Generally, in our personal version of heaven we live in a system that is similar to our current system, except that it's more sophisticated and things work better. Many classical Buddhists seem to believe that the ultimate achievement on the Dharma journey comes only after this life is over. That we are stuck with these impure surroundings and bodies, therefore we must die in order to fully succeed. Only after death will we experience the divine or enlightened state. So the best thing we can do in this life is prepare for it. What we do now will determine whether we go to heaven or to hell. Some people have already lost hope. They believe they are inherently bad or evil and don't deserve to go to heaven, they are predestined for the netherworld. Similarly, many Buddhists know intellectually that everyone has the same potential and the same nature as the Buddha, yet emotionally they believe that they don't have the qualities or abilities to gain access to the golden gates of enlightenment. At least not in this life.

For the Buddha, the ultimate resting place of heaven or nirvana isn't a place at all. It's a release from the straightjacket of confusion. If you demand that a physical place be specified, then it can be where you are sitting right now. The Buddha's version of freedom is non-exclusive. It is realizable in this life, depending on courage, wisdom and the effort of the individual. There is no one who doesn't have this potential. It was not the Buddha's aim to be happy. His journey does not ultimately lead to happiness. Instead it is a direct route to freedom from worry, freedom from confusion. Thus nirvana is neither, happiness or unhappiness. It goes beyond all such dualistic concepts.

Chapter Twenty One: Practicalities

Depressive thinking, emotional stress and psychological anxiety, appear to be the plague of modernity within western culture. This is why, it is suggested here, that the no worries, secular western approach to Buddhism, meditation, life and actuality provides a helpful response to this level of worrying within our society. It does this by removing the religious dogma, the institutionalized hierarchical structures of elitism and the rites and rituals of cultural superstitions and beliefs. It promotes a context that aims to get back to the very simple, down-to-earth and practical aspects of what the Buddha communicated. In this final chapter we will explore how this context can be practically applied in relation to those areas of greatest concern within our society, which for ease of communication will be spoken of in this chapter as depression.

In 2016 a world-wide study was published which claimed, that for the third year in succession, Australia was found to be the happiest place on earth to live. This study was based on income, jobs, housing and health. Two weeks earlier the West Australian health department released statistics that claimed Western Australia had the highest levels, per head of capita in the western world, of depression. It became clear that the criteria for the first study was based on apparent happiness linked to material worth and physical health but it failed to see beyond to the possible consequences of such a materialistic lifestyle that, according to the Buddha, could never sustain genuine, long-term happiness. It seemed clear to me that we in the west have, over time, created a system in which our materialistic growth actually fuels the growth of our worries and as a result we have a ticking time-bomb of despair just waiting to explode.

According to my dictionary, depression is an emotional state, characterised by experiences of gloom and inadequacy. If you have ever experienced any form of depressive episode, I am sure that you would see this description as being just a little bit derisory, especially when you recall, or consider, the level of pain and distress you have experienced, or are still experiencing. The secular western approach to depression is aligned to the very first teaching of the Buddha over 2,500 years ago in a deer park in Sarnath, Northern India It is the first of the four principle assignments, the existence of worry.

It needs to be understood from the outset that this book and certainly not this chapter, is not designed to be an explanation of, or a cure for depression. It should also not be assumed that it is being suggested that you shouldn't seek treatment or counseling. The main focus of this chapter is to show you how depression, like everything else in life, can be a helpful experience if you are willing to find compassion for yourself in the midst of the dull pain of it. Essential to this discovery is a willingness to look closely and to go beyond our own pre-conditioned ideas and beliefs. In this chapter you will read many things that will seem to go against what you have been conditioned to believe and think. When something sounds unhelpful or doesn't make sense, just try, as best as you can to put any immediate unhelpful reactions to one side and come back to the subject matter later, when you might see things differently, after you've had the opportunity to consider it for a while. It's helpful to also bear in mind that if the answers you already have were working for you, you wouldn't still be looking for an answer. Always remember that it takes a lot of courage to step into uncharted territory and although this journey we will be exploring might, at times, be emotional and maybe a bit scary, I am sure that if you stay with it you will find it very worthwhile.

This chapter has four primary aims. The first is to try and help you to see what the cause of your depression is, the second is to try and help you to accept where you are, the third is to help you to embrace yourself with compassion and finally the fourth is to try and help you to let go and end the depression. We begin with something for you to consider and it is this: **'The state of depression is not the problem.'** It is the process of depressing that is the problem. If you are depressed try asking yourself "What am I depressing?" You might find that a pattern begins to emerge very quickly. Do you tend to try and deny the experience you are having or do you indulge it? The solution to the problem of depression, as with everything else the Buddha taught is to be found by turning our attention inwards.

The important thing to understand about depression, in general, is that it is not random. You experience, think, say and believe the same things every time. Perhaps what you are depressing changes but how you depress remains the same. The only way we can know what is going on is to sit down with an open mind and pay attention. If we watch closely enough, we will notice that there are sensations in our bodies that go with depression. They don't vary. They're the same every time. We have a labeling system that goes with those sensations. In this case the label we have given it is depression. With this label comes a learned reaction the self-talk – everything we've been taught to believe about depression. What it is, what it means, what I am for experiencing it, what will happen as a result or how the future will be. When self-talk starts, we have an emotional reaction to it. I don't want this, I am afraid, this is too painful, oh no, not this again. This is followed by a conditioned behaviour pattern which is usually avoidance of some kind. I should quit my job, I've got to leave town, I need a drink, I want a divorce, I'm going to kill myself, I can't function etc. The important thing to notice is that there is a sequence. First there is a sensation, followed by a thought, followed by an emotion, followed by a behaviour pattern. This sequence is going on all the time not just in depression and it doesn't vary.

There is a lovely saying within the Zen tradition that I find helpful to explain what approach we need to be taking to bring an end to depression and it is this: **"Train as if your hair is on fire"**. It means don't wait. Get immediately into the present moment and do what the moment requires. If your hair was on fire it would not be helpful to panic and race around in all directions would it? Neither would it be a good idea to have a quick nap. The most helpful thing to do would be to get present, assess the situation and then move to the nearest source for help. Dunk your head under the water, grab a fire extinguisher, smother the flames, yell for help. In other words if you think you are depressed, see your doctor, see a therapist, start an awareness practice, learn to meditate and most important of all become the worlds leading authority on depression - especially your own.

Bear in mind that the advice of the Buddha is that each of us is solely responsible for ourselves and that we must work out our own solution diligently. Your G.P is a trained professional. Be open to their suggestions but don't just accept them as a matter of blind faith. Try what they suggest. See if it works for you. Be open to what a therapist has to offer because you are in a 'leave no stone unturned' process here, but don't just take it as gospel because they have a lot of letters behind their name. A Buddhist teacher might say this or that and it might seem to make sense but don't agree or disagree – find out. Assume nothing. Look everywhere.

As you begin to take this approach to depression you will find that your life will begin to change. It will change for many reasons, but I would suggest that the main reason for the change is that someone is putting interested, kind, caring, supportive time and energy into you and right now that's what you need more than anything. Can meditation cure depression? No. But it is recognised to be helpful. But few appear to be willing to take that route. Why? Because we want quick fixes. We want to take a pill and never have to face the issues that are resulting in depression.

As children, we learned that when we operated from who we are, we got into trouble. We learned that there is something wrong with us. Because we don't want to experience that again we try harder and harder to be the person we're supposed to be. If we could only realize that there was nothing wrong with us in the first place we'd be heading in the right direction. It's OK to be who you are. It's OK to have all your emotional experiences. That's what human beings have – experiences. Being depressed is like wearing sunglasses with black lenses. When you have them on everything looks dark. When we respond to the circumstances of our lives by putting on the dark glasses of depression, we are responding from a lifetime of conditioning. We have learned that certain situations require certain reactions, and the very thought of not reacting the way we 'should' frightens us, if we even think of it at all. When we find ourselves wearing those glasses, it is possible, through a process of acceptance and compassion, to take them off. Even though this notion of ending the depression sounds very appealing, to a part of us it seems like death. It leaves a hole in our identity, an empty space that usually appears unbearably uncomfortable.

You may, by now, be wondering if this chapter is for you, after all, you are not depressed. Well, you don't think you are at least. Remember that this chapter is about the secular western Buddhist approach to the problems of human existence of which worry plays an integral part. Within this context, this experience that we have labelled depression is little more than an exaggerated form of what each and every one of us experiences almost all of the time. Let's remind ourselves of what the Buddha had to say about depression. He taught that worrying exists because old age, sickness and death are inescapable. Another way of describing worry is that we want what we don't get, aren't satisfied with what we do get, are separated from those or that which we love and are forced to endure those and that which we do not love. Does that sound familiar? Depressed or not this chapter is for you.

There is a very helpful exercise that you might like to engage with to help you to understand this a bit deeper. Imagine that you are someone that you have no reason to dislike. Pay attention to all your thoughts, sensations emotions and begin to write them down as you experience them. Don't try analysing the experience. Just allow it to come out like a volcano. Spew it out. Express it in any way you can. Stay tuned into this person that you like until you express everything that you need to express. Go through all the thoughts and emotions that arise until it seems like you get to the end of it. The point of this exercise is to begin to see your individual patterns. If you pay attention to this exercise closely and often you will see the steps you take that lead to self-rejection and depression. You will notice your fears and assumptions and conditioned reactions to circumstances. It will become clear that depression is something you do, not some larger-than-life monster to which you are a victim. What we are moving towards with this exercise is letting go of everything that keeps us from being present with our authentic selves.

Two of the most unhelpful phrases in the English language are **'what if'** and **'yes but'**. They create doubt, indecision and close the mind to things we might otherwise find helpful. One other area that causes confusion for us is that we fail to understand the difference between what we call feelings (emotional experiences) and thoughts and it is vital that we do understand the difference if we are to make progress. When someone asks us how we're feeling we say **"I'm feeling depressed"**. That isn't a feeling. That's a thought. If you turn your attention to what you are actually experiencing, rather than what you're thinking, you will find all manner of things going on that have little or no connection with depression. A common example is **"I'm feeling tearful"**. No you're not. You're either tearful or you are not. The tears arise only as a result of a depressed thought.

A common pattern emerges when we confuse thoughts with emotional experiences. Even the most severely depressed individual isn't in a state of depression all of the time. Like everything else, depression isn't a permanent experience. It moves in and out with our thought process. When we are distracted, our attention is turned away from our depression. For a while we are not aware of the depression. As soon as the distraction stops our thought process kicks in with **"Oh, I forgot I'm depressed. I have no reason to be feeling good"** and off we go again until the next distraction. We have come to believe that depression is the only helpful reaction to this situation in our life. We think that anyone would be depressed if they were in the same position as us and as a result the depressing thoughts re-emerge and we are officially depressed again.

We don't need to be looking for excuses or justification for what our experience is. It is better to just stay focused on how we experience something. Then why we experience that way will become apparent. Trying to figure out in our heads why we are emoting a certain way just takes us further and further away from ourselves. It is never helpful to use a thought to figure out an emotional reaction. For example: when grieving, give yourself permission to experience whatever you are experiencing physically, emotionally and psychologically instead of having standards about how you should be. It's not true that certain emotions are OK and others are not. OK and not OK are thoughts. When we put thoughts in charge of emotions we get into trouble. It's not the emotion we're having that's a problem - it's our judgment about that emotion. We could be experiencing anything and if we weren't telling ourselves it was wrong in some way, there would be no problem. The problem comes when we reject ourselves for what we're experiencing.

Our emotions are the most intimate experience we have of ourselves. Very often we think we need to blame ourselves for our emotions, or experience guilt about them and then punish or discipline ourselves. But really, what we do about our emotions determines the quality of our relationship with ourselves. We are responsible to how we experience rather than for how we experience. If we can create a safe, loving place within ourselves for how we experience, then we can create it for all the aspects of who we are. Get used to looking to see how you experience. Don't assume you know. As long as we're depressed, we don't know how we're actually are. It's only when we say yes to ourselves and stop depressing that how we're experiencing becomes available to us.

The reason that the Buddha gave as to why human experience is tainted by worry is that we want things to be other than they are. This is a huge problem for us as we have a conditioned reaction to the world around us. We are sensory beings. We see, hear, taste, touch, smell. The problem of wanting arises because we also think. When we engage with any one of our senses there is an automatic response of "I like" or "I don't like". Rarely are we indifferent to a sense experience and even if we were, it wouldn't take too long before we would want it to be something we like. If we now link this teaching to the subject of depression we can perhaps see how accurate it is.

If you came to me and said you were feeling depressed it would be natural for me to say something like: "What's going on" or "Why do you think you are depressed" and then we would start talking about it. First you would talk about the 'what's, the external elements of your situation. This isn't working, that isn't working and I feel this and I feel that. Then we would start talking about what is going on under that and you would say "Well, this is going on and that is going on". Then we'd talk about what's under that and as we worked our way through the multi-layers we would eventually get to the actuality: "I don't like this, I don't want this, I don't want to be having this experience".

Well, you are. So, now, how can you sit still with that? How can you be with that? In our practice we take the next step of how can you embrace that? How can you be with that as though you were being with one of your children who came to you and said "Mom, I'm depressed". You wouldn't say "Get out of here. I don't want to hear that kind of talk". The practice is to develop the same relationship with yourself that you would be willing to have with someone you love or even perhaps with someone you hardly know.

You might be surprised to learn that there are some people who don't even find depression particularly troubling. They have more difficulty with things like happiness or anger. So it's just whatever a person has identified as a really big problem that becomes a problem for them. The strangest thing about depressive episodes is that the very thing that arises with them, is the very thing that will prevent us from overcoming them. It is the fear and hatred of it that will keep you stuck and not the depression. Initially this might sound preposterous or absurd because our automatic reaction would be to say "Why would I want to maintain depression? I hate depression. I don't want to be depressed. I want to get over it. I don't want to experience this ever again." Well, the answer might just sound too simplistic but sit with it for a while - Stop hating it!

But then you'll say "How can I stop hating it? If I do that I'll be depressed all the time. The only thing that's keeping me from being constantly depressed is that I hate depression". When dealing with depression, the biggest problem of all is trying to teach a person to be open to the possibility that what they think is going on might not actually be going on. Everything in our conditioning tells us that the way to get rid of something is to hate it – hate it out of existence, resist it out of existence and to propose that it is our own resistance that is maintaining the problem can be too hard for people to accept. We are conditioned to believe that there is something wrong with depression. We need to hide it, reject it or deny it. As soon as we can understand that it is OK we become free to explore exactly what it is. We can only begin to do this if we are at least open to the possibility that it's nothing like our previously fixed idea of what we believed it was. We have to learn to let go - to stop resisting and this will involve a practical element.

What follows is a meditative exercise that has been specifically designed to help you to engage with the subject matter in this chapter. Give it a go. Remember, this is a leave no stone unturned approach. Begin by finding a sitting position that is comfortable and one that will keep you alert to the practice. A position where the back is upright and the hands supported - gently close the eyes and take two or three very deep breaths, filling the entire body with new breath until you are almost at bursting point and then letting go with some force. See if you can keep your attention focused on the breath as it enters your body, as it fills your body and as it leaves your body. Nothing to do but breathe. Having no concern for anything other than breathing in and breathing out.

Now, just allow your breath to return to its own normal pattern. Not trying to change or alter it in any way. Spend a few moments checking in with your body, allowing your awareness to expand to include your entire body from head to toe, Being open to the body. Aware of it. Sensitive to it in a way that will allow it to tell you what is going on.

Now, taking a longer, deeper breath, shift your awareness to what you are experiencing emotionally. Once again being open, being available to what you experience. See if you can just be open to any insights your emotions might hold for right now. Allow for some silent learning space and repeat as many times as you are comfortable with.

Now, another deep breath. Allow your awareness to expand to include your thought process. Not trying to change anything, improve anything – just noticing. Allow for some silent learning space and repeat as many times as you are comfortable with.

Now, taking another deep breath and just let go. Just allow yourself to let go completely and absolutely. Let yourself experience what it is like when you let go completely.

What is this like for you? Is it like laughing, dancing, running? Perhaps as you let go, you are aware that there is something that stops you from letting go completely. Allow yourself to become aware of that as completely as you can for now. What is it that keeps you from letting go? Where is it in your body? What does your body experience when you're holding on, when you're resisting? What happens with you emotionally when you can't let go? What keeps you from letting go? Is it your emotions? What is it like in your mind when you can't let go? How does your mind keep you from letting go? When you find something within you that keeps you from letting go, see if you can simply acknowledge it. Thank it for taking care of you and protecting you in the way that it does. Allow for some silent learning space and repeat as many times as you are comfortable with.

Take another deep breath and let go. Just experience yourself let go. No restraint. No concern. Relaxing completely. What is that experience like? Is it calm? Is it peaceful? Letting go totally. See if you can take it to an even deeper level. If you run into something that stops you, once again see if you can just acknowledge it, just allow it, simply breathing in and breathing out. Nothing separating you from all that is. Allow for some silent learning space and repeat as many times as you are comfortable with.

Just stay with these things and when you are ready, taking as much time as you wish, slowly bring your attention back into the room and slowly open your eyes.

One of the processes that we pay close attention to in our practice goes like this: there is movement, sensation; a label goes with that sensation, an emotional reaction and then a conditioned behaviour pattern. We do this so we can begin to let go of the labeling system we have developed to go with the particular sensation. We don't need to change anything. We just need to realize that sensations don't mean anything and certainly not what we have always thought they meant.

In Eastern philosophy there is the concept of what are called chakras. Let me say straight away there is apparently no medical or scientific evidence to support this concept, but bear with me as it can be useful to see that there may be a connection with depression that we might find useful. In all, there are apparently seven chakras, ranging from the tip of the spine to the crown of the head but there are three in particular which seem to me, to play a big role in the relationship between worry and depression as they reflect the typical behaviour patterns that arise with depression.

The sixth chakra, located in the head, is where our social conditioning resides. The sixth chakra knows how everything should be and is very concerned with control. The third chakra, located n the solar plexus, near the stomach, is the will centre, the centre that enables us to exert our influence in the world. The third chakra is the 'do' chakra. The second chakra, located in the belly just below the navel, is the emotional centre. As we are being socialised, we learn to have the sixth chakra (how we have been taught we should be) use the third chakra (the will) to control the second chakra (emotion). There is a continual downward pressure of control, a need to keep our emotions in check so that we can continue to do what the control is saying we should be doing. Taking control, getting ourselves under control or controlling our behaviour are all a process of depressing. Numbing ourselves with food, drugs, alcohol, sex etc is also a process of depressing

For example: we start to get upset about something and we get nervous. The worry builds and the voices in your head are going crazy with all the things that are going to happen if you don't get a grip on yourself. Your stomach is in a knot. This is where you're likely to pour yourself a good stiff drink. It is at this point we will do almost anything to numb or dissipate those physical sensations and most of the things we do will be unhelpful to us. One thing that is widely recognised as being helpful for us in these situations is exercise. Exercise frees energy blocked in the solar plexus and dissipates it in a healthy way. Meditation will calm that energy without deadening, dissipating or depressing it. As we sit still, attending closely to what we are experiencing, we realize that what we have learned to call worry (and learned to be afraid of) is simply sensation in the body. Energy, the life force that animates us, moves and we experience the effects of that movement as sensation.

As we become familiar with the sensation in the third chakra, we also become more comfortable with it. As we sit quietly, we see that sensations don't mean anything. At some point in the conditioning process something happened and two things got put together that, in fact, don't go together. 1. that sensation in my stomach 2. means something is wrong. As we sit in meditation, watching the sensations come and go and watching what we label those sensations and continuing to simply sit, we realize we don't need to cling to that old reaction to a current situation. Nothing is threatening. You are not in any danger. You're sitting in meditation. This is just sensation in my body. I don't need to do anything. If I leave it alone it will pass. Try and understand that depression is a label. In actuality, you are simply experiencing what is happening. The big question is how much of your problem is with the way you actually experience and how much is with what you are telling yourself about how you experience.

One of the most commonly depressed emotions is anger. When we are children, anger is frightening because it is so unacceptable to adults. We experience anger, but it's more threatening to have it than not to have it so we learn to depress it because we are afraid. We often turn this anger inward against ourselves. As adults we can react with guilt, fear, self-hate, illness, aggression etc. What is helpful to be doing is treating our emotions like house guests. If we give them the master bedroom with the hot tub and flat screen TV they're never going to want to leave. But if we throw a sleeping bag on the floor of the garage they won't think that they are too welcome. We need to find the place in-between where they think they are welcome but know they're not invited to stay forever. In Buddhist terms we are seeking here to find the middle path. Remember, don't meet the guests at the door with a shotgun. They'll only come down the chimney and creep up behind you. What we resist, persists.

The dilemma of human existence according to the Buddha is that we want what we can't have. As soon as we make something forbidden, it becomes the most desirable thing in the world. An emotion that is rejected gets stronger. It becomes like a dog that you don't feed enough or a child who doesn't get enough attention. It becomes desperate. Don't be afraid of your emotional experiences. Learn to express them to yourself. It is always safe to express what and how you experience to yourself. Don't worry, you won't lose control. The reason we lose control is that we haven't expressed our thoughts and emotions. We think we have to keep them damned up or else there will be a flood. But, if we never damned them up in the first place, a flood would be much less likely.

You can try opening up to yourself a little at a time until the pressure is down. All you have to do is acknowledge how you are and then treat yourself as you would treat a friend who was the same way. This is a common time for one of those useless saying to appear: yes but... I should know better... yes but... I have no right to be like this... yes but... I've done something wrong... yes but... I've brought this on myself... yes but.... It's all my fault. Rubbish! The most likely reason you're having this experience is that you haven't loved yourself enough. A good beating never helped anything, except possibly a rug and aren't you tired of being one yet?

Adopting the Buddhist approach to depression involves learning to trust yourself and we don't trust people who beat us up. If we're going to find out who we are, we have to stop beating ourselves up long enough to open up to ourselves in order to find out who we are. My top four tips to help you change your relationship with depression are:

1. Set limits. Say no if life is making more demands than you can meet. Instead of doing and doing until you can't take anymore and you explode, learn to recognise the signs sooner
2. Stop beating yourself up
3. Take care of yourself. Do this not in a minimal, miserly sort of way because you think that's all you deserve, but in a loving, generous way. Be kinder to yourself than you think you should be
4. Develop awareness. Sit quietly. Focus on your breath. Observe your thoughts, physical sensations and emotions, holding onto nothing, pushing nothing away. If you notice yourself tensing up, stop and return to the breath, no judgments

Here is another practical exercise you can try. It's more about developing an attitude of mind rather than following a list of things to do. When doing this keep in mind that, if you are kind and caring towards yourself, nothing you do will be unhelpful. Is there anything more important than bringing compassion to the one person you know really needs it? And if that old fear of becoming self-indulgent rises up, just remind yourself that you are training to be able to be unconditionally compassionate towards all of life. If you cannot be kind to the one person whose worrying you can actually experience, you will never be able to be kind to anyone. This is the most unselfish work a human being can do. See how you get on. Try and include as many as you can in each day for a while and pay attention to what happens.

1. Consciously put yourself first at least once a day
2. Do something each day just because you enjoy it
3. Break any big task into several small steps and do one at a time
4. Ask yourself how you experience and listen to the answer
5. Stop assuming you know yourself
6. Lower your standards

424

7. Rest a while

8. Congratulate yourself each time you accomplish anything

9. Make time for people who help you to develop a helpful state of mind

10. Say kind things to yourself

11. Give yourself time off from hard things. No big decisions. No big changes

12. Let yourself say "Me first"

13. Practice not believing the unhelpful critical voices in your head

14. Go for a walk and take in as much of nature as you can

15. Let yourself know you are worth any amount of effort

16. Find people who can give you support

17. Trust yourself

18. Just sit and be for at least ten minutes every day

Acceptance plays a crucial role in alleviating our worries and it is aligned to the third principal assignment that the Buddha sets out in his primary communication. We have learned of the existence of worry and of the cause of that worry. With acceptance, we now learn that it can be alleviated or eradicated. Acceptance precedes even recognition. You will not be willing to see what you are experiencing until you are willing to accept what you are experiencing. As long as we're trying to avoid being who we are or seeing who we are at any level, we are doomed to remain in these conditioned habitual patterns of behaviour that will keep us trapped. Each time we grasp our willingness to see these things, without judgment, if possible, we take one step closer to freedom.

If you see something you don't like about the way you are and you beat yourself up for it, pretty soon you will have trained yourself to stop looking. The only thing that gives these unhelpful thoughts any power is our fear of them. If you were to welcome them eagerly with open arms, they wouldn't appear. The more you genuinely try to invite them in, the more unavailable they are. It goes something like this: OK, I'm ready. I'm going to face this. I'm willing. I'm really going to see how this works. OK, come on depression. Come on. Where are you? Talk to me? What have you got to say? Big silence! But the moment I forget and the willingness to be open isn't there, and I think I've let go of depression, and I'm hoping I'm better and I'm hoping I'll never be depressed again, the moment I forget not to resist, it's back!

There are a number of things that will always be helpful and unhelpful to you. It will be unhelpful to raise your standards to a level where you're going to be dissatisfied. Not doing what gives your life meaning or repressing how you are and with that depressing the life you know you could be living. Things you will find helpful are staying present, not trying to change anything, accepting what is. We tend to believe that if we accept things as they are without trying to change them they'll always be with us. In our experience the opposite is true. We maintain our depression by resisting it. As long as we're resisting, we're putting our energy into whatever it is we don't want. As soon as we accept the depression, in that moment it is different.

We can actually use depression as a tool for self discovery because we depress what we're experiencing for a reason. For example, I'm angry; I depress that anger and in focusing on the depression I don't need to see that under that anger is hurt and under that hurt is disappointment and under the disappointment is fear. i.e the boss criticises me, makes me angry. I can't express anger because I might lose my job. I'm disappointed because I thought the boss was a friend. Underneath that, I'm afraid because what I thought was firm is revealed to be shaky. I'm afraid I'm not going to make it. Like everything in life depression

426

is an ally, a gift. It has something to teach us. Just for a little while be open to the possibility that there is nothing wrong with you.

The Buddha taught that all life is little more than an on-going flow of arising and ending experiences resulting from a previous condition. In effect he taught that in actuality the past no longer exists and cannot be changed or trouble us and the future is just a projected fantasy. All we will ever have is each moment of existence as it arises. This teaching is really useful in relation to depression. This moment is the only moment you have, so have it. Don't be afraid to experience your experience. There is nothing to fear. There is nothing in the universe that wants you to worry. Rather than focusing on what you want to have, or get, or do, focus on how you are, now, because how you are now is all you'll ever experience.

You believe that what you are experiencing is real. If you can just let go of that belief and get centred into the present moment you will realize that the present moment is quite manage-able. After all, nothing awful is going on except the way you think and react and if you didn't hate the thought or the emotion that arises it wouldn't be awful. Coming back to the present allows you to focus on what is really going on instead of overwhelming yourself with imaginings. The experience is only an experience. It's the label that's upsetting.

Another helpful meditative exercise could be to explore cen-tring as a theme. Begin by setting up as you would normally do for any other meditation session. Spend a bit of time settling in and resting in an awareness of the breath and then when you think you are ready begin shifting your awareness to your physical body.

See if you can have a sense of the outline of your body as it rests against the chair or stool. Beginning at the base of the left foot, move your attention around the entire body. Become aware of any physical discomfort in any part of the body and make an effort to release it and become relaxed.

Take one deep and full breath and let go with a sigh and then turn your attention to the emotional tones. What are you experiencing right now? Calm, anxiety, anger joy? Whatever emotional tone you recognise look to see if you can discover where in the body you are experiencing it. Ask yourself what would be the opposite of this emotional experience. See if you can be aware of yourself going to that opposite emotional tone in order to recognise and know it. Where in your body do you sense this opposite tone? Allow for some silent learning space and repeat as many times as you are comfortable with.

Take one deep and full breath and let go with a sigh and shift your awareness to your thought process. How are you able to see your mind? Who is it that is able to see your mind? Just observe the activity that is going on in your mind right now. Allow for some silent learning space and repeat as many times as you are comfortable with.

Take one deep and full breath and let go with a sigh. Now focus on the word centre, on the concept centre and then the experience of centre. Has your attention shifted to that place of emotional tone that is your centre? If not, focus there now and just experience your centre as fully as possible. Can you become aware of the energy, the vitality, the life that is the centre. See if you can experience that. Allow for some silent learning space and repeat as many times as you are comfortable with.

428

Take one deep and full breath and let go with a sigh. Now let that energy begin to grow, to expand and move through your body. Experience it in your back, in your shoulders, your abdomen, your chest, upper arms, forearms and hands. Experience this life energy in your legs, your feet, your toes. Can you experience it in your neck, your scalp, your face? See if you can experience this life energy throughout your entire body all at once. Allow for some silent learning space and repeat as many times as you are comfortable with.

Notice if you are shifting your attention from place to place in your body to experience this. Or have you moved back from yourself in order to experience it everywhere at once. Look to see how you are experiencing these thoughts, sensations and emotions. Continue to focus on this life force, this vitality throughout your body. Where do you experience it most strongly? Do you know how you are able to experience this? See if you can increase this experience, intensify the sensation and when you're ready slowly bring the session to a close and open your eyes.

How you treat yourself in depression is more important than getting over it or what you'll do when it's over. Hating and reject-ing yourself in a moment of depression is not helpful if you are going to learn to love an accept yourself. When you stop depress-ing the thoughts and emotions, you can begin to take care of the parts of you that you experience as being isolated, vulnerable and afraid. If you stay in depression you will never see what is under-neath it. We don't need to be afraid of our thoughts and emotions because of how we think they're going to make us act. Life keeps giving us opportunities to take responsibility and end our worries, but we keep turning them down. Some faith or belief systems say that many are called but few are chosen, within Buddhism we say that everyone is called, almost no one listens.

By taking responsibility, I mean starting out right now. Things such as depression, stress, anxiety, grief, loss and illness provide an ideal opportunity for us to practice what we have learned. The best way of moving forward with this is to adopt a different attitude. An attitude where we accept that only we can do it. It's like all of our life we have been going along never having experienced ourselves as being strong or supported and suddenly, someone comes into our life who wants to help, who wants to give you support, who wants to listen and talk and explore things with you. On top of that, this is someone who loves you unconditionally and is willing to be with you all of the time. Wouldn't it be wonderful if heaven would open up and drop someone like that into your life, but have you noticed how seldom that happens? So, realize that you can be that person yourself. You can always come back to a centred place, move into unconditional love and acceptance and have the same attitude toward yourself that you have towards anyone else you love. You can let go and be free in a moment. But will you? Probably not. But that just means we won't, it doesn't mean we can't.

The difference between allowing yourself to experience real pain or depressing that pain is the difference between being cut by a knife or enveloped by fog. The cut will heal usually quicker than you think and life can go on. But you can live your whole life in the fog, buffered against the experience of pain. The sadness is that when protected from pain we are also protected from joy. Being depressed and unhappy sometimes is just part of life. It doesn't mean that something has gone wrong with life any more than rain is something that has gone wrong with the weather, or night is something that has gone wrong with day.

We're conditioned from childhood. Growing up is a process of having one's autonomy removed in order to be socially acceptable and compliant. Generally speaking, the better you learn that, the worse off you are. Finding yourself, following your own direct experience, doesn't mean you're going to become socially unacceptable. Think about heroes, pioneers, geniuses, inspirational people. They are focused on that which gives their life meaning, not on being socially acceptable. First is commitment to being authentic, second maybe, to what the world expects.

The most important piece of advice in relation to depression is this: Everyone has one person to take care of. Be sure you take care of you before you try taking care of someone else. Learn to say yes to you before saying yes to others and take care of your needs before attempting to take care of another's. It won't make you more selfish, it will make you more generous.

Here's another helpful exercise to try. Put a tick against the things you would say to your best friend if he/she were depressed and came to you for help.

1. You shouldn't be that way. It's a sign of weakness
2. Would a big hug from someone who loves you help?
3. Are you being kind and gentle with yourself?
4. Just stop being that way. It's all your fault anyway. You asked for it
5. You're probably going to be depressed forever
6. Can you just let yourself be depressed without hating it?
7. I don't want to be around you when you're depressed

Now go back over the list and put a tick next to the things you say to yourself when you are experiencing a depressed episode.

It is helpful to recognise that the expectations of others, the standards they expect us to meet, are really our own projections. We judge ourselves by our standards, project them out onto other people then believe that they think those things about us. It goes something like this: I'm depressed; I hate being depressed. I look at my friends; I think they hate it when I'm depressed; I think they are judging me. In fact they may have no reaction at all. They may not even notice. It's your standards that aren't being met. Yes but.... what if they tell me they hate my depression? If your friends tell you they hate your depression, you can know that it's their problem just as it would be your problem if you hated theirs. We hate in others what we're not willing to face in ourselves, when in actuality, when we see a problem it's ours. Our eyes saw it; it appeared in our head and it came out of our mouth.

The ways we think the world expects us to be are the ways we've been taught to believe we should be. People are judging and criticising and dismissing us all the time, but as long as we're meeting our standards of how we should be, we don't even notice. As soon as we don't meet our standards, we think other people know that we're not and are judging us as harshly as we're judging ourselves. Are we really willing to give up our lives for what we think other people might be thinking? Has giving up your own life brought you the acceptance and approval you've always wanted? Has not being who you really are brought the joy and fulfillment you've been seeking?

We deny ourselves our life, close our options, because we think society expects us to, we think people will judge us. We think it's too selfish to do otherwise. We take the path that seems safest. Then, because we're depressing our passion, our desire for life, we eventually move into despair and ask ourselves, why go on? This is a very valid question in this frame of mind because we end up with just the hard stuff, the I should, the I have to, the things we were trying to avoid in the first place. We end up with emptiness, exhaustion and meaningless.

The good news is that none of what society or culture tried to get us to believe was true in the first place. There never have been any limits. There never was anything wrong with you and there still isn't. You can be whatever you choose, and the proof of that is that you are now. When you're feeling good, you are a good person. When you're feeling bad you're a bad person. If you're happy, you're OK. If you're not happy you're not OK. The choice of words in our language shows the priority that 'happy' has. Depression can happen when we try not to be unhappy. We want to go from one peak to the next without travelling through the valleys below. Peaks/valleys, up/down, right/wrong can't exist without the other.

If what we think is wrong with us were really wrong with us, we would have been able to fix it by now. The fact that we haven't been able to fix it is the proof that it's not really the problem. The problem is that we have been taught to believe there's a problem. It's like being told that something is broken and trying to fix it and never succeeding because it isn't broken. There is no problem. Stop creating one.

Experiencing guilt over being how you are does nothing but rob you of your life. It's OK to experience whatever is happening, think whatever you think, be however you are. Guilt and fear keep us from knowing our authentic being, our intrinsic purity and potential for compassionate living. Whatever we are doing we need to love ourselves for doing it. Whatever we are thinking, love yourself for thinking it. If you don't like it, love yourself for not liking it. Try and remain open to the possibility that if you were who you really are you would have the approval and acceptance you've always wanted, from yourself if from no one else. The only approval we really care about is our own. If we think we've done a good job, we're OK. If not, we don't. It doesn't actually matter to us what others think.

If we are really living the kind of life we want to live it'll be clear that nobody owes us anything and from that place of being satisfied we can be much more generous. Whatever you do, recognise that you are doing it for you and enjoy it. If you realize you no longer want to do it, stop. Yes but... isn't that irresponsible? You'll never know until you stop and find out. You could practice with some of the many little things you do and hate but continue to do because you believe you should or someone told you that you should. If you're responsible because you're afraid not to be, you're not responsible, you're afraid.

We have to face eventually that we don't want to be un-depressed. Terrible things might happen to us if we're not depressed. We have our own identity in this process of depressing. We are afraid that if we stop, we won't know how to be, won't know who to be, won't know what life will expect. It is safer and more comfortable to continue with the depressing than to risk freedom. Is this depressing? Can you realize that you reject well-

434

being without being depressed about it? After all, it must be depressing to realize that you've spent your whole life depressing yourself. The most depressing part is that you've always thought it was external. Now you're learning to see that it's something you've learned to do and now do to yourself. To say this is depressing information is like saying that you are on a sinking ship and have just discovered a lifeboat. If you choose to, you can stand there and be upset that the ship is sinking, or you can take the lifeboat. The lifeboat here is the Buddha's solution to the problem.

The miracle cure for depression is compassion. The compassion I'm talking about might not look nice and polite. It doesn't necessarily mean doing what others want us to do or being how they want us to be. The compassion I'm talking about begins with yourself because everything else springs from that. It is not selfish to love yourself. It's the most helpful thing a human being can do. If you can't find compassion for yourself, you'll never find it for anyone else, you won't know how. You will never be truly generous to anyone else while depriving yourself.

The aim of this book was not to be telling anyone what they should do because nobody will begin to take this medicine until they are ready themselves. All I'm suggesting here is that when you're ready, here's the Buddha's solution to the problem. This solution is definitely not another stick with which to beat yourself up with. When you've suffered enough just remember that you already have the solution available to you. It doesn't really matter what you have thought, believed, experienced or done before. This is a new day. Along with those two most useless of sayings 'yes but' and 'what if' go the three worst excuses of all time: 'but I've always done it this way', but I've always been this way', 'this is how I am'.

So, let's bring this chapter to a close with a summary of the four most important things to bear in mind.

1. **Get to know your emotions and learn to have them in a healthy way. Learn to express the energy of emotion in ways that take care of you and those around you. No guilt or blame**
2. **Rest, eat well, exercise regularly and prove to yourself that tension does not lead to control.**
3. **Take up an awareness practice that enables you to let go of false beliefs and assumptions about how you are and how the world should be. This will enable you to live in the current moment.**
4. **Recognise that it's OK to change. It's OK to try something new. It's OK to try something rather radically new such as the Buddha's approach.**

If you try something and don't like it, you can always return to how you were doing it before. No problem. No 'I should'. Trying something once or twice doesn't mean you ever have to do it again if you don't find it helpful. Not taking a risk because you are afraid is a grave disservice to yourself. Fear is not the problem. You can have fear and allow it to stop you, or you can have your fear and risk it anyway. Either way, the fear is there. The choice is yours.

Finally, there comes the link with the Buddha's teaching. Depression is nothing more than the actuality of the existence of worrying. The reason we experience worry is that we want things to be other than they are. We don't need to experience worry. There is a way of life available to us that will help us to realize the actuality of what the Buddha taught the world. What's stopping us from fully committing ourselves to the journey of freedom and joy? We are! How are we stopping ourselves fully committing ourselves to the path of freedom and joy? We keep saying yes but... what if.... but I've always done it this way... but I've always been this way... this is how I am... I'm scared... It's too irresponsible... I have a job... I'm a parent... I'm just not good enough.... The list is endless. We are not.

About the Author

In this age of instant access to information and data, it would not take long for you to track me down and identify me. I am sure that for some, there will be a compulsion to do that. I chose to publish this book using a pseudonym not because I have anything to hide, nor because of the inevitable hostile backlash from within classical Buddhism. I chose to do that to emphasise that the contents of this book are nothing to do with me. The likelihood is that much of what I have written has been picked up, memorised, learned and accumulated from a very wide variety of sources over the years on this actualization journey. Everything I have learned and found helpful along the way has been recycled, reformulated and regurgitated to fit with what I communicate today within a secular western Buddhist context. Everything I have found to be unhelpful has been discarded. If, after reading this book, you choose to be upset because you have an idea that you somehow own any of the words in it, I hope you will accept that I won't lose any sleep over that. I have never quite understood the concept of being able to own the Dharma or anything that points towards it. Conversely, if you find anything in this book to be helpful, you are free to lift it, claim it as your own if you wish and pass it on to others. It makes no difference to me.

The communication of the Dharma has never been and never will be about the communicator. If you waste valuable time exploring the finger all the time, you miss what it is pointing to. I can assure you that I am not infallible or special and if anyone tries to project those things onto me they will be very disappointed. You will have noticed that I am not a scholar, or an intellectual. This is about Mr Joe Average who, due to a particular set of circumstances, experienced something that included the realization that nobody was having the experience. What followed and is happening now is just the on-going actualization of that as a lived experience that I share with others, because an integral part of that experience is that it cannot be contained and needs to be communicated.

CPSIA information can be obtained
at www.ICGtesting.com
Printed in the USA
BVOW09s2114130717
489256BV00001B/77/P